Soil Mechanics in Foundation Engineering

Volume 2   Theory and Practice

ZENON WIŁUN

Professor of Foundation Engineering
Technical University of Warsaw

and

KRZYSZTOF STARZEWSKI

Ph.D., B.Sc., C.Eng., M.I.C.E.

Lecturer in Civil Engineering
The University of Aston in Birmingham

A Halsted Press Book

John Wiley & Sons
New York—Toronto

Published in the U.S.A. and Canada by Halsted Press, a Division of
John Wiley & Sons, Inc., New York

First published 1972

ISBN 0 470–82077–2

Library of Congress
catalog card no. 72–5120

Printed in Great Britain

Preface

Our purpose in writing this book has been to present the fundamentals of soil mechanics and foundation engineering in a manner understandable to all those concerned with the design and construction of foundations. Only a small group of men specialize in this field, yet, because foundations form an essential part of every building, structure or pavement, it is important to students and professional men in the fields of civil, structural and municipal engineering, building engineering and architecture. The common need of all is an understanding of the fundamental principles and problems encountered in the field as a whole. For those directly concerned with the design and construction of foundations it is essential to be able to apply the fundamental principles and design methods to an inexhaustible variety of practical problems. Thus, this book is an effort to make available a unified presentation of the fundamental principles of soil mechanics (Volume 1) and their application to real foundation problems (Volume 2).

All foundation problems, such as the determination of allowable bearing stresses or analysis of stability of slopes, are very complex and require a comprehensive knowledge of the material contained in both volumes of this book. The determination of, for example, allowable bearing stresses involves the following.

(1) Investigation of soil and ground water conditions on the site.
(2) Geotechnical analysis of physical and mechanical properties of the soils.
(3) Analysis of the problem on the basis of the findings from the above investigations and with reference to the proposed structure.

In Volume 1 the contents of Chapters 1, 3, and 6 cover the problems associated with site investigation work, identification of soils, and geological interpretation of the results; Chapter 4 covers the problems associated with the groundwater. Classification of soils and the determination of their physical properties is dealt with in Chapters 3 and 7; Chapter 2 deals with special problems associated with the mineralogical composition of soils and discusses interparticle forces in cohesive soils. Determination of mechanical properties of soils is discussed in detail in Chapters 5 and 6. A graphical correlation method for the determination of generalized characteristic soil properties is presented in Chapter 6.

In Volume 2 methods of evaluation of overburden stresses in soils and the determination of stress increments induced by applied loading are presented in Chapter 1. Methods of determination of allowable bearing stresses, with the consideration of ultimate bearing capacity and settlement and rates of settlement, are given in Chapter 2 and are further illustrated in Appendix A. Stability of natural and artificial slopes is discussed in Chapter 3 and determination of thrust on retaining structures and their stability in Chapter 4. A discussion of the effects of frost and preventive measures is contained in Chapter 5. Chapter 6 deals with the very important problem of compaction of soils, Chapter 7 contains many useful suggestions for design engineers and contractors and for observations of the settlement of structures. A comprehensive list of references, some of which are probably quite new to the Western reader, are included in both volumes.

Our thanks are due to Mr. John Corbett and Mrs. Audrey Bennett, who have kindly read the script and to Mr. D. H. Bennett for his many valuable comments. We are indebted to Dr. R. S. Johnson of the Department of Geology at the University of Aston in Birmingham for his valuable comments on the contents of Chapter 1 (Volume 1). We are also indebted to many members of the Civil Engineering Department at the University of Aston who have directly or indirectly assisted in the preparation of this book. We are particularly grateful to Mrs. Helena Starzewska who, apart from being a constant source of encouragement, has typed the script.

Z. Wiłun

K. Starzewski

1972

List of Contents

List of Figures

List of Tables

1

Stresses Within a Soil Mass

1.1. General Considerations

1.1.1. HALF-SPACE CONCEPT

A soil mass can be considered as a half-space bounded from the top by a horizontal plane (ground surface) and extending indefinitely in both depth and width.

It will be assumed in all further considerations in determining stresses induced by external loading that the soil mass is elastic (deforming linearly), isotropic, and homogeneous. These assumptions considerably simplify the determination of stresses and deformations but obviously introduce an error, the magnitude of which depends on how far the true stress–strain behaviour of the soil diverges from Hooke's law.

Within the practical range of working loads (considerably smaller than loads which produce plastic deformations of soils) it can be assumed that the deformations of the soil mass are linearly related to the stresses produced by the loads.

1.1.2. PRINCIPLE OF SUPERPOSITION

In the evaluation of stresses in a soil mass, by treating it as an elastic medium, the principle of superposition can be used, i.e. that the stress induced at a given point M due to the action of a number of point loads Q can be evaluated as the sum of the stresses induced at that point by each load acting on its own (Figure 1.1(a)).

Distributed loading q on the surface of the half-space can approximately be replaced by an equivalent system of point loads (Figure 1.1(b)).

1.1.3. OVERBURDEN AND FINAL STRESSES

In the evaluation of stresses in soils it is necessary (with a few exceptions) to consider the effect of the self-weight of the soil. The stresses which exist in the soil due to the weight of the overlying strata are called *overburden or geostatic stresses* and will be denoted by σ_o.

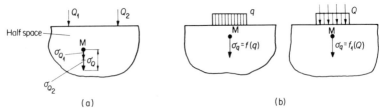

Figure 1.1. Application of the principle of superposition to (a) two concentrated loads; (b) distributed loads.

According to the principle of superposition the final stress σ within the soil will be the sum of the overburden stress σ_o and the stress increment $\Delta\sigma_q$ induced by the applied loading q:

$$\sigma = \sigma_o + \Delta\sigma_q \qquad (1.1)$$

In the case of the application of external loading which is not on the surface of the half-space but is at the bottom of an excavation (Figure 1.2), the stress at any point is computed as the sum of the overburden pressure σ_o decreased by unloading due to excavation $\Delta\sigma_o$ and the stress increment $\Delta\sigma_q$ induced by the applied loading q:

$$\sigma = (\sigma_o - \Delta\sigma_o) + \Delta\sigma_q \qquad (1.2)$$

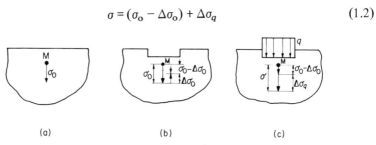

Figure 1.2. Stresses at a point M beneath excavation: (a) overburden stress; (b) stress after excavation; (c) final stress.

1.2. Determination of Overburden Stresses

In most practical problems it is only necessary to determine the vertical overburden stresses σ_{oz} but in certain cases the knowledge of the horizontal overburden stresses σ_{ox} and σ_{oy} may also be required.

1.2.1. DETERMINATION OF VERTICAL OVERBURDEN STRESSES

In the most general case of layered soils the overburden stress σ_{oz} is determined from the following expressions:

(a) in terms of total stresses

$$\sigma_{oz} = \sum_{i=1}^{n} (g\rho_i)h_i = \sum_{i=1}^{n} \gamma_i h_i \qquad (1.3)$$

and (b) in terms of effective stresses

$$\sigma'_{oz} = \sigma_{oz} - u_z \qquad (1.4)$$

where ρ_i = density of soil in layer i in kg/m³ or t/m³ = g/ml
         γ_i = unit weight of soil in layer i in kN/m³
         h_i = thickness of layer i in m
         n = number of layers above depth z
         u_z = pore water pressure at depth z, equal to piezometric head, at the
              time of consideration times unit weight of water in kN/m²

Example. It is necessary to determine total and effective overburden stresses for
ground conditions as shown in Figure 1.3. Owing to Artesian pressure in the
gravel (piezometric level 2 m higher than in the sand) there is upward seepage
of water and because of the low permeability of the silt it can be assumed that
the excess head is wholly dissipated in this soil under a uniform hydraulic
gradient of

$$i = \frac{\Delta H}{l} = \frac{2 \cdot 0}{4 \cdot 0} = 0 \cdot 5$$

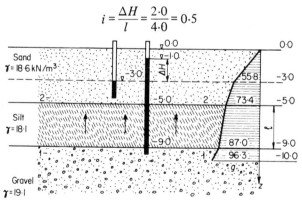

Figure 1.3. Vertical overburden stresses in soils.

A change in the ground water level may have a considerable influence on the
effective overburden stresses. According to Archimedes' principle the soil below
the ground water level is subject to an uplift which decreases its unit weight by
approximately 9·8 kN/m³ (62·4 lbf/ft³, 1000 kgf/m³); practically in all
cohesive soils either joints (or fissures) or thin permeable layers are present
which make it necessary to consider the above uplift regardless of whether the
soil itself is of the high or low permeability type. The effects of this uplift can
be allowed for either by considering the submerged unit weight of the soil (and

Depth z	$\sigma_{oz} = \sum\limits_{i=1}^{n} \gamma_i h_i$	u_z	$\sigma'_{oz} = \sigma_{oz} - u_z$
3	$18 \cdot 6 \times 3 = 55 \cdot 8*$	0	$55 \cdot 8$
5	$55 \cdot 8 + 18 \cdot 6 \times 2 = 93 \cdot 0$	$9 \cdot 8 \times 2 = 19 \cdot 6$	$73 \cdot 4$
9	$93 \cdot 0 + 18 \cdot 1 \times 4 = 165 \cdot 4$	$9 \cdot 8 \times 8 = 78 \cdot 4$	$87 \cdot 0$
10	$165 \cdot 4 + 19 \cdot 1 \times 1 = 184 \cdot 5$	$9 \cdot 8 \times 9 = 88 \cdot 2$	$96 \cdot 3$

* All stresses in kN/m^2.
Vertical overburden pressures are usually plotted horizontally against depth, on the left-hand side of the z axis.

the effects of any seepage forces present) or simply by using the effective stress Equation (1.4) as illustrated in the above example. In the case of a rise in the ground water level the effective overburden stresses will be decreased (Figure 1.4) while a drop in the ground water level will produce an increase in the stresses which may be quite considerable, particularly if the soil is of the fine-grained type and a full passive capillary zone develops (see Volume 1, Section 2.5).

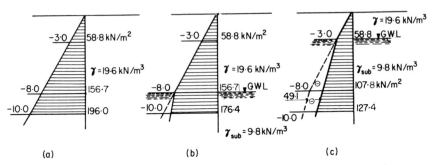

Figure 1.4. Change in vertical overburden stresses due to rise in ground water level: (a) vertical overburden stresses above ground water level; (b) with ground water level at $8 \cdot 0$ m depth; (c) with ground water level at $3 \cdot 0$ m depth.

1.2.2. DETERMINATION OF HORIZONTAL OVERBURDEN STRESSES

At any point within the soil mass vertical overburden stresses will be accompanied by horizontal stresses (Figure 1.5), the magnitude of which can be computed from the following expression:

$$\sigma'_{ox} = \sigma'_{oy} = K_0 \sigma'_{oz} \tag{1.5}$$

where K_0 = coefficient of lateral stress at rest (dimensionless)
   σ'_{oz} = vertical effective overburden stress at a given point in kN/m^2 (lbf/ft^2, kgf/cm^2)

The coefficient of lateral stress at rest K_0 depends on the type of soil and on its past geological history (Figure 1.6); for normally consolidated soils it varies between 0·4 and 0·5 for sands and between 0·5 and 0·7 for silts and silty clays, while for heavily overconsolidated soils it can be as high as 2·5 (Skempton, 1961) or even 3.

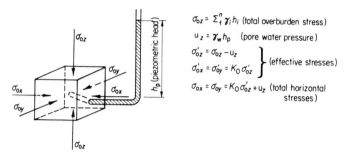

$\sigma_{oz} = \sum_1^n \gamma_i h_i$ (total overburden stress)

$u_z = \gamma_w h_p$ (pore water pressure)

$\sigma'_{oz} = \sigma_{oz} - u_z$

$\left. \begin{array}{l} \sigma'_{ox} = \sigma'_{oy} = K_0 \sigma'_{oz} \end{array} \right\}$ (effective stresses)

$\sigma_{ox} = \sigma_{oy} = K_0 \sigma'_{oz} + u_z$ (total horizontal stresses)

Figure 1.5. Effective and total vertical and horizontal overburden or geostatic stresses.

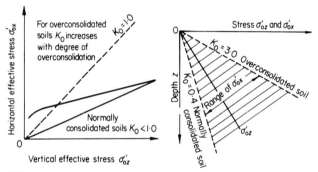

Figure 1.6. Effect of overconsolidation on coefficient of lateral stress at rest.

1.3. Determination of Distribution of Stresses in a Soil Mass Due to Applied Loading

The distribution of stresses in a soil mass due to applied loading is determined on the basis of a simplified assumption that the soil mass can be represented by a weightless elastic isotropic homogeneous half-space of known elastic properties E and ν. For practical purposes the stresses induced by the applied loading are treated as *stress increments* and where necessary are added to stresses in the soil according to the principle of superposition outlined in Section 1.1.2. For the sake of clarity the notation $\Delta\sigma$ and $\Delta\tau$ which indicates incremental changes in stresses have been omitted from the Sections 1.3.1 to 1.3.9 but has been used in all practical examples and considerations.

1.3.1. DISTRIBUTION OF STRESSES IN A SOIL MASS DUE TO VERTICAL POINT LOAD

The problem of the distribution of stresses in an elastic isotropic homogeneous half-space due to a point load applied to its surface has been solved by Boussinesq (1885), without consideration of the self-weight of the medium. In the first instance it is assumed (Biezukhov, 1953) that the radial stress at a point M, having polar coordinates R and β (Figure 1.7) is given by

$$\sigma_R = kQ \cos \beta / R^2 \qquad\qquad (a)$$

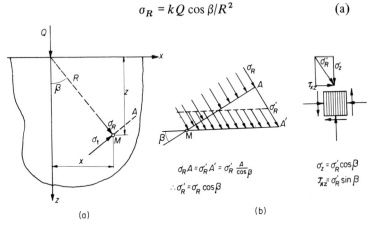

(a)   (b)

Figure 1.7. Stresses at point M induced by a point load: (a) radial stress σ_R; (b) determination of vertical stress σ_z.

Vertical stress σ_z at the same point is given by (Figure 1.7(b))

$$\sigma_z = \sigma_R \cos^2 \beta = kQ \cos^3 \beta / R^2 \qquad\qquad (b)$$

Substituting $\cos \beta = z/R$ into the equation (b)

$$\sigma_z = kQz^3 / R^5 \qquad\qquad (c)$$

In order to determine the value of the coefficient k an elemental force acting on an infinitesimally narrow annulus (according to Figure 1.8) of width dr and of radius r is considered:

$$\sigma_z \, dA = \sigma_z 2\pi r \, dr \qquad\qquad (d)$$

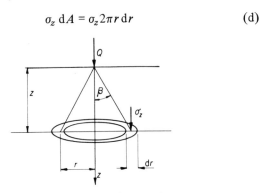

Figure 1.8. Stress acting on an elemental surface of an annulus.

The applied force Q must be equal to the sum of the vertical stresses acting on an infinite horizontal plane at a depth z, i.e.

$$Q = 2\pi \int_0^\infty \sigma_z r \, dr = 2\pi k Q z^3 \int_0^\infty \frac{r \, dr}{R^5} \qquad \text{(e)}$$

Differentiating the expression $R^2 = z^2 + r^2$ with respect to r

$$2R \, dR = 2r \, dr \qquad \text{(f)}$$

Hence on substitution of $r \, dr = R \, dR$ in (e) and on integration (with appropriate change of limits) the following is obtained:

$$Q = 2\pi k Q z^3 \int_z^\infty \frac{dR}{R^4}$$

or

$$1 = 2\pi k z^3 \left[\frac{1}{-3R^3} \right]_z^\infty = \frac{2}{3} \pi k$$

hence

$$k = \frac{3}{2\pi} \qquad \text{(g)}$$

Substituting in (a) the expression for radial stress σ_R is obtained:

$$\sigma_R = \frac{3 \, Q \cos \beta}{2\pi R^2} \qquad \text{(1.6)}$$

Vertical stress σ_z in cylindrical coordinates can be obtained from the equation (c) on substitution for k and $R^2 = z^2 + r^2$:

$$\sigma_z = \frac{3Qz^3}{2\pi R^5} = \frac{3Qz^3}{2(z^2 + r^2)^{5/2}} = \frac{3Qz^3}{2\pi z^5 \{1 + (r/z)^2\}^{5/2}}$$

hence

$$\sigma_z = \frac{3Q}{2\pi z^2 \{1 + (r/z)^2\}^{5/2}} \qquad \text{(1.7)}$$

If $c_z = (3/2\pi) \{1 + (r/z)^2\}^{-5/2}$ is substituted in (1.7), then the following simple expression is obtained:

$$\sigma_z = \frac{Q}{z^2} c_z \qquad \text{(1.8)}$$

Values of c_z are given in Figure 1.9. It can clearly be seen that maximum values of c_z occur at $x/z = 0$, i.e. on the vertical line passing through the point of application of force Q; away from the z axis the stresses decrease very rapidly.

A similar decrease can be observed in stresses σ_{z_i} with depth z. The curves plotted in Figure 1.10 are geometrical loci of points of equal value of stress σ_z; such curves are known as stress isobars.

Values of horizontal normal radial stresses σ_r and circumferential stresses σ_δ and also of shear stresses τ_{zr} (Figure 1.11) can be evaluated from the following formulae:

$$\left.\begin{array}{l}
\sigma_r = \dfrac{Q}{2\pi}\left\{\dfrac{3zr^2}{R^5} - \dfrac{1-2v}{R(R+z)}\right\} \\[2mm]
\sigma_\delta = -(1-2v)\dfrac{Q}{2\pi}\cdot\left\{\dfrac{z}{R^3} - \dfrac{1}{R(R+z)}\right\} \\[2mm]
\tau_{zr} = \dfrac{3Q}{2\pi}\cdot\dfrac{z^2 r}{R^5} \\[2mm]
\tau_{z\delta} = \tau_{\delta r} = 0
\end{array}\right\} \qquad (1.9)$$

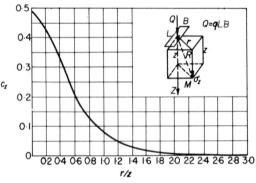

Figure 1.9. Nomogram for determination of c_z.

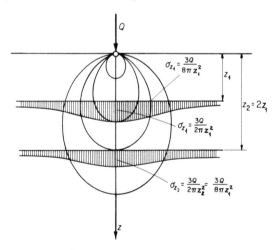

Figure 1.10. Isobars of normal vertical stresses.

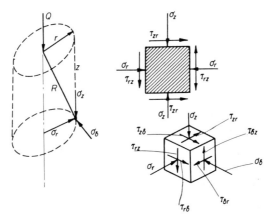

Figure 1.11. Horizontal normal and shear stresses.

In cases where it is necessary to consider the combined effects of stress increments $\Delta\sigma_z$, $\Delta\sigma_r$, and $\Delta\sigma_\delta$ due to applied loading and the overburden stresses σ'_{oz}, σ'_{ox}, and σ'_{oy} the latter are expressed with reference to the cylindrical coordinates z, r, and δ:

$$\left.\begin{aligned}
\sigma'_{oz} &= \sigma'_{oz} \\
\sigma'_{or} &= \sigma'_{o\delta} = \sigma'_{ox} = \sigma'_{oy} = K_0\sigma'_{oz} \\
\tau'_z &= \tau'_{r\delta} = 0
\end{aligned}\right\} \tag{1.10}$$

The stress components given by Equation (1.9) can be expressed in terms of rectangular coordinates:

$$\left.\begin{aligned}
\sigma_x &= \frac{3Q}{2\pi}\left[\frac{zx^2}{R^5} + \frac{1-2v}{3}\left\{\frac{R^2-Rz-z^2}{R^3(R+z)} - \frac{x^2(2R+z)}{R^3(R+z)^2}\right\}\right] \\
\sigma_y &= \frac{3Q}{2\pi}\left[\frac{zy^2}{R^5} + \frac{1-2v}{3}\left\{\frac{R^2-Rz-z^2}{R^3(R+z)} - \frac{y^2(2R+z)}{R^3(R+z)^2}\right\}\right] \\
\sigma_z &= \frac{3Q}{2\pi}\cdot\frac{z^3}{R^5} \\
\tau_{xy} &= \frac{3Q}{2\pi}\left[\frac{xyz}{R^5} - \frac{1-2v}{3}\left\{\frac{xy(2R+z)}{R^3(R+z)^2}\right\}\right] \\
\tau_{yz} &= -\frac{3Q}{2\pi}\cdot\frac{yz^2}{R^5} \\
\tau_{zx} &= -\frac{3Q}{2\pi}\cdot\frac{xz^2}{R^5}
\end{aligned}\right\} \tag{1.11}$$

If the point load is not applied at the origin of the coordinate axes but at a point $(\xi, \eta, 0)$, then Equations (1.11) should be modified by substituting $(x - \xi)$ for x and $(y - \eta)$ for y.

Stresses σ_x (or σ_y) can be computed from the following equation:

$$\sigma_x = \frac{Q}{z^2} c_x \qquad (1.12)$$

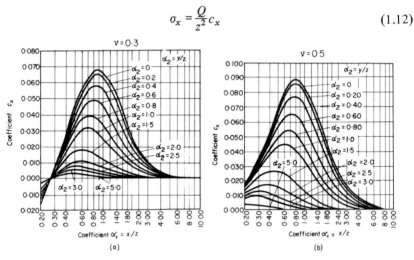

Figure 1.12. Coefficient c_x (after Glushkov, 1954): (a) for $\nu = 0.3$; (b) for $\nu = 0.5$.

Values of c_x (Florin, 1959) are given in Figure 1.12 for values of $\nu = 0.3$ and $\nu = 0.5$ and in terms of coefficients $\alpha_1 = x/z$ and $\alpha_2 = y/z$.

The sum of normal stresses at any point is known as the first invariant and is equal to

$$I_1 = \sigma_x + \sigma_y + \sigma_z = \frac{Q}{\pi}(1 + \nu)\frac{z}{R^3} \qquad (1.13)$$

1.3.2. DISTRIBUTION OF STRESSES IN A SOIL MASS DUE TO CONTINUOUS DISTRIBUTED LOAD

The formulae derived for the point load effects can be used in the evaluation of the stresses due to continuous distributed loading by applying the principle of superposition.

A loaded area can be divided into small elements which can then be replaced by equivalent point loads applied at their centres. For practical purposes sufficient accuracy is achieved when the condition $R_i \geqslant 2L_i$ is satisfied, where L_i is the length of each of the small elements (Figure 1.13(a)).

Vertical normal stresses can be computed by summation of the effects of individual equivalent point loads:

$$\sigma_z = \frac{Q}{z^2} \sum c_{zi}$$

The above application of the principle of superposition to individual cases is laborious and time consuming and therefore various formulae, tables, and nomograms have been prepared which simplify the work.

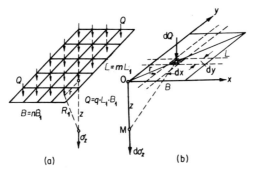

Figure 1.13. Determination of vertical normal stresses due to continuous distributed loading by consideration of a system of equivalent point loads.

Vertical normal stress at any point within a soil mass due to continuous distributed loading applied over an area on the surface of the half-space can be computed by integration of Boussinesq's equation, Equation (1.7):

$$\sigma_z = \frac{3Q}{2\pi z^2 \{1 + (r/z)^2\}^{5/2}}$$

Within a given area A, an infinitesimally small element of an area $dA = dx\, dy$ is considered; the corresponding elemental point load $dQ = q\, dA$ induces at a point M (Figure 1.13(b)) a vertical stress component given by

$$d\sigma_z = \frac{3\, dQ}{2\pi z^2 \{1 + (r/z)^2\}^{5/2}}$$

The vertical stress induced at that point by the load q acting over the entire area A is the given by

$$\sigma_z = \int_0^L \int_0^B \frac{3q\, dx\, dy}{2\pi z^2 \{1 + (x^2 + y^2)/z^2\}^{5/2}}$$

The problem of the determination of stresses under the corner of a rectangular uniformly loaded area has been solved by Steinbrenner; equations for determination of stresses under the centre of a rectangular uniformly loaded area have been derived by Newmark and Polshin.

1.3.2.1. Method of Corner Points

The method of corner points (Steinbrenner, 1936) permits the determination of vertical stress σ_z, and the sum of the principal stresses I_1, at any depth below a corner of a uniformly loaded rectangular area $L \times B$:

$$\sigma_z = \frac{q}{2}\left\{\frac{LBz(L^2 + B^2 + 2z^2)}{(L^2 + z^2)(B^2 + z^2)\sqrt{(L^2 + B^2 + z^2)}} + \arctan\frac{LB}{z\sqrt{(L^2 + B^2 + z^2)}}\right\} = q \cdot \eta_c$$

(1.14)

$$I_1 = (1 + \nu)\frac{q}{\pi}\arctan\frac{LB}{z\sqrt{L^2 + B^2 + z^2}} = (1 + \nu)q\eta_1$$

(1.15)

where η_c = coefficient which for any given ratios $L : B$ and $z : B$ can be obtained from nomogram in Figure 1.14(a)

η_I = coefficient from nomogram in Figure 1.14(b)

q = uniformly distributed load in kN/m^2 (lbf/ft^2, kgf/cm^2)

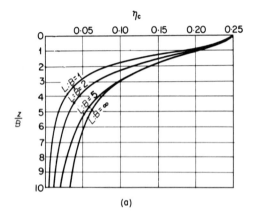

(a)

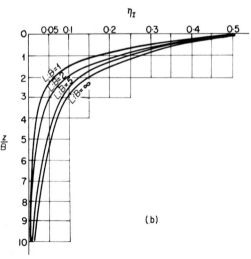

(b)

Figure 1.14. Nomograms for determination of (a) coefficient η_c; (b) coefficient η_I.

In cases where it is necessary to determine stresses at any points other than the corners of rectangular areas the principle of superposition is used as illustrated in the following example.

Example. Loaded area L = 20 m, B = 8 m, uniformly distributed loading q = 70 kN/m^2. Determine the vertical stress increment $\Delta\sigma_z$ at depth z = 5·0 below point E outside the loaded area (Figure 1.15).

Construct rectangles BB'EE' and B'CE"E; another two rectangles AA'EE' and A'DE"E are obtained with common corners at the point E. Rectangles AA'EE' and A'DE"E are symmetrical with respect to E; their dimensions are as

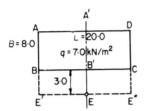

Figure 1.15. Application of method of corner points to determination of stress increments at any points.

follows: length L' = 8 + 3 = 11 m, width B' = 20 : 2 = 10 m, therefore $L : B$ = 1.1; $z : B$ = 5 : 10 = 0·5 and hence η_c' = 0·23 and $\Delta\sigma_z'$ = 0·23 x 70 = 16·1 kN/m^2.
   Similarly rectangles BB'EE' and B'CE"E have L'' = 20 : 2 = 10 m; B'' = 3·0 m; $L : B$ = 10 : 3 = 3·33; $z : B$ = 5 : 3 = 1·67; η_c'' = 0·15; $\Delta\sigma_z''$ = 0·15 x 70 = 10·5 kN/m^2.
   Applying now the principle of superposition the required stress increment is obtained:

$$\Delta\sigma_z = 2 \times 16{\cdot}1 - 2 \times 10{\cdot}5 = 32{\cdot}2 - 21{\cdot}0 = 11{\cdot}2 \text{ kN/m}^2$$

1.3.2.2. Method of Centre Points

The method of centre points (Newmark, 1940) permits the determination of the vertical stress σ_z at any depth z below the centre of a uniformly loaded rectangular area $L \times B$:

$$\sigma_z = q\eta_0 \tag{1.16}$$

Coefficients η_0 are given in Figure 1.16.
   Vertical stress σ_z beneath the centre can also be computed using the principle of superposition by considering it as a corner point common to four rectangular loaded areas of sides $L/2$ and $B/2$.

1.3.3. DETERMINATION OF STRESSES UNDER EMBANKMENTS

Vertical stresses under embankments (Figure 1.17) can be computed from equation

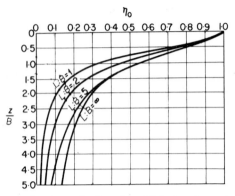

Figure 1.16. Nomogram for determination of coefficient η_0 for evaluation of stresses below the centre of uniformly loaded rectangular area.

$$\sigma_z = \sigma_{z_1} + \sigma_{z_2} + \sigma_{z_3} = q\,(\eta_1 + \eta_2 + \eta_3) \qquad (1.17)$$

where η_1 and η_3 = coefficients corresponding to strip loading of triangular distribution from Table 1.1

η_2 = coefficient corresponding to strip loading of rectangular distribution from Table 1.2

q = γh = maximum intensity of loading kN/m^2

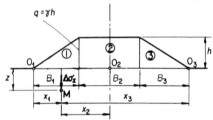

Figure 1.17. Schematic diagram of necessary details for evaluation of vertical normal stresses in the soil mass below embankment.

Example. Given (Figure 1.17): $B_1 = 6.0$ m; $B_2 = 10.0$ m; $B_3 = 6.0$ m; $h = 4.0$ m; $x_1 = 4.0$ m; $x_2 = 7.0$ m; $x_3 = 18.0$ m; $\rho = 1800$ kg/m^3; $z = 3.0$ m. Determine $\Delta\sigma_z$.

Evaluate parameters necessary for the determination of η_1, η_2 and η_3:

$x_1/B_1 = 4.0/6.0 = 0.67; x_2/B_2 = 7.0/10.0 = 0.7; x_3/B_3 = 18.0/6.0 = 3.0$
$z/B_1 = 3.0/6.0 = 0.50; z/B_2 = 3.0/10.0 = 0.30; z/B_3 = 0.50$

Therefore from Tables 1.1 and 1.2

$$\eta_1 = 0.44; \quad \eta_2 = 0.30; \quad \eta_3 = 0$$

Therefore $q = (1800 \times 9.81) \times 4/1000 = 70.7$ kN/m^2

$$\Delta\sigma_z = 70.7\,(0.44 + 0.30) = 52.2 \text{ kN/m}^2$$

Tables 1.1 and 1.2 can also be used for the computation of stress increments under strip trapezoidal loading (Figure 1.18) by the summation of stress increments due to rectangular and triangular strip loads:

$$\Delta\sigma_z = \eta_2 q_2 + \eta_3 q_3$$

The distance x_3 (Figure 1.18) will be negative if the point M is to the right of point O_3.

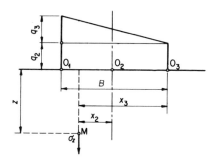

Figure 1.18. Schematic diagrams of necessary details for evaluation of vertical normal stresses in the soil mass due to strip loading of trapezoidal distribution.

Table 1.1. Values of coefficient η_1 (or η_3) for evaluation of stresses due to infinitely long continuous strip load of triangular distribution (Figure 1.17)

Ratio of depth z to width B_1 (or B_3) $z : B$	Coefficient η_1 (or η_3) for different values of $x_1 : B_1$ (or $x_3 : B_3$)												
	−1·5	−1·0	−0·5	0·0	0·25	0·50	0·75	0·99	1·00	1·01	1·5	2·0	2·5
0·00	0·00	0·00	0·00	0·00	0·25	0·50	0·75	0·99	0·50	0·00	0·00	0·00	0·00
0·10	0·00	0·00	0·00	0·05	0·25	0·49	0·73	0·53	0·47	0·46	0·00	0·00	0·00
0·25	0·00	0·00	0·00	0·08	0·26	0·48	0·64	0·37	0·42	0·40	0·02	0·00	0·00
0·50	0·00	0·00	0·02	0·13	0·26	0·41	0·48	0·37	0·35	0·33	0·06	0·02	0·00
0·75	0·01	0·02	0·04	0·15	0·25	0·34	0·36	0·31	0·29	0·29	0·11	0·02	0·01
1·00	0·01	0·03	0·06	0·16	0·22	0·28	0·28	0·25	0·25	0·25	0·13	0·05	0·01
1·50	0·02	0·05	0·08	0·15	0·18	0·20	0·20	0·19	0·19	0·18	0·12	0·06	0·04
2·00	0·03	0·06	0·09	0·13	0·15	0·16	0·16	0·15	0·15	0·15	0·11	0·07	0·05
3·00	0·05	0·06	0·08	0·10	0·10	0·10	0·11	0·10	0·10	0·10	0·09	0·07	0·05
4·00	0·05	0·06	0·07	0·08	0·08	0·09	0·08	0·08	0·08	0·08	0·08	0·06	0·05
5·00	0·05	0·05	0·06	0·06	0·06	0·06	0·06	0·06	0·06	0·06	0·06	0·05	0·04
6·00	0·04	0·04	0·05	0·05	0·05	0·05	0·05	0·05	0·05	0·05	0·05	0·05	0·04

Note: x = distance from a point at which $q = 0$, i.e. from O_1 for triangle 1 and from O_3 for triangle 3 (x is taken as positive in direction in which q increases)

b = width of strip loading

1.3.4. DETERMINATION OF VERTICAL STRESSES BELOW THE CENTRE OF UNIFORMLY LOADED CIRCULAR AREA

By reference to Figure 1.19 and Boussinesq's equation for vertical normal stress:

Table 1.2. Values of coefficients η_2 for evaluation of stresses due to infinitely long continuous strip load of rectangular distribution

Ratio of depth z to width B_2	Coefficient η_2 for different values of $x_2 : B_2$								
$z : B_2$	0	0·25	0·49	0·50	0·51	0·75	1·0	1·5	2·0
0·00	1·00	1·00	1·00	0·50	0·00	0·00	0·00	0·00	0·00
0·10	0·99	0·98	0·56	0·50	0·44	0·04	0·00	0·00	0·00
0·25	0·96	0·90	0·52	0·50	0·48	0·31	0·02	0·00	0·00
0·50	0·82	0·74	0·50	0·48	0·46	0·34	0·08	0·02	0·00
0·75	0·67	0·61	0·46	0·45	0·40	0·35	0·15	0·04	0·02
1·00	0·55	0·51	0·42	0·41	0·40	0·34	0·19	0·07	0·03
1·25	0·46	0·44	0·38	0·37	0·37	0·32	0·20	0·10	0·045
1·50	0·40	0·38	0·34	0·34	0·33	0·30	0·21	0·115	0·06
1·75	0·35	0·34	0·31	0·31	0·31	0·27	0·22	0·13	0·07
2·00	0·31	0·31	0·29	0·28	0·28	0·25	0·21	0·14	0·08
3·00	0·21	0·21	0·20	0·20	0·19	0·18	0·17	0·135	0·10
4·00	0·16	0·16	0·15	0·15	0·14	0·14	0·14	0·12	0·10
5·00	0·13	0·13	0·12	0·12	0·12	0·12	0·12	0·11	0·09
6·00	0·11	0·11	0·10	0·10	0·10	0·10	0·10	0·10	0·09
10·00	0·064	0·064	0·062	0·062	0·062	0·062	0·062	0·062	0·059

$$\sigma_z = \frac{3Qz^3}{2\pi R^5}$$

the elemental stress component $d\sigma_z$ due to elemental point load dQ can be computed:

Therefore
$$dQ = q\, dA = q\rho\, d\phi\, d\rho$$

$$\therefore\ d\sigma_z = \frac{3q\rho z^3\, d\phi\, d\rho}{2\pi R^5}$$

Integrating the above expression to obtain σ_z below the centre of the circular area,

$$\sigma_z = \int_0^r \int_0^{2\pi} d\sigma_z = \int_0^r \int_0^{2\pi} \frac{3q\rho z^3\, d\phi\, d\rho}{2\pi R^5} = 3qz^3 \int_0^r \frac{\rho\, d\rho}{R^5}$$

Considering that $R^2 = z^2 + \rho^2$ and hence $2R\, dR = 2\rho\, d\rho$ and substituting in the above expression

$$\sigma_z = 3qz^3 \int_z^{\sqrt{(z^2+r^2)}} \frac{dR}{R^4} = 3qz^3 \left[\frac{1}{-3R^3}\right]_z^{\sqrt{(z^2+r^2)}} = q\left[1 - \frac{1}{\{1 + (r/z)^2\}^{3/2}}\right]$$

$$(1.18)$$

In a general form

$$\sigma_z = q\eta \qquad (1.19)$$

Values of coefficient η are shown in Figure 1.20 and in the following table.

z/D	0·125	0·25	0·50	0·75	1·00	1·25	1·50	1·75
η	0·986	0·911	0·646	0·424	0·285	0·200	0·146	0·111
z/D	2·00	2·25	2·50	3·00	3·50	4·00	4·50	5·00
η	0·087	0·070	0·057	0·040	0·030	0·023	0·018	0·015

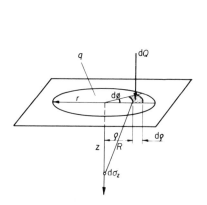

Figure 1.19. Elemental stress component below the centre of a circular loaded area.

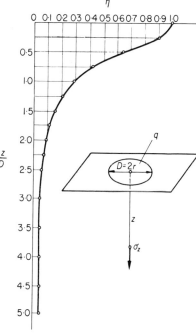

Figure 1.20. Nomogram for determination of coefficient η for evaluation of stresses below the centre of circular loaded area.

1.3.5. NEWMARK'S NOMOGRAM

The surface of a uniformly loaded half-space can be divided by concentric circles of radii r_i into ring loads which induce equal vertical stress increments at a given depth below their common centre.

In accordance with Equation (1.18)

$$\text{for } r = \infty \quad \eta = 1 \text{ and hence } \sigma_z = q$$

and

$$\text{for } r = 0 \quad \eta = 0 \text{ and hence } \sigma_z = 0$$

Assuming in Equation (1.19) that $\eta_1 = 1/n$, the radius of the first (i.e. innermost) circle, inducing stress increment $\sigma_z = q/n$ can be found.

From Equations (1.18) and (1.19)

$$r_1 = z\sqrt{\left\{\frac{1}{(1-\eta_1)^{2/3}} - 1\right\}}$$

Values of radii for following circles can now be so selected that the loading on any of the rings contained between two adjacent circles induce the same stress increments $\sigma_z = q/n$, i.e. that the difference between influence coefficients is $\Delta\eta = \eta_{i+1} - \eta_i = \text{constant} = 1/n$.

Considering stresses at a given depth only, i.e. assuming $z = \text{constant}$, an expression for the variable r_i can now be obtained:

$$r_i = z\sqrt{\left\{\frac{1}{(1-\eta_i)^{2/3}} - 1\right\}} \tag{1.20}$$

where

$$\eta_i = i\left(\frac{1}{n}\right) \tag{1.21}$$

Example. Evaluate ratios r_i/z for $n = 10$. Results obtained from Equations (1.20) and (1.21) are compiled in Table 1.3.

Note. The tabulated results can conveniently be used for plotting Newmark's nomograms to any required scale.

Table 1.3. Influence coefficient η_i and corresponding ratios r_i/z

Annulus No. i	η_i	r_i/z
0	0·0	0·000
1	0·1	0·270
2	0·2	0·400
3	0·3	0·518
4	0·4	0·637
5	0·5	0·766
6	0·6	0·918
7	0·7	1·110
8	0·8	1·387
9	0·9	1·908
10	1·0	∞

The circles in Figure 1.21 have been plotted using the results from Table 1.3 and assuming unit length of z as shown adjacent to the nomogram.

By dividing the surface area of the circles into $m = 20$ sectors, $m \times n =$

= 20 x 10 = 200 equivalent areas are obtained which can be considered as influence areas.

Influence coefficient is then equal to

$$\alpha = \frac{1}{mn} = \frac{1}{200} \qquad (1.22)$$

This diagram is known as Newmark's nomogram (Newmark, 1942) and it can be used for the determination of the vertical stress σ_z below any point of a uniformly loaded area of any shape from the following equation:

$$\sigma_z = q \alpha N \qquad (1.23)$$

where N = number of influence areas
         α = influence coefficient
         q = uniform loading

In using the nomogram the point, under which it is required to determine the stress σ_z, must be positioned over its centre while the outline of the loaded area must be plotted on it to a scale corresponding to the depth z (Figure 1.21(b)).

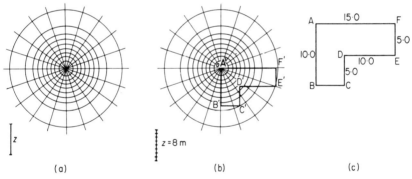

Figure 1.21. Newmark's nomogram: (a) nomogram network; (b) loaded area in z scale; (c) dimensions of loaded area.

Example. Given dimensions of loaded area according to Figure 1.21(c), uniform loading $q = 200$ kN/m². Determine the stress increment $\Delta\sigma_z$ at a depth $z = 8$ m below point A.

By dividing the unit length of z into 8 equal parts the length of 1 m in z scale is obtained.

With the point A over the centre of the nomogram the shape of the loaded area is now plotted in the z scale.

The number of influence areas contained within the loaded area are now counted: $N = 36$.

8 m below corner A stress increment $\Delta\sigma_z$ is equal to

$$\Delta\sigma_z = q\alpha N = 200 \times \frac{1}{200} \times 36 = 36 \text{ kN/m}^2$$

1.3.6. DISTRIBUTION OF STRESSES UNDER INFINITELY RIGID FOUNDATION

In all the above-considered cases the distribution of stresses within the soil mass was determined on the assumption that the applied loading is transmitted to the soil through a perfectly flexible foundation which can take up the deformation of the soil surface. In practice this happens in the cases of embankment loading or distributed loading transmitted to the soil through a hard core or through a flexible concrete raft.

In the case of masonry or concrete foundations of considerable flexural stiffness (about horizontal axes) the distribution of stresses at the foundation level will not be uniform; this will also apply to the stresses in the soil within the immediate vicinity of that level (approximately to a depth equal to half the foundation width).

The theoretical stress distribution beneath a circular rigid footing is given by the following equation:

$$\sigma = \frac{q}{2\sqrt{(1 - \rho^2/r^2)}} \tag{1.24}$$

where ρ = distance from the centre of foundation to the point under consideration

        r = radius of the foundation

According to Equation (1.24) for $\rho = 0$ (at the centre of the footing) $\sigma = 0.5q$; for $\rho = r$ stress $\sigma = \infty$ (Figure 1.22). Because the stress in the soil beneath the edge of the foundation cannot increase above a certain critical value, the soil beneath the edge deforms and some of the load is taken up by the soil further away from it. This leads to a change in the distribution of stresses at the foundation level; the actual distribution of stresses is indicated in Figure 1.22(a) by a solid line; the shape of the stress diagram is that of an inverted saddle.

As the loading is further increased, the stresses in the soil continue to increase towards the centre of the foundation and the pressure diagram becomes parabolic in shape (Figure 1.22(b)).

It can be seen from the above that the stress distribution at the foundation level depends to a large extent on the strength of the soil, on the magnitude of loading, and, undoubtedly, on the width of the foundation; under relatively narrow foundations the stress distribution is in most cases parabolic, while under wide foundations it is saddle like.

1.3.7. DETERMINATION OF STRESSES BY 'CHARACTERISTIC POINT' METHOD

In the case of a structure of large plan dimensions and founded on a continuous raft, the stresses in the raft and in the structure are computed by taking into consideration the elastic deformations of the soil mass (design of slabs and beams on elastic foundations).

However, in calculating the average settlement of the structure an approximate method of determination of average stresses within the soil mass, the

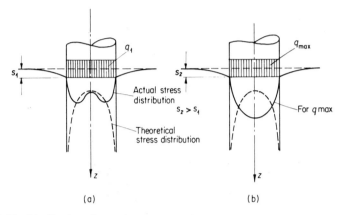

Figure 1.22. Distribution of stress beneath a rigid foundation: (a) during initial loading stages; (b) at limiting loading.

method of characteristic points, can be used (Grasshof, 1955). Stresses beneath the characteristic point M (Figure 1.23) are taken as being the representative stresses for evaluation of settlement. They are computed using the corner point method, by dividing the loaded area into four rectangles with a common corner at M.

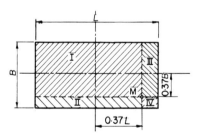

Figure 1.23. Characteristic point for a rectangular foundation.

1.3.8. DISTRIBUTION OF STRESSES DUE TO HORIZONTAL LOADING APPLIED TO SURFACE OF THE HALF-SPACE

In design of hydraulic and other structures which are subject to large horizontal forces it is necessary to determine stresses within the soil mass induced by this type of loading; the knowledge of the component of vertical stress and of the sum of normal stresses (the first stress invariant I_1) is usually sufficient.

In the case of application of a horizontal point load (Figure 1.24) at the surface of a soil half-space the vertical stress component is given by

$$\sigma_z = \frac{3P}{2R^2} \cos \psi \sin \beta \cos^2 \beta = \frac{3P}{2\pi R^5} xz^2 \tag{1.25}$$

and the sum of the normal stress components by

$$I_1 = \frac{(1 + \nu)P}{R^2} \cos \psi \sin \beta = \frac{(1 + \nu)Px}{R^3} \tag{1.26}$$

where $R^2 = x^2 + y^2 + z^2$

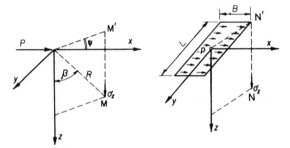

Figure 1.24. Schematic diagram of horizontal loading of a half-space.

If the force P is applied at a point on the surface $(z = 0)$ having coordinates ξ and η, then in order to be able to use the above expressions it is necessary to substitute $(x - \xi)$ for x and $(y - \eta)$ for y.

In the case of the application of continuous uniform loading distributed over a rectangular area the vertical stress component at any point beneath the loaded area is given by the following expression:

$$\sigma_z = \frac{3pz^2}{2\pi} \int_{-B/2}^{+B/2} \int_{-L/2}^{+L/2} \frac{(x - \xi)\,d\xi\,d\eta}{\{(x - \xi)^2 + (y - \eta)^2 + z^2\}^{5/2}} \tag{1.27}$$

and the sum of the normal stresses

$$I_1 = \frac{(1 + \nu)p}{\pi} \int_{-B/2}^{+B/2} \int_{-L/2}^{+L/2} \frac{(x - \xi)\,d\xi\,d\eta}{\{(x - \xi)^2 + (y - \eta)^2 + z^2\}^{3/2}} \tag{1.28}$$

Under the corner points, i.e. for $x = \pm L/2$ and $y = \pm B/2$, the following expressions are obtained:

$$\sigma_{zc} = \mp \frac{p}{2\pi} \left\{ \frac{n}{\sqrt{(m^2 + n^2)}} - \frac{nm^2}{(1 + m)\sqrt{(1 + m^2 + n^2)}} \right\} = \mp p \cdot \eta_{hz} \tag{1.29}$$

$$I_1 = \mp \frac{(1 + \nu)}{\pi} p \left[\ln \frac{\sqrt{(1 + m^2)}}{m} \times \frac{n + \sqrt{(m^2 + n^2)}}{n + \sqrt{(1 + m^2 + n^2)}} \right] = \mp (1 + \nu) p \cdot \eta_{hI}$$

$$(1.30)$$

where $n = L/B$ and $m = z/B$

The sign before each expression is governed by the x coordinate; for $x < 0$ the expression assumes a negative value, while for $x > 0$ it is positive.

Values of η_{hz} and η_{hI} are given in Tables 1.4 and 1.5.

Table 1.4. Coefficients η_{hz}

$m = \dfrac{z}{B}$	Ratio of sides $n = L : B$						
	0·2	0·4	0·6	1·0	2·0	3·0	10·0
	Coefficient η_{hz}						
0·0	0·1592	0·1592	0·1592	0·1592	0·1592	0·1592	0·1592
0·2	0·1114	0·1401	0·1479	0·1518	0·1529	0·1530	0·1530
0·4	0·0672	0·1049	0·1211	0·1328	0·1361	0·1371	0·1372
0·6	0·0432	0·0746	0·0933	0·1091	0·1160	0·1168	0·1170
0·8	0·0290	0·0527	0·0691	0·0861	0·0955	0·0967	0·0970
1·0	0·0201	0·0375	0·0508	0·0666	0·0774	0·0790	0·0796
2·0	0·0045	0·0088	0·0127	0·0192	0·0277	0·0303	0·0318
5·0	0·0004	0·0007	0·0011	0·0018	0·0032	0·0043	0·0060
10·0	0·00005	0·0001	0·0001	0·0002	0·0005	0·0007	0·0014

Table 1.5. Coefficients η_{hI}

$m = \dfrac{z}{B}$	Ratio of sides $n = L : B$						
	0·2	0·4	0·6	1·0	2·0	3·0	10·0
	Coefficient η_{hI}						
0·0	∞	∞	∞	∞	∞	∞	∞
0·2	0·2185	0·3377	0·4010	0·4599	0·5004	0·5101	0·5177
0·4	0·0944	0·1649	0·2111	0·2602	0·2975	0·3069	0·3145
0·6	0·0499	0·0918	0·1233	0·1613	0·1943	0·2033	0·2107
0·8	0·0293	0·0553	0·0765	0·1050	0·1333	0·1417	0·1490
1·0	0·0184	0·0353	0·0498	0·0710	0·0947	0·1024	0·1095
2·0	0·0033	0·0066	0·0097	0·0152	0·0244	0·0290	0·0347
5·0	0·0002	0·0005	0·0007	0·0012	0·0023	0·0032	0·0056
10·0	0·00005	0·0001	0·0001	0·0002	0·0003	0·0005	0·0011

1.3.9. APPROXIMATE DISTRIBUTION OF STRESSES IN A SOIL MASS DUE TO DISTRIBUTED LOADING

In the case of less important structures founded on compressible soils vertical stresses can be computed on the assumption that their distribution takes place at an angle of $27°$ to the vertical, i.e. at $2 : 1$ inclination (Figure 1.25); for sands and for soils of low compressibility the distribution of stresses can be assumed to take place at an angle of $45°$.

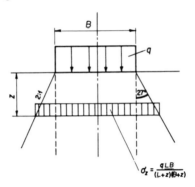

$$\sigma_z = \frac{qLB}{(L+z)(B+z)}$$

Figure 1.25. Approximate distribution of vertical stresses at an angle of $27°$.

1.4. Determination of Stress Increments Under Foundations

For most practical purposes the determination of stress increments beneath foundations and pavements is carried out using the method of centre points and on the assumption that at all depths the vertical stress increments are uniformly distributed and are equal to the stress increments beneath the centre of the foundation.

This is a conservative assumption which gives a certain margin of safety. In determining the settlement of different points of the same structure the method of corner points is used.

In structural foundations the loading is not applied to the ground surface but to the bottom of the excavation. In such cases the unloading of the soil due to removal of the excavated material should be considered. The effects of the unloading are computed in the same manner as those due to applied loading by changing the sign of the loading to negative and by assuming that it is acting in the plane of the bottom of the excavation.

In the case of an isolated footing, which has the same plan dimensions as the excavation, the changes in stresses within the soil follow the progress of the construction.

(a) Before commencement of excavation only the overburden stresses exist in the soil and their values σ'_{oz} vary with depth as indicated in Figure 1.26(a) by the hatched area between lines $ABCD$ and $AB_1C_1D_1$.

(b) On completion of the excavation a load equal to the weight of the excavated material has been removed and hence the stresses in the soil have been reduced by amounts $\Delta\sigma_{oz} = \eta\sigma_{oD}$ to their minimum values $\sigma_{oz\,min}$ as indicated in Figure 1.26(b) between lines BCD and BC_2D_2.

(c) After the foundation has been constructed and backfilled to the original ground level, the stresses in the soil are approximately returned to their initial overburden values; the increases of stress from the minimum value $\sigma_{oz\,min}$ to the overburden value σ'_{oz} are known as *reloading stress increments* $\Delta\sigma_{rz}$ and are shown between lines BC_2D_2 and $B_1C_1D_1$ in Figure 1.26(c).

(d) On completion of the structure and on application of the live load the stresses in the soil reach their maximum values σ_z as shown in Figure 1.26(d) between lines BCD and $B_3C_3D_3$; the increases in the stresses from σ'_{oz} to σ_z

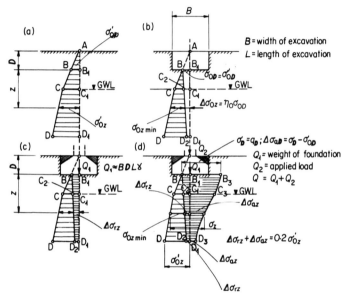

Figure 1.26. Stress distribution; (a) effective overburden stresses; (b) minimum overburden stresses; (c) reloading to initial conditions; (d) additional applied and final stresses.

are referred to as *additional applied stresses* increments and are shown in Figure 1.26(d), as $\Delta\sigma_{az}$ between lines $B_1C_1D_1$ and $B_3C_3D_3$; the final stresses in the soil are computed from equation $\sigma_z = \sigma'_{oz} + \eta\Delta\sigma_{aD}$ and the additional applied stresses from equation $\Delta\sigma_{az} = \eta(\sigma_D - \sigma_{oD}) = \eta\Delta\sigma_{aD}$.

Example. A rectangular pier foundation, 10 m x 6 m in plan is founded at a depth of 2·5 m in a sandy soil of density $\rho = 1800$ kg/m³. The average bearing stress due to combined dead and live loading is $q = 200$ kN/m² (Figure 1.27). It is required to determine stresses at a depth of 3 m below the foundation level, i.e.

$$\sigma'_{oz}\,\sigma_{oz\,min},\ \Delta\sigma_{rz},\ \Delta\sigma_{az},\ \text{and}\ \sigma_z\ \text{for}\ z = 3\cdot0\ \text{m}$$

Overburden stresses:

at depth $D = 2 \cdot 5$ m:

$$\sigma'_{oD} = (\rho g)D = \frac{1800}{1000} \times 9 \cdot 81 \times 2 \cdot 5 = 44 \cdot 1 \text{ kN/m}^2$$

at depth $D + z = 5 \cdot 5$ m:

$$\sigma'_{oz} = 44 \cdot 1 + \frac{1800}{1000} \times 9 \cdot 81 \times 3 = 97 \cdot 1 \text{ kN/m}^2$$

The decrease in stress due to removal of the excavated material at $D = 2 \cdot 5$ m is $\sigma'_{oD} = 44 \cdot 1$ kN/m^2. The decrease in stress $\Delta\sigma_{oz}$ at $z = 3 \cdot 0$ m is (value of η_0 is obtained as shown in Figure 1.27)

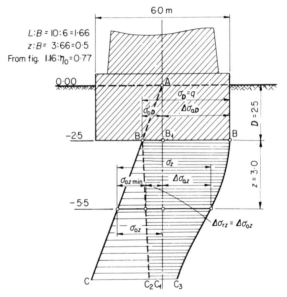

Figure 1.27. Stresses beneath a pier foundation.

$$\Delta\sigma_{oz} = \eta\sigma'_{oD} = 0 \cdot 77 \times 44 \cdot 1 = 34 \cdot 0 \text{ kN/m}^2$$

The minimal value of stress at $D + z = 5 \cdot 5$ m (after excavation) is

$$\sigma_{oz \text{ min}} = \sigma'_{oz} - \Delta\sigma_{oz} = 97 \cdot 1 - 34 \cdot 0 = 63 \cdot 1 \text{ kN/m}^2$$

The increase of stress at that depth due to the applied bearing stress is

$$\Delta\sigma_z = \eta_0 \times q = 0 \cdot 77 \times 200 = 154 \cdot 0 \text{ kN/m}^2$$

Final stress:

$$\sigma_z = \sigma_{oz \text{ min}} + \Delta\sigma_z = 63 \cdot 1 + 154 \cdot 0 = 217 \cdot 1 \text{ kN/m}^2$$

Additional applied stress increment:

$$\Delta\sigma_{az} = \sigma_z - \sigma'_{oz} = 217 \cdot 1 - 97 \cdot 1 = 120 \cdot 0 \text{ kN/m}^2$$

Reloading stress increment:

$$\Delta\sigma_{rz} = \Delta\sigma_{oz} = 34 \cdot 0 \text{ kN/m}^2$$

Check:

$$\sigma_z = \sigma_{oz\ min} + \Delta\sigma_{rz} + \Delta\sigma_{az} = 63 \cdot 1 + 34 \cdot 0 + 120 = 217 \cdot 1 \text{ kN/m}^2$$

1.5. Significantly Stressed Zone

For practical purposes the stresses beneath foundations need only to be considered to a depth at which the sum of the reloading stress increment and the additional applied stress increment due to the foundation loading is equal to 20% of the overburden stress:

$$\Delta\sigma_{rz} + \Delta\sigma_{az} = 0 \cdot 2\sigma'_{oz} \tag{1.31}$$

It can be assumed that the influence of the applied foundation loading on the deformation of the soil ends there; the stressed zone of the soil between that depth and the foundation level is referred to as the *significantly stressed zone*.

2

Deformation and Bearing Capacity of Soils

2.1. Deformation of Soils

The deformation of the soil is the main criterion in the design of structural foundations and road pavements. Small deformations of the soil do not even produce hair cracks in buildings or pavements, whereas large and particularly uneven (differential) deformations usually result in considerable damage to them.

The increase in the deformation of the soil can best be illustrated on a simple case of loading of an isolated footing (Figure 2.1).

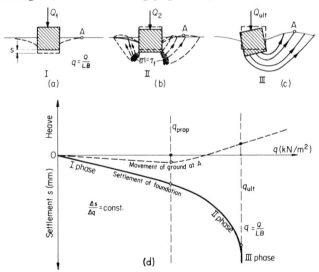

Figure 2.1. Settlement of foundation and deformation of soil with increasing loading: (a) phase I, settlement proportional to stress; (b) phase II, local yielding of soil under edges of the foundation; (c) phase III, displacement of soil from underneath the foundation with increasing loading; (d) load–settlement curve.

28

The loading on an isolated footing, founded below the ground level, is gradually increased. At the same time its settlement and the vertical displacement of the point A on the ground surface are observed. In phase I of the loading (Figure 2.1(a)) the settlements of the foundation and of the ground surface at A are approximately proportional to the increase in the loading. In phase II, a more rapid increase in the settlement of the foundation is observed, while at the same time the ground surface at A begins to rise. When the loading approaches the ultimate value q_{ult} the foundation settles rapidly and displacement (plastic flow) of the soil from underneath takes place, usually leading to its tilting (Figure 2.1(c)).

The settlement in phase I is due to the compressibility of the soil; in phase II there is an increasing influence of the zones of the soil in the state of limiting equilibrium below the edges of the foundation; the settlement and tilting of the foundation in phase III is almost entirely due to the displacement or plastic flow of the soil from underneath it.

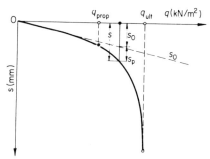

Figure 2.2. Settlement of foundation due to compressibility and plastic flow of the soil: s_0, settlement due to compressibility of soil; s_p, settlement due to plastic flow or displacement of soil from underneath the foundation; s, total settlement; $s = s_0 + s_p$.

Generalizing the problem of the deformation of the soil underneath a foundation it can be said that it results from two basic causes: (a) the settlement proper (due to the compressibility of the soil); (b) the displacement of the soil from underneath the foundation.

The proportions of the two effects in the total deformation of the soil depends on the intensity of the applied loading and can be illustrated as shown in Figure 2.2.

The deformation of the soil due to its compressibility can be taken as proportional to the loading, whereas the deformations due to the displacement increases exponentially as the loading intensity approaches the ultimate value.

The following conclusion can be drawn from the above considerations: the allowable intensity of loading at the foundation level should not exceed the limit of proportionality (q_{prop}), which is usually between a third and a half of the value of the ultimate loading. This will ensure that there is no deleterious displacement of the soil from underneath building foundations or road pavements:

$$q_{safe} \leqslant \frac{q_{ult}}{F} \tag{2.1}$$

where F = load factor or factor of safety, generally between 2 and 3

Additionally two conclusions can be drawn from the consideration of the uniform settlement of the structure as a whole and of its individual foundations.

(a) Structures or pavements which are not sensitive to differential movements can tolerate large total settlements and large differences between settlements of individual points within them.

(b) On the other hand, structures or pavements which are sensitive to differential movements should have their total settlements limited, because the greater they are, the greater can be the differences between settlements of individual points within them.

It follows from the above that the total settlement s_{max} of a given structure or pavement should not exceed the total allowable settlement s_{all} for the given type of construction:

$$s_{max} \leqslant s_{all} \tag{2.2}$$

while the differential settlement between individual points of distance l apart within it, expressed in terms of angular distortion α, should not exceed the allowable angular distortion α_{all} for the given type of construction (Figure 2.3):

$$\alpha_{max} = \left| \frac{s_1 - s_2}{l_1} - \frac{s_2 - s_3}{l_2} \right| \leqslant \alpha_{all} \tag{2.3}$$

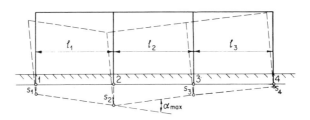

Figure 2.3. Maximum and differential settlement of foundation bases: (i) maximum angular distortion occurs between bays 1–2 and 2–3 at base 2; (ii) maximum settlement occurs at base 2.

2.2. Bearing Capacity Failure

In the case of a perfectly rigid foundation, which is quite common in practice, very high stresses are induced below the edges (in a narrow zone along its perimeter) even under relatively small loading. This leads to the formation of localized plastic zones under the edges and to a certain amount of displacement of the soil from underneath them, until the high stresses decrease to the critical value. In the initial stages of the loading (Figure 2.4(a)) the effects of the plastic flow are, however, so small that they have practically no influence on the settlement of the foundation which can be considered to take place almost entirely due to the compressibility of the soil.

When the average applied loading reaches the critical value the extent of the plastic zones is considerably increased, but they are still situated outside the foundation (Figure 2.4(b)).

As the loading increases above the critical value the plastic zones, not only increase in size, but begin to extend below the foundation (Figure 2.4(c)), which undoubtedly leads to a more intensive displacement of the soil from underneath it.

The greater the extent of the plastic zones under the foundation the greater is its settlement.

When the average applied loading reaches the ultimate value (Figure 2.4(d)) the plastic zones merge and there is a continuous displacement or plastic flow of the soil from underneath the foundation. This is accompanied by large settlement and usually tilting of the foundation.

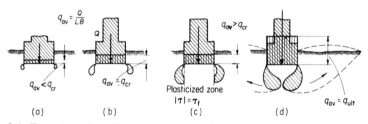

Figure 2.4. Formation of plastic zones below the edges of a rigid footing.

2.3. Determination of Critical Loading

The critical loading is defined as the loading under which the soil beneath the edges of the loaded area begins to yield, i.e. under which the local plastic zones begin to form. The soil within the plastic zones is in the state of limiting or plastic equilibrium and is not capable of offering any resistance to the increasing shear stresses, i.e. in terms of the mechanical properties it behaves like a viscous fluid.

The limiting equilibrium is considered to exist at a given point within the soil when on any plane through that point the shear and the normal stress components satisfy Coulomb's failure criterion (Volume 1, Section 5.4.7):

$$|\tau| = \sigma_n \tan \phi + c \qquad (2.4)$$

where τ = shear stress component within the plane

σ_n = direct stress component normal to the plane (normal stress)

ϕ = angle of internal shearing resistance

c = cohesion

The conditions necessary for the existence of the state of plastic equilibrium at a point within the soil can also be expressed in terms of the principal stresses:

$$(\sigma_1 + \sigma_3) \sin \phi = (\sigma_1 - \sigma_3) - 2c \cos \phi \qquad (2.5)$$

Equation (2.5) is referred to as the Coulomb—Mohr failure or yield criterion; it is independent of the intermediate principal stress $\sigma_2 (\sigma_1 > \sigma_2 > \sigma_3)$.

The principal stresses σ_1 and σ_3 are computed from the consideration of the overburden stresses and the stresses induced by the applied uniformly distributed loading q acting at the foundation level AB (Figure 2.5).

Using the Coulomb—Mohr failure criterion and the assumption that the critical loading is the maximum possible loading which does not induce yielding at any point within the soil an expression for the intensity of the critical loading can be derived (Maag, 1938):

$$q_{cr} = \frac{\pi(\gamma_0 D + c \cot \phi)}{\cot \phi + (\phi - \pi/2)} + \gamma_0 D \qquad (2.6)$$

where γ_0 = unit weight of the soil above foundation level in kN/m^3

D = depth of foundation in m

c = cohesive resistance of soil below foundation level in kN/m^2

ϕ = angle of internal shearing resistance of soil below foundation in radians

Equation (2.6) can be rewritten in a different form:

$$q_{cr} = cM_c + \gamma_0 D M_q \qquad (2.7)$$

where

$$M_c = \cot \phi \left\{ \frac{\cot \phi + (\phi - \pi/2)}{\cot \phi + \phi - \pi/2} - 1 \right\}$$

and

$$M_q = \frac{\cot \phi + (\phi + \pi/2)}{\cot \phi + (\phi - \pi/2)}$$

The coefficients M_c and M_q are dependent only on the angle of internal shearing resistance ϕ of the soil; their values are given in Table 2.1.

Maslov (1950) has suggested that for the state of stress as shown in Figure 2.4(c) a third term should be included in Equation (2.7) to allow for the effects of the width of the foundation and the weight of the soil below it:

$$q_{cr} = cM_c + \gamma_0 D M_q + \gamma_1 B M_\gamma \qquad (2.8)$$

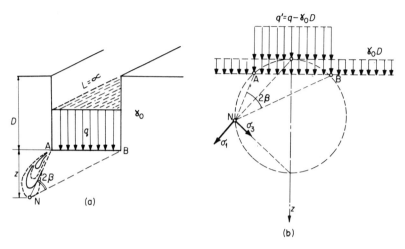

Figure 2.5. Determination of critical loading: (a) section through foundation trench; (b) schematic diagram of loading at the foundation level and of the principal stresses σ_1 and σ_3 at point N.

Table 2.1. Coefficients M_c, M_q, and M_γ

ϕ (deg)	$\tan \phi$	M_c	M_q	M_γ
0	0	3·14	1·00	0·00
10	0·176	4·15	1·73	0·13
15	0·268	4·85	2·30	0·35
20	0·365	5·65	3·06	0·75
25	0·470	6·60	4·11	1·46
30	0·580	7·95	5·59	2·65
35	0·700	9·60	7·71	4·70
40	0·840	11·70	10·85	8·30
45	1·000	14·60	15·68	14·60

where γ_1 = unit weight of the soil below the foundation level
M_c, M_q, and M_γ = coefficients dependent on ϕ of the soil below the foundation level, given in Table 2.1

$$M_\gamma = \tan \phi \left\{ \frac{\cot \phi + (\phi + \pi/2)}{\cot \phi + (\phi - \pi/2)} - 1 \right\} \qquad (2.9)$$

It is suggested that the critical loading can be taken as the allowable bearing capacity of the soil.

Example. Determine the critical loading for a strip footing using Equation (2.8) and coefficients from Table 2.1.

$$D = 0\cdot5 \text{ m}; \quad B = 2\cdot5 \text{ m}$$

For slightly cohesive clayey sand $\rho_0 = 2.0 \ t/m^3$;

$$\phi' = 20°; \quad c = 15 \ kN/m^2$$

$$\gamma_0 = g\rho_0 = \gamma_1 = 9.81 \times 2.0 = 19.6 \ kN/m^3$$

From Table 2.1

$$M_c = 5.65; \quad M_q = 3.06; \quad M_\gamma = 0.75$$

$$q_{cr} = 15 \times 5.65 + 19.6 \times 0.5 \times 3.06 + 19.6 \times 2.5 \times 0.75$$

$$= 157.4 \ kN/m^2 \approx 157 \ kN/m^2$$

2.4. Determination of Ultimate Loading

2.4.1. GENERAL CONSIDERATIONS

As the applied loading approaches the ultimate value the local plastic zones merge below the foundation to form a large single zone within which the soil is fully plastic, i.e. is in the state of plastic equilibrium. In other words, the foundation is now resting on a soil which can undergo large plastic deformations under even the slightest increase in the loading.

If the deformations of the soil prior to reaching the state of plastic equilibrium are ignored, i.e. if the soil is treated as a rigid plastic material then the theory of perfect plasticity, based on the Coulomb–Mohr failure criterion, can be used to determine the intensity of loading necessary to maintain this state of equilibrium within the soil. From our point of view this loading will be equivalent to the ultimate loading or the ultimate bearing capacity of the soil.

In one way or another all the existing solutions to the bearing capacity problems (and other problems such as stability of slopes or active and passive pressures on retaining walls) are based on the above approach.

The rigorous solution to the bearing capacity and other soil stability problems was presented by Sokolovsky (1960). In the plane strain case (two-dimensional problems) and, given boundary conditions, it reduces to the solution of hyperbolic partial differential equations which are derived from the conditions of static equilibrium and the Coulomb–Mohr failure criterion as given below:

$$\left.\begin{array}{c} \dfrac{\partial \sigma_x}{\partial x} + \dfrac{\partial \tau_{xz}}{\partial z} = 0 \\[2mm] \dfrac{\partial \sigma_z}{\partial z} + \dfrac{\partial \tau_{xz}}{\partial x} = \gamma \\[2mm] (\sigma_z - \sigma_x)^2 + 4\tau_{xz}^2 = (\sigma_x + \sigma_z + 2c \cot \phi)^2 \sin^2 \phi \end{array}\right\} \quad (2.10)$$

According to the theory of plasticity of soils, originally developed by Drucker and Prager (1952), all the other solutions of limiting stability problems can be classified as special cases of lower or upper bounds to the solution. For example, Terzaghi's method of determination of the bearing capacity is a special case of an upper bound solution to this problem whereas Bell's (1915) method is a special case of a lower bound solution.

The two *plastic limit theorems* applicable to any body or assemblage of bodies of perfectly plastic materials are as follows.

Theorem 1 (lower bound). If an equilibrium distribution of stress can be found which balances the applied load and nowhere violates the yield criterion which includes c and ϕ, the soil mass will not fail or will be just at the point of failure.

Theorem 2 (upper bound). The soil mass will collapse if there is any compatible pattern of plastic deformations for which the rate of work of the external loads exceeds the rate of internal energy dissipation.

In most of the present-day engineering solutions of the soil stability problems an indirect application of the upper bound theorem is made. A plausible collapse mechanism is chosen and assuming that the shear strength of the soil is developed along the discontinuities (slip surfaces) the equilibrium of the external and internal forces is considered. The reliability of these solutions have been confirmed by observation of the slip surfaces in simple model tests and in actual failure cases but it can also be checked theoretically by comparing them with lower bound or rigorous solutions.

2.4.2. PRACTICAL METHODS OF DETERMINATION OF ULTIMATE LOADING

Practical experience and model tests have shown that none of the existing methods of determination of the ultimate loading give reliable results over the complete range of the types of soil and depths and shapes of foundations. The methods presented below have been selected on the basis that they cover most of the practical cases and are simple in application.

2.4.2.1. General Case of Shallow Foundations

A foundation is considered to be shallow when the depth at which it is founded is less than its width $(D \leqslant B)$. In these circumstances the contribution of the shear strength of the soil above the foundation level can be neglected (Figure 2.6).

Prandtl and Sokolovsky have obtained identical solutions to the bearing capacity problem of a shallow strip footing, founded at a depth D below the ground level, by neglecting the effects of the self-weight of the soil below the foundation level:

$$q_{\text{ult}} = c \cot \phi \left\{ \tan^2\left(45 + \frac{\phi}{2}\right) e^{\pi \tan \phi} - 1 \right\} + \gamma_0 D \tan^2\left(45 + \frac{\phi}{2}\right) e^{\pi \tan \phi} \tag{2.11}$$

The effects of the self-weight of the soil are included in Prandtl–Caquot–Kérisel's (Caquot and Kérisel, 1949) approximate solution:

$$q_{ult} = c \cot \phi \left\{ \tan^2 \left(45 + \frac{\phi}{2} \right) e^{\pi \tan \phi} - 1 \right\} + \gamma_0 D \tan^2 \left(45 + \frac{\phi}{2} \right) e^{\pi \tan \phi}$$

$$+ \frac{\gamma_1 B}{4} \tan^2 \left(45 + \frac{\phi}{2} \right) e^{(3\pi/2) \tan \phi} \tag{2.12}$$

where B = width of strip footing in m

γ_0 = unit weight of soil above foundation level in kN/m^3

γ_1 = unit weight of soil below foundation level in kN/m^3

c, ϕ = strength parameters of the soil below foundation level in kN/m^2
and degrees respectively

In both the above solutions the base of the foundation has been assumed to be perfectly smooth.

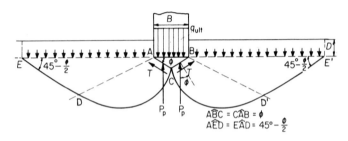

Figure 2.6. Schematic representation of external and internal forces in the soil at ultimate loading of rough strip foundation.

The most commonly used solution is that developed by Terzaghi (1943). It was originally developed for shallow strip footings but, on the basis of experimental and field evidence, it has subsequently been modified to cover rectangular, square, and circular footings. Terzaghi has assumed (Figure 2.6) that the wedge ABC of the soil situated below a rough strip foundation is in the state of limiting equilibrium and that the forces acting on it are as follows.

    (1) From the top and within.

        (a) Foundation load $Q = q_{ult} \times B$.

        (b) Weight of the wedge ABC of soil.

    (2) From underneath.

        (a) Passive resistance P_p of soil within areas ACDE and BCD'E'.

        (b) Cohesive resistance T along planes AC and BC:

$$Q_{ult} + \gamma_1 \frac{B^2}{4} \tan \phi - 2P_p - cB \tan \phi = 0$$

On evaluation of the passive resistance P_p Terzaghi obtained an expression for the ultimate bearing capacity of a strip footing of any width B. A more general expression is obtained by introduction of correction terms suggested by

Schultze which extend the range of applicability of the Terzaghi's bearing capacity equation to rectangular foundations of any sides ratio $B : L$:

$$q_{ult} = \left(1 + 0.3\frac{B}{L}\right)cN_c + \gamma_0 DN_q + \left(1 - 0.2\frac{B}{L}\right)\frac{\gamma_1 B}{2}N_\gamma \qquad (2.13)$$

where γ_0 and γ_1 = as defined in Equation (2.12)
$\quad\quad B$ = width of foundation in m
$\quad\quad L$ = length of foundation in m
N_c, N_q, and N_γ = bearing capacity coefficients dependent on the angle of internal shearing resistance of the soil below foundation level, given in Table 2.2 (dimensionless)

In the case of a circular footing of radius R

$$q_{ult} = 1.3cN_c + \gamma_0 DN_q + 0.6\gamma_1 RN_\gamma \qquad (2.14)$$

The first term on the right-hand side of Equation (2.13) represents the contribution of the cohesive resistance c to the bearing capacity, the second the contribution of the surcharge $\gamma_0 D$, and the third the contribution of the self-weight γ_1 of the soil below the foundation level. The angle of internal shearing resistance ϕ governs the size of the wedge ABC and areas ACDE and BCD'E' and therefore influences all three terms through the presence of the bearing capacity factors N_c, N_q, and N_γ.

Table 2.2. Terzaghi's bearing capacity factors N_c, N_q, and N_γ (rough foundation)

ϕ	N_c	N_q	N_γ
0	5.7	1.0	0.0
5	7.0	1.6	0.14
10	9.5	2.7	0.7
15	13.0	4.5	2.0
20	17.0	7.5	4.8
25	24.0	13.0	9.8
30	37.0	23.0	20.0
35	58.0	42.0	43.0
40	98.0	77.0	98.0

The soil strength parameters c and ϕ used in Equation (2.13) must be obtained from tests which, as closely as possible, correspond to the *in situ* stressing and drainage conditions of the soil. For free draining cohesionless soils the drained strength parameters c_d and ϕ_d are used. For highly imperme-able soils the bearing capacity for undrained loading is generally less than for drained loading and therefore in the case of cohesive soils the undrained strength parameters c_u and ϕ_u are used. In the first case the strength parameters are obtained in terms of effective stresses and therefore effective stresses must be used in the evaluation of the bearing capacities. In the second case the total stresses are used throughout.

The application of the theory of plasticity to the stability problems is really limited to the soils whose behaviour approaches that of the idealized rigid plastic materials as in the case of overconsolidated clays and dense sands. It is, however, convenient when dealing with soft normally consolidated soils to introduce empirical corrections to their strength parameters so that the use of the existing solutions can be extended to these soils.

According to Terzaghi the cohesion and angle of internal friction for soft soils can be modified as follows:

$$c_1 = \tfrac{2}{3} c$$

and   (2.15)

$$\tan \phi_1 = \tfrac{2}{3} \tan \phi$$

For small values of angle ϕ it can be assumed that $\phi_1 = \tfrac{2}{3}\phi$. The bearing capacity factors N_c, N_q, and N_γ are taken from Table 2.2 for the new value of ϕ_1.

Example. Determine the ultimate loading of a strip footing using Terzaghi's equation and soil properties as in example in Section 2.3:

$$D = 0.5 \text{ m}; \quad B = 2.5 \text{ m}$$
$$\gamma_0 = \gamma_1 = 19.6 \text{ kN/m}^3; \quad c = 15 \text{ kN/m}^2; \quad \phi = 20°$$

From Table 2.2,

$$N_c = 17.0; \quad N_q = 7.5; \quad N_\gamma = 4.8$$
$$q_{ult} = 15 \times 17.0 + 19.6 \times 0.5 \times 7.5 + 19.6 \times 2.5 \times 4.8 = 449 \text{ kN/m}^2$$

The net bearing capacity of the soils is

$$q'_{ult} = q_{ult} - \gamma_0 D = 44.9 - 9.8 \approx 440 \text{ kN/m}^2$$

The solution developed for shallow foundations ($D \leqslant B$) are generally used for determination of the ultimate loading of foundations of intermediate depths ($B < D \leqslant 2.5 B$), which cannot be classed as either shallow or deep. Meyerhof (1950) has shown that, as the depth of the foundation increases, the shear strength of the soil above the base level begins to contribute significantly to the total bearing capacity of the soil. Therefore, by adopting solutions which neglect this effect the bearing capacity of the soil is generally underestimated. One exception to this is when the foundations are on dense and very dense sands and gravels which in any case are subject to settlement limitations and not ultimate loading.

Example. Using Terzaghi's solution (Equation (2.13)) determine the ultimate loading of a square footing shown in Figure 2.7 founded in a soft normally consolidated soil of $\gamma_0 = \gamma_1 = 19.8 \text{ kN/m}^3$.

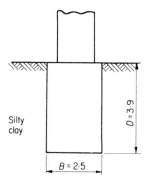

Figure 2.7. Foundation details.

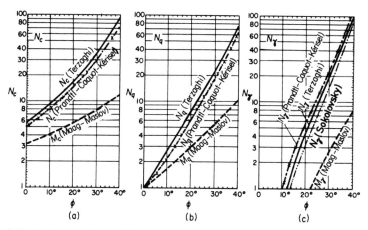

Figure 2.8. Bearing capacity coefficients M and N: (a) coefficients M_c and N_c; (b) M_q and N_q; (c) M_γ and N_γ.

The following strength parameters were obtained from direct shear box tests:

$$c' = 9 \text{ kN/m}^2 \text{ and } \phi' = 20°$$

For normally consolidated soils Equations (2.15) is used to determine the modified strength parameters:

$$c_1 = \frac{2}{3} 9 = 6 \text{ kN/m}^2; \quad \phi_1 = \frac{2}{3} 20 = 13°20'$$

Bearing capacity factors are taken from Table 2.2 for $\phi = 13°20'$:

$$N_c = 11·8, \quad N_q = 3·8, \quad \text{and} \quad N_\gamma = 1·5$$

The ultimate loading is obtained from Equation (2.13):

$$q_{ult} = 1 \cdot 3 \times 6 \times 11 \cdot 8 + 19 \cdot 8 \times 3 \cdot 9 \times 3 \cdot 8 + 0 \cdot 8 \times \frac{19 \cdot 8 \times 2 \cdot 5}{2} \times 1 \cdot 5$$

$$= 403 \ kN/m^2$$

The net bearing capacity of the soil is

$$q'_{ult} = q_{ult} - \gamma_0 D = 403 - 77 = 326 \ kN/m^2$$

Reducing Sokolovsky's, Prandtl's, and other solutions to the form of Equation (2.13) corresponding bearing capacity factors N_c, N_q, and N_γ can be obtained; these are plotted in Figure 2.8.

British Standard Code of Practice CP 2004 recognizes Terzaghi's solution as the most practical for the $c - \phi$ soils. In the case of $\phi = 0$ soils (undrained condition) the use of Skempton's semi-empirical method is considered as more appropriate.

2.4.2.2. General Case of Foundations in $\phi = 0$ Soils

In the case of sudden applications of loading to foundations on saturated clay soils (e.g. rapid filling of grain silos or oil storage tanks) the soil is behaving in an undrained manner and ϕ (i.e. ϕ_u) can be taken as equal to zero. Under these circumstances the bearing capacity for the undrained loading may be the governing design criterion.

A semi-empirical solution of the above problem, which makes allowance for the shear strength of the soil above the foundation level, has been presented by Skempton (1951):

$$q_{ult} = cN_c + \gamma_0 D \tag{2.16}$$

The values of N_c are partly based on laboratory tests, on theory, and on observation of full-scale failures and can be obtained from the following equation:

$$N_c = 5\left(1 + 0 \cdot 2 \frac{B}{L}\right)\left(1 + 0 \cdot 2 \frac{D}{B}\right) \tag{2.17}$$

where the maximum value of D/B is taken as $2 \cdot 5$. It should be noted that the maximum value which N_c can have, for a square or circular footing at a depth which is great compared with its width, is 9.

Example. Determine the ultimate loading of a rectangular footing assuming $\phi_u = 0$ condition.

$$B = 1 \cdot 5 \ m; \quad L = 3 \cdot 0 \ m; \quad D = 4 \cdot 5 \ m$$
$$c_u = 30 \ kN/m^2 \ and \ \phi_u = 0; \quad \gamma_0 = 19 \cdot 8 \ kN/m^3$$

Since $D/B = 3$ the maximum value of 2·5 is taken. Using Equation (2.17)

$$N_c = 5(1 + 0\cdot2 \times 0\cdot5)(1 + 0\cdot2 \times 2\cdot5) = 8\cdot25$$

Substituting into Equation (2.16) the ultimate loading is

$$q_{ult} = 30 \times 8\cdot25 + 19\cdot8 \times 4\cdot5 = 336 \text{ kN/m}^2$$

For comparison, Terzaghi's method gives

$$q_{ult} = (1 + 0\cdot3 \times 0\cdot5)\,30 \times 5\cdot7 + 19\cdot8 \times 4\cdot5 = 286 \text{ kN/m}^2$$

2.5. Ultimate Bearing Capacity of Stratified Deposits

In practice one frequently encounters stratified deposits. The most common case is that of a weak stratum, immediately below the foundation, overlying stiffer and stronger strata at greater depths. Sometimes, however, reverse conditions are encountered.

In the case of the weaker stratum being immediately below the foundation (Figure 2.9(a)) a simplifying assumption is made that the entire soil below the foundation consists of the weaker material and then the bearing capacity is determined in the usual manner. This results in a certain additional margin of safety.

Skempton recommends, in the case of the $\phi = 0$ analysis, that, if the shear strength for a depth of $0\cdot67B$ beneath the foundation does not depart from the average by more than ± 50%, then that average may be used in the calculations.

In the case in which the weaker soil is not immediately beneath the foundation, but deeper (Figure 2.9(b)), then the bearing capacity at the foundation level is computed from Equation (2.18) which is based on Equation (2.13) but takes account of the distribution of stresses through the stiffer stratum:

$$q_{1\,ult} = \left\{ \left(1 + 0\cdot3\frac{B}{L}\right)cN_c + (\gamma_0 D + \gamma_1 z)N_q - \gamma_1 z + \left(1 - 0\cdot2\frac{B}{L}\right)\frac{\gamma_2 B}{2}N_\gamma \right\}\frac{1}{n_0} + \gamma_0 D$$

$$(2.18)$$

For soils having $\phi < 5°$ a simplified equation can be used:

$$q_{1\,ult} = \left\{ \left(1 + 0\cdot3\frac{B}{L}\right)cN_c + \gamma_0 D \right\}\frac{1}{n_0} + \gamma_0 D \qquad (2.19)$$

In Equations (2.18) and (2.19)

$$c = \text{cohesive resistance of the weaker soil}$$
$$B \text{ and } L = \text{width and length of the foundation}$$
$$\gamma_0 = \text{unit weight of the soil adjacent to foundation}$$
$$\gamma_1 = \text{unit weight of the stronger soil below foundation}$$
$$D = \text{depth of foundation below ground level}$$

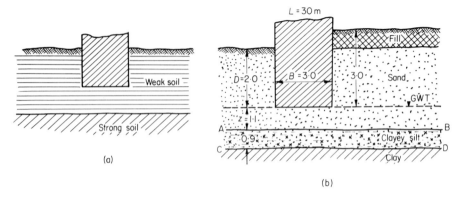

Figure 2.9. Foundations on stratified soils: (a) weak soil immediately below foundations; (b) weak soil at depth z below foundation.

z = vertical distance between the underside of the foundation and the top of the weaker layer

γ_2 = unit weight of the weaker soil below foundation

N_c, N_q, and N_γ = bearing capacity coefficients from Table 2.2 for the weaker soil

η_0 = stress distribution coefficient obtained for L/B and z/B from Figure 1.16

Example. Determine the ultimate loading of the foundation shown in Figure 2.9(b). Because there is a weaker stratum at a depth z below the foundation the bearing capacity will be evaluated from Equation (2.18) or (2.19).

Description of soils
above AB: fine medium dense river sand
below AB: firm clayey silt (alluvium)
below CD: stiff clayey sand (boulder clay)
ground water table: at the foundation level

Physical and mechanical properties of soils
sand: $\rho = 1 \cdot 9$ T/m^3, $\gamma_0 = 18 \cdot 6$ kN/m^3, $\gamma_{sub} = 8 \cdot 8$ kN/m^3, $\phi' = 30°$
silt: $\rho = 1 \cdot 8$ T/m^3, $\gamma_2 = 17 \cdot 7$ kN/m^3, $\gamma_{sub}^* = 7 \cdot 9$ kN/m^3, $c_u = 20$ kN/m^2, $\phi_u = 0°$
boulder clay: $\rho = 2 \cdot 1$ T/m^3, $\gamma = 20 \cdot 6$ kN/m^3, $\gamma_{sub}^* = 10 \cdot 8$ kN/m^3, $c_u = 70$ kN/m^2, $\phi_u = 25°$

Solution
The weakest soil is the clayey silt; because $\phi_u = 0° < 5°$, Equation (2.19) can be

* Because this is an approximate method submerged units weights are taken for all soils below GWL.

used for evaluation of $q_{1\,ult}$. From Table 2.2 for $\phi = 0°$ we obtain $N_c = 5\cdot7$. From Figure 2.9(b), $D = 2\cdot0$ hence $\gamma_0 D = 18\cdot6 \times 2 = 37\cdot2$ kN/m², $z = 1\cdot1$ m; therefore $z : B = 1\cdot1/3\cdot0 = 0\cdot37$; from Figure 1.16 for $L : B = 10$ and $z : B = 0\cdot37$ we obtain $\eta_0 = 0\cdot90$. Substituting in Equation (2.19)

$$q_{1\,ult} = \left\{ (1 + 0\cdot03) \times 20 \times 5\cdot7 + 37\cdot2 \right\} \frac{1}{0\cdot9} + 37\cdot2 \approx 209 \text{ kN/m}^2$$

The ultimate loading of the foundation is therefore taken as $q_{ult} = 210$ kN/m². The net bearing capacity of the soil is

$$q'_{ult} = q_{ult} - \gamma_0 D = 210 - 37 = 173 \text{ kN/m}^2$$

2.6. Ultimate Loading of Foundations Subject to Lateral Loads

If a horizontal load is acting on a foundation (Figure 2.10), then the soil has to resist a combined action of the vertical and horizontal loads; the resultant loading is taken as inclined at an angle δ to the vertical (Figure 2.10).

In such cases the displacement of the soil from underneath the foundation is only counteracted by the passive resistance of the soil within the area $BCD'E'F'$, on which in addition to the vertical load Q_z, a horizontal load Q_x is acting. This obviously considerably decreases the bearing capacity of the soil in relation to that evaluated from Equation (2.13). The bearing capacity depends now on the ratio of the horizontal load Q_x to the vertical Q_z (expressed in terms of angle δ as shown in Figure 2.12) as well as on the cohesion and angle of internal shearing resistance of the soil:

$$q_{ult} = cN'_c + \gamma_0 DN'_q + \frac{\gamma_1 B}{2} N'_\gamma \qquad (2.20)$$

where N'_c, N'_q, and N'_γ = bearing capacity factors from Figure 2.11
other symbols as in Equation (2.13)

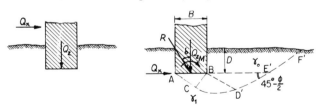

Figure 2.10. Combined vertical and horizontal loading.

Equation (2.20) is directly applicable to strip foundations but its use can be extended to cover rectangular and square foundations by empirical modifications of the bearing capacity factors N'_c and N'_γ as in Equation (2.13); this leads to an increased margin of safety as the $B : L$ ratio approaches $1\cdot0$.

According to Schultze the decrease in the ultimate loading should be considered only in the case when the horizontal loading is acting laterally on a strip

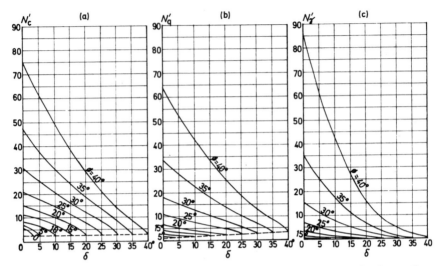

Figure 2.11. Nomogram for determination of bearing capacity coefficients N'_c, N'_q and N'_γ (after Sokolovsky (Harr, 1966)).

foundation; its effects can be neglected when it is acting longitudinally on a strip foundation or on a square footing. In the latter case the ultimate loading should be determined as for a vertically loaded strip foundation which ensures that the passive resistance E_p of the soil within the shaded volume (Figure 2.12(b)) is sufficiently large to compensate for the omission of the horizontal loading.

The ultimate loading evaluated from Equation (2.20) should be treated as an average loading: $q_{ult} = Q_z/B$.

If the horizontal load exceeds 25% of the vertical load, then the stability of the foundation against sliding and overturning must be checked.

British Standard Code of Practice CP 2004 suggests a simple empirical procedure for the design of foundations under non-vertical loads. The inclined load is resolved into vertical and horizontal components and if the following rule is satisfied then the design is considered to be satisfactory:

$$\frac{Q_z}{Q_{z\,all}} + \frac{Q_x}{Q_{x\,all}} < 1 \tag{2.21}$$

where Q_z = vertical component of the inclined load
           Q_x = horizontal component of the inclined load
           $Q_{z\,all}$ = allowable vertical load
           $Q_{x\,all}$ = allowable horizontal load

The allowable vertical load is evaluated according to Equations (2.1) to (2.3); the allowable horizontal load is taken as the allowable passive resistance of the ground in contact with the vertical face of the footing, plus the allowable friction and/or adhesion on the horizontal base of the footing corresponding to the applied vertical component.

In practice the above rule gives results on the safe side, with exception of shallow footing on cohesionless soils (with $D : B < 0.25$), which require a more conservative approach.

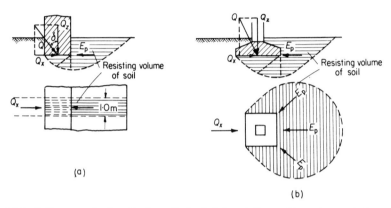

Figure 2.12. Collapse mechanism for laterally loaded foundations: (a) section and plan of a strip footing; (b) section and plan of a square footing.

It is suggested that, if there is a horizontal load acting on a foundation, then, regardless of its magnitude and of the method of design, the stability of the foundation against overturning should be checked.

The British Standard Code of Practice CP 2004 permits the neglect of the effects of wind loading if individual foundation loads due to wind are less than 25% of the loadings due to dead and live loads. Where this ratio exceeds 25%, foundations may be so proportioned that the stress due to combined dead, live, and wind loads does not exceed the allowable bearing stress by more than 25%.

The eccentric or horizontal loading due to any cause other than wind pressure should be fully taken into consideration and the maximum stress should not exceed the allowable bearing stress.

The authors suggest that in the case of free standing structures with high centre of gravity, e.g. chimneys, water towers, etc., the above requirement should also include the wind loading.

2.7. Determination of Allowable Bearing Capacity

The safe bearing capacity of soil beneath a given foundation can be determined from the following equation:

$$q_{safe} = \frac{q'_{ult}}{F} + \gamma_0 D = \frac{q_{ult} - \gamma_0 D}{F} + \gamma_0 D \qquad (2.22)$$

Table 2.3. Presumed bearing values under vertical static loading
(based on British Standard Code of Practice CP 2004 (1971 Draft, Table 1)

Group	Class	Types of rocks and soils	Presumed bearing value tonf/ft²	kN/m² (approx.)	Remarks
I — Rocks	1	hard igneous and gneissic rocks in sound condition	100	10 000	These values are based on the assumption that the foundations are carried down to unweathered rock. *(From 1.223.1 (f)): 'very weakly cemented sandstones which are so friable that they can easily disintegrate between fingers may be found. Frequently beds of stronger sandstone are weathered to this condition near the surface. A presumed bearing value of 10 tonf/ft² (1000 kN/m²) would be appropriate. For important structures, a reliable assessment of the allowable bearing pressure requires loading tests.'
	2	hard limestones and hard sandstones	40	4000	
	3	schists and slates	30	3000	
	4	hard shales, hard mudstones and soft sandstones	20*	2000*	
	5	soft shales and soft mudstones	6–10	600–1000	
	6	hard sound chalk, soft limestone	6	600	
	7	thinly bedded limestones, sandstones, shales	to be assessed after inspection		
	8	heavily shattered rocks			
II — Non-cohesive soils	9	compact gravel, or compact sand and gravel	>6	>600	Classes 9–14: width of foundation (B) not less than 1 m (3 ft); GWL assumed to be at a depth not less than B below the base of the foundation.
	10	medium dense gravel, or medium dense sand gravel	2–6	200–600	
	11	loose gravel, or loose sand and gravel	<2	<200	
	12	compact sand	>3	>300	SPT: >30 blows per 1 ft (0·30 m)
	13	medium dense sand	1–3	100–300	SPT: 30–10 blows per 1 ft (0·30 m)
	14	loose sand	<1	<100	SPT: <10 blows per 1 ft (0·30 m)

Table 2.3 (continued)

Group	Class	Types of rocks and soils	Presumed bearing value		Remarks
			tonf/ft²	kN/m² (approx.)	
III — Cohesive soils	15	very stiff boulder clays and hard clays	3–6	300–600	This group is susceptible to long-term consolidation settlement. (See 1.142.2.)
	16	stiff clays	1·5–3	150–300	
	17	firm clays	0·75–1·5	75–150	
	18	soft clays and silts	<0·75	<75	
	19	very soft clays and silts	not applicable		For consistencies of clays see Table 2—1.223.3.
IV	20	peat and organic soils			(See 1.223.4.) 'All these soils are highly compressible, and even lightly loaded foundations are subject to considerable settlement over a long period if placed on them. For this reason these soils are not suitable for carrying the loads from important structures'.
V	21	made ground or fill			(See 1.223.5.) 'All made ground should be treated as suspect, because of the likelihood of extreme variability. Any proposal to found a structure on made ground should be investigated with extreme care. . . . Loading tests may be completely misleading because of the variability of such deposits. Where a filling operation is adequately controlled by placing selected suitable fill material in sufficiently thin layers, properly compacted, then the methods described in this Code may be used to assess the allowable bearing pressure.'

Note. These values are for preliminary purposes only, and may need alteration upwards or downwards. (No addition has been made for the depth of embedment of the foundation.) (See 1.142.) Reference must be made to other parts of the Code when using this table.

Table 2.4. Allowable bearing stresses (after Polish Code of Practice: PN-59/B-03020)

Class	Group	Type	Allowable bearing values q_2, kN/m² at depth $H = 2 \cdot 0$ m beneath original ground level and $D = 0 \cdot 5$ m beneath lowest adjoining ground level [i][ii]					Remarks
Rocks	**hard**	igneous and metamorphic	massive [iii]: 4000*	lightly jointed [iii]: 2000	heavily jointed [iii]: 1000			Value of q_2 is taken according to the degree of jointing, regardless of width or depth of foundation. If in doubt with regards to the strength of rock its compressive strength σ_c should be determined. It should be checked if for massive rock the condition $0 \cdot 14\sigma_c \geqslant q_2$ is satisfied and, if not, then the value of q_2 should be reduced according to the degree of jointing, proportional to the tabulated values.
		sedimentary: limestones and sandstones	2000	1000	600			
	soft	chalky marls, clay shales, weakly cemented sandstones, etc.	1000	500	300			
Natural inorganic soils	**stony soils**	head, residual rock debris, etc. (with voids filled with cohesionless or cohesive soils)	cohesionless soils $I_D = 1 \cdot 0$: 700–350	$0 \cdot 33$: 400	cohesive soils $I_c = 1 \cdot 0$: 400–200	$0 \cdot 5$: 200–100	0: 0	Value of q_2 is taken according to the type and state of soil filling the voids between coarser grains. Interpolate linearly to obtain q_2 for intermediate values of density index I_D and consistency index I_c.
		gravels, tills, hoggins, etc. (regardless of their water content)	600–300	350	350–200	200–100	0	
	gravelly soils	cohesionless soils $I_p \leqslant 1 \cdot 0$ coarse and medium sands (regardless of their water content)	dense $I_D = 1 \cdot 0$: 500–400	medium $0 \cdot 67$: 400–300	loose $0 \cdot 33$: 300–200	0: 0		Interpolate linearly to obtain q_2 for intermediate values of density index I_D. It can be assumed that fine sands and silty sands to within 0·5 m above the GWT are wet and above that level are moist; the highest position of the GWT should be taken.
	fine grained soils	fine and silty sands damp	400–350	350–250	250–150			
		moist	350–280	280–200	200–120			
		wet	250–200	200–150	150–100			

Table 2.4 (continued)

		very hard	very stiff or hard	stiff	firm	soft to very soft	0	Notes
			$w=w_3$ $I_c=1.0$	0.75(iv)	0.5(iv)		0	
Natural inorganic soils — fine grained soils	cohesive soils $I_p > 1.0$ slightly clayey sands, silts, clayey soils, clays, etc.	450 / 350	450–300 / 350–250	300–200 / 250–150	200–120 / 150–80	[120–0](v) / [80–0](v)		Interpolate linearly to obtain q_2 for intermediate values of consistency index I_c. Upper values of q_2 (above the line) are used if at least three of the following conditions are satisfied. (1) Live load does not exceed 30% of the dead load. (2) The structure is not sensitive to differential settlement (statically determinant structures and steel, timber, masonry or brick (with R.C. ring beams) construction or structures very rigid about horizontal axes. (3) The soil is of glacial or even earlier origin. (4) Foundation level is above GWT. Lower values of q_2 (below the line) are used if at least three of the following conditions are satisfied. (1) Live load exceeds 50% of the dead load. (2) The structure is sensitive to differential settlement, e.g. one-to two-storey R.C. construction (masonry or brickwork without R.C. ring beams), etc. (3) The soil is of post-glacial or even more recent origin. (4) Foundation level is below GWT. For intermediate conditions average values of q_2 are taken. (i), (ii), etc., see Footnotes on p. 50
	metastable soils	for metastable soils of stable structure the same values of q_2 are taken as for the corresponding cohesive soils of the same consistency index I_c; for metastable soils of unstable structure allowable bearing values are determined on the basis of compressibility tests and evaluation of ultimate loading or settlement						
Natural organic soils — soils with traces of organic matter	recent alluvial, clayey silts (mud)	as for metastable soils of unstable structure						
organic muds	organic sands (as lenses of thickness less than 0.5 m)			$\left[\dfrac{200}{50}\right]$(v)				
	organic silts (as lenses of thickness less than 0.5 m)			$\left[\dfrac{150}{0}\right]$(v)				
	organic clayey silts (as lenses of thickness < 0.5 m)			$\left[\dfrac{100}{0}\right]$(v)				
peat	peaty soils and peats (as lenses of thickness less than 0.5 m)			$\left[\dfrac{50}{0}\right]$(v)				
Fill A	sandy fills	as for corresponding sands —depending on I_D						
B	inorganic cohesive fills			$\left[\dfrac{100}{0}\right]$(v)				
C	organic soil fills	not suitable for founding on directly						

Footnotes to Table 2.4

(i) In cases when H is less than $2 \cdot 0$ m then the allowable bearing values $q_H < 2 \cdot 0$ should be computed from the following expression: $q_H < 2 \cdot 0 = 0 \cdot 5 q_2 (1 + 0 \cdot 5H)$.

In cases when H is greater than $2 \cdot 0$ m then the allowable bearing values $q_H > 2 \cdot 0$ are greater than q_2. To take full advantage of this the allowable bearing stress should be computed from Equations (2.22), (2.2), and (2.3).

(ii) In cases when $D = 2 \cdot 0$ m the given values of q_2 should be increased by 20 kN/m²; in cases when $0 \cdot 5 < D < 2 \cdot 0$ m the given values are increased by 10 kN/m².

(iii) The classification of rocks in relation to the degree of jointing can be taken as follows.

(a) Massive (intact) — if there are no opened joints and closed joints are not clearly grouped within a distance of $0 \cdot 50$ m.

(b) Lightly jointed — if the width of opened joints does not exceed 2 mm and the so-formed blocks have not moved and their smallest dimension is greater than $0 \cdot 2$ m, i.e. the rock can be considered as a dry masonry structure.

(c) Heavily jointed — if the width of opened joints is between 2 and 10 mm and the so-formed blocks have not moved and their smallest dimension is less than $0 \cdot 20$ m.

Jointed rocks with opened joints greater than 10 mm or with displaced blocks are considered as natural stony soils.

(iv) When constructing foundations on cohesive soils of consistency index $I_c < 0 \cdot 75$, and on organic soils, a layer of 'nofines' concrete blinding of thickness between 100–150 mm should be placed below foundations for more rapid consolidation.

(v) Values of q_2 in square brackets are only indicative and can only be used in the case of structures insensitive to differential settlement and even then only in cases when the weak soils are not immediately below the foundation but are in the form of layers or lenses of thickness smaller than $0 \cdot 5$ m and $0 \cdot 2 B$ (B = width of foundation); in all other cases the allowable bearing stress should be computed from Equations (2.22), (2.2), and (2.3).

* For approximate conversion from kN/m² to lbf/ft² multiply by 21 and to kgf/cm² by $0 \cdot 01$.

where q_{ult} = ultimate loading evaluated in accordance with Sections 2.4–2.6

q'_{ult} = net ultimate loading: $q'_{ult} = q_{ult} - \gamma_0 D$

γ_0 = unit weight of soil above foundation level

D = foundation depth

F = factor of safety normally of the order of 2 to 3; the lower value is taken when the soil is allowed to consolidate during application of the loading, i.e. when its shear strength increases with increase in the intensity of the loading

In special cases, such as an isolated foundation in a basement excavation or an isolated bridge pier in an excavated area, etc., the effects of the immediately adjoining dead loads must be considered.

A semi-empirical method of determination of safe bearing capacity using the results of Menard's pressure meter test is given in Volume 1, Section 6.3.4.

The limitation of the bearing stress to the safe bearing value, evaluated with regards to the stability (shear failure) of the soil, *does not ensure* that the settlement of the foundation will be within the allowable limits for the given type of construction. Therefore the conditions stated in Equations (2.2) and (2.3) must also be satisfied:

$$s_{max} \leqslant s_{all}$$

and

$$\alpha_{max} \leqslant \alpha_{all}$$

In practice the detailed determination of allowable bearing stresses according to Equations (2.22), (2.2), and (2.3) is usually carried out only in the final stages of the design. In the initial stages presumed values of allowable bearing stresses are used (Table 2.3, after British Standard Code of Practice CP 2004 (1971, Draft)). These are selected on the basis of the knowledge of the type of the soil and its state of consistency or compaction.

For conventional types of foundations, varying in width between 0·6 and 4·0 m and founded at depths greater than 0·5 m, allowable bearing values given in Table 2.4 can be used provided the following requirements are satisfied.

(a) A sufficiently detailed site investigation is carried out for accurate classification of the soils (according to the methods given in Volume 1, Chapter 3), and for establishment of a clear picture of the ground conditions, including the position of the ground water table.

(b) The encountered soils are not of the weaker type for which the bearing values are given in square brackets and are reasonably uniform so that there is no danger of excessive differential settlement.

(c) All the requirements specified in Table 2.4 are followed.

The allowable bearing values in Table 2.4 have been computed on the basis of the typical physical properties of soils given in Table 3.3 and mechanical properties given in Tables 5.2 and 5.7 in Volume 1. The safe bearing stresses have been determined using Equation (2.22) and factor of safety of 2 for 0·6 m wide footings founded at a depth of 2·0 m below the original ground level and with the final foundation depth $D = 0·5$ m. The allowable stresses have been also computed with respect to settlement on the basis of 30 mm maximum settlement of 2·0 m wide strip footings founded at a depth of 2·0 m below the original ground level; in calculation of settlements the soil was treated as homogeneous and isotropic.

In addition to satisfying the above design criteria, which obviously for the sake of universality are on the conservative side, the allowable bearing stresses given in Table 2.4 have been verified as satisfactory by many years of documented field observations of the performance of buildings and other structures, prior to their adaptation in 1959 in the Polish Standard PN-59/B-03020. They also compare well with the values which are being used in other countries and which are based on several decades of practical experience.

The value of the allowable bearing stress does not only depend on the soil and water condition on a given site but also on the type of construction and dimensions of the structure. It is a complex problem and it has been treated as such in preparation of Table 2.4.

2.8. Determination of Settlement of Foundations

Settlement with reference to foundations is the vertical component of deformation of the soil due to its compressibility.

The basic equation for determination of the settlement (the change in thickness) of a single layer of soil is derived directly from Equation (5.1) in Volume 1:

$$E'_{oed} = \frac{\Delta \sigma h}{\Delta h}$$

Assuming $s = \Delta h$ the following expression is obtained:

$$s = \frac{\Delta \sigma h}{E'_{oed}} \tag{2.23}$$

where s = settlement of one layer in m
$\Delta \sigma$ = increase in stress in kN/m^2
h = thickness of the layer in m
E'_{oed} = first loading oedometric modulus of the layer in kN/m^2

Before the application of Equation (2.23) to evaluation of settlements of soil layers in situ it is necessary to eliminate the errors inherent to the oedometer test (Volume 1, Section 5.22), i.e. the oedometric modulus E'_{oed} is replaced with stiffness modulus E' where

$$E' = \kappa_f E'_{oed}$$

Equation (2.23) does not allow for the unloading of the soil during the excavation for foundations and for the subsequent reloading stage (see Section 1.1.3) during which the reloading stiffness modulus is operative (Volume 1, Section 5.22). In connection with this the settlement of the layer should be calculated from the following expression:

$$s_i = \left(\frac{\Delta\sigma_{rz}}{E''} + \frac{\Delta\sigma_{az}}{E'} \right) h_i \qquad (2.24)$$

where $\Delta\sigma_{rz}$ = reloading stress increment at mid-depth of the layer i in kN/m^2
$\quad\quad h_i$ = thickness of layer i in m or mm
$\quad\quad \Delta\sigma_{az}$ = additional stress increment in kN/m^2
$\quad\quad E''$ = reloading stiffness modulus ($E'' = \kappa_r E''_{oed}$) in kN/m^2
$\quad\quad E'$ = first loading stiffness modulus ($E' = \kappa_f E''_{oed}$) in kN/m^2

In the case of soils which in the past have been subjected to stresses higher than the existing overburden stresses (i.e. overconsolidated soils) the stress range over which reloading is taking place should be determined on the basis of the previous loading.

For soils heavily preconsolidated by the weight of ice sheet or subsequently removed overburden (e.g. London clay) the design stresses are generally much smaller than those previously experienced and Equation (2.24) transforms to

$$s_i = \frac{\Delta\sigma_{rz} + \Delta\sigma_{az}}{E''} h_i \qquad (2.25)$$

The settlement of a foundation is equal to the sum of the settlements of individual layers of the underlying soil:

$$s = \sum_{i=1}^{n} s_i \qquad (2.26)$$

The underlying soil is divided into layers of thickness smaller than 0·5B but not greater than approximately 2·0 m; each layer should be homogeneous. The depth of the significantly stressed zone is taken as equal to that depth at which $\Delta\sigma_{rz} + \Delta\sigma_{az} = 0\cdot2\sigma'_{oz}$. An example of settlement calculations is given in Table 2.5 (see also Appendix A).

2.9. Settlement of Soil Half-space Under Surface Loading

If the soil is treated as an elastic, homogeneous, isotropic body, extending indefinitely below the ground level, i.e. as a half-space, then the settlement of its surface can be evaluated using the methods of analysis developed in the mechanics of solids theory. According to Florin (1959) the effects of non-homogeneity need only to be considered in the case of considerable differences in the compressibility of the individual strata. The vertical displacement of a point within the half-space (having coordinates r and β) due to a point load applied to its surface (Figure 2.13) is given by the following expression (Terzaghi, 1943):

$$\zeta = \frac{Q}{2\pi r}\frac{1+\nu}{E_\nu}\{\cos^2\beta + 2(1-\nu)\}\sin\beta \tag{2.27}$$

The radial displacement is

$$\zeta = \frac{Q}{2\pi r}\frac{1+\nu}{E_\nu}\left\{\cos^2\beta + \cos\beta + (1-2\nu)\right\}\sin\beta\tan\frac{\beta}{2} \tag{2.28}$$

Corresponding displacements of a point on the surface of the half-space can be obtained by substituting $\beta = 90°$, $\cos\beta = 0$, $\sin\beta = 1\cdot0$ and $\tan\beta/2 = 1\cdot0$:

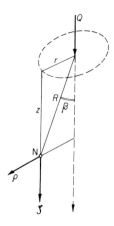

Figure 2.13. Vertical and horizontal (radial) displacements of a point N situated within an elastic, homogeneous, isotropic, semi-infinite body, due to a point load applied to its surface.

$$\zeta_0 = \frac{Q}{\pi r}\frac{1-\nu^2}{E_\nu} \tag{2.29}$$

and

$$\zeta_0 = \frac{Q}{2\pi r}\frac{1-\nu-2\nu^2}{E_\nu} \tag{2.30}$$

In the case of uniformly distributed loading, applied over a limited area, the settlement of a given point on the surface of the half-space can be determined by integration of its vertical displacements due to the elemental point loads acting over the given area. The result can be presented in the following general form:

$$s = \frac{qB\omega(1-\nu^2)}{E_\nu} \tag{2.31}$$

Table 2.5. Calculations of foundation settlement

Details of ground conditions and physical properties of soils	z_{GL} (m)	h (m)	γ or γ_{sub} (kN/m³)	σ'_{oz} (kN/m²)	Average σ'_{oz} (kN/m²)	z (m)	$z:B$	η	$\Delta\sigma_{zz} = \eta\rho_{oD}$ (kN/m²)	$\Delta\sigma_{az} = \eta\Delta\sigma_{aD}$ (kN/m²)	E'' (MN/m²)	E' (MN/m²)	s_r (mm)	s_a (mm)	s_i (mm)
Ground level	0·0	0·0	—	—	—	—	—		—	—	—	—	—	—	—
Fine sand ρ = 1·9 t/m³ GWL at z_{GL} = 2·0 m	2·0	2·0	18·6	37·2	37·2	0	—	$L = 12\cdot0$ m $B = 3\cdot0$ m $L:B = 4\cdot0$ 1·000	37·2	112·8	—	—	—	—	—
Fine sand ρ_{sat} = 2·0 t/m³ I_D = 0·40	3·1	1·1	9·8	48·0	42·6	0·55	0·18	0·978	36·4	111·3	60	33	0·67	3·71	4·38
Clayey silt ρ_{sat} = 1·8 t/m³ I_c = 0·55	4·0	0·9	7·9	55·1	51·6	1·55	0·52	0·805	29·9	91·6	16	5	1·68	16·48	18·16
Clayey sand (boulder clay) ρ_{sat} = 2·1 t/m³ I_c = 0·95	5·0	1·0	10·8	65·9	60·5	2·50	0·83	0·625	23·2	71·1	53	26	0·44	2·74	3·18
	6·0	1·0	10·8	76·7	71·3	3·50	1·17	0·470	17·5	53·5	53	26	0·33	2·06	2·39
	7·0	1·0	10·8	87·5	82·1	4·50	1·50	0·372	13·8	42·4	53	26	0·26	1·63	1·89
	8·0	1·0	10·8	98·3	92·9	5·50	1·83	0·297	11·0	33·8	53	26	0·21	1·30	1·51
	9·0	1·0	10·8	109·1	103·7	6·50	2·17	0·243	9·0	27·7	53	26	0·17	1·07	1·24
	10·0	1·0	10·8	119·9	114·5	7·50	2·50	0·202	7·5	23·0	53	26	0·14	0·89	1·03
	11·0	1·0	10·8	130·7	125·3	8·50	2·83	0·168	6·2	19·1	53	26	0·12	0·73	0·85

$q = 150$ kN/m²

$v = \Sigma s_i = 34\cdot63$

Foundation dimensions: length L = 12·0 m, width B = 3·0 m, foundation depth D = 2·0 m.

where q = uniformly distributed surface loading

B = width of the loaded area (foundation)

ν = Poisson's ratio (Volume 1, Table 5.3)

E_ν = elastic modulus of the semi-infinite body; in the case of soils—deformation modulus for laterally unrestrained compression (see Volume 1, Section 5.2.5)

ω = influence coefficient which depends on shape of the loaded area (foundation) and its stiffness and also on the position of the given point with relation to the loaded area (Table 2.6)

Table 2.6. Influence coefficients

Shape of foundation	Flexible foundation			Rigid foundation
	Settlement of centre	Settlement of corner	Mean settlement	Settlement
	ω_0	ω_c	ω_m	ω_{0r}
circular	1·00	0·64 point on perimeter	0·85	0·79
square	1·12	$\omega_c = \frac{1}{2}\omega_0$	0·95	0·88
rectangle				
$L:B = 2$	1·53		1·30	1·22
$L:B = 5$	2·10		1·83	1·72
$L:B = 10$	2·53		2·25	2·12
$L:B = 100$	4·00		3·69	—

The use of coefficients ω from Table 2.6 in Equation (2.31) enables one to determine the settlement s of the surface of the soil half-space (i.e. for $z = \infty$).

In practice, Equation (2.31) is used in the determination of the deformation modulus E_ν from the results of plate-loading tests and in computation of settlements in the half-space conditions as well as of the individual layers. In the case of layered soils settlements Δs of individual layers are computed from Equation (2.31a) which is obtained by substitution of $\Delta\omega = \omega_2 - \omega_1$ for ω in Equation (2.31):

$$\Delta s = \frac{qB\Delta\omega(1 - \nu^2)}{E_\nu} = \frac{qB\Delta\omega(1 - \nu^2)}{\delta E'} \qquad (2.31a)$$

The values of ω_2 and ω_1, corresponding to ratios $z_2 : B$ and $z_1 : B$ are taken from Table 2.7 or Figure 2.14 (Vasiljev, 1955)

where z_2 = depth below base of foundation to underside of the given layer

z_1 = depth to top of the layer

B = width of foundation

The values of ω_z are given for a rigid foundation and for $\nu = 0.3$ a mean value for soils ($\nu = 0.2-0.4$). In the case of $\nu \neq 0.3$ the values of ω_z are slightly different but for practical purposes this can be neglected.

If both the effects of reloading and first loading are considered in Equation (2.31a), then it should have the following form:

$$\Delta s = \left(\frac{\Delta \sigma_{rD}}{\delta E''} + \frac{\Delta \sigma_{aD}}{\delta E'} \right) B \Delta \omega (1 - \nu^2) \qquad (2.31b)$$

where $\Delta \sigma_{rD}$ = reloading stress increment at foundation base level

$\Delta \sigma_{aD}$ = additional stress increment at the same level

E'' = reloading stiffness modulus

E' = first loading stiffness modulus

δ = coefficient dependent on Poisson's ratio for the given soil

$$\delta = \frac{(1 + \nu)(1 - 2\nu)}{1 - \nu}$$

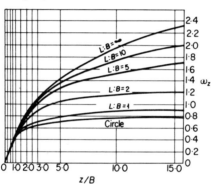

Figure 2.14. Nomogram for determination of coefficients ω_z (for $\nu = 0.3$).

Table 2.7. Coefficients ω_z (for $\nu = 0.3$)

$\dfrac{z}{B}$	Circular foundation	Ratio of length to width of foundation				
		$L : B = 1$	$L : B = 2$	$L : B = 5$	$L : B = 10$	$L : B = \infty$
0	0	0	0	0	0	0
0.25	0.12	0.13	0.13	0.13	0.13	0.13
0.5	0.23	0.25	0.25	0.26	0.26	0.26
0.75	0.33	0.37	0.38	0.38	0.39	0.39
1.0	0.41	0.45	0.47	0.48	0.50	0.51
1.5	0.52	0.56	0.66	0.67	0.70	0.73
2.0	0.58	0.63	0.77	0.83	0.86	0.89
2.5	0.62	0.68	0.86	0.96	1.00	1.03
3.0	0.65	0.71	0.91	1.06	1.11	1.14
5.0	0.70	0.78	1.05	1.31	1.37	1.45
10.0	0.75	0.84	1.16	1.56	1.80	1.96
∞	0.79	0.88	1.22	1.72	2.12	∞

Example. For data given in Table 2.5 evaluate settlement of the clayey silt stratum using Equation (2.31b).

Firstly determine ω_2 and ω_1: depth to underside of silt stratum $z_2 = 2\cdot0$ m, to top $z_1 = 1\cdot1$ m. The width of foundation $B = 3\cdot0$ m. Ratio $z_2 : B = 0\cdot66$ and $z_1 : B = 0\cdot37$; coefficients ω_2 and ω_1 are obtained, for foundation sides ratio $L : B = 12 : 3 = 4$, from Table 2.7; interpolating $\omega_2 = 0\cdot33$ and $\omega_1 = 0\cdot20$.

The stress increment at the foundation base level in the reloading stress range is $\Delta\sigma_{rD} = \sigma'_{oD} = 37\cdot2$ kN/m^2 and in additional stress range $\Delta\sigma_{aD} = q_D - \sigma'_{oD} = 150 - 37\cdot2 = 112\cdot8$ kN/m^2.

The value of Poisson's ratio is taken from Volume 1, Table 5.3 as for a firm clay $v = 0\cdot4$. Then the coefficient

$$\delta = \frac{(1 + 0\cdot4)(1 - 0\cdot8)}{(1 - 0\cdot4)} = 0\cdot47$$

According to Equation (2.31b) the settlement of the clayey silt stratum is

$$\Delta s = \left(\frac{\Delta\sigma_{rD}}{\delta E''} + \frac{\Delta\sigma_{aD}}{\delta E'}\right) B\Delta\omega(1 - v^2)$$

$$= \left(\frac{37\cdot2}{0\cdot47 \times 16\,000} + \frac{112\cdot8}{0\cdot47 \times 5000}\right) 3\cdot0 \times 0\cdot13 \times 0\cdot84$$

$$= (0\cdot0049 + 0\cdot0476) = 0\cdot0172 \text{ m} \approx 17 \text{ mm}$$

A semi-empirical method of the determination of settlement of foundations using the results of Menard's pressuremeter test is given in Volume 1, Section 6.3.4.

2.10. Settlement of Soil Half-space Under Internal Loading (Deep Foundation)

The use of Equations (2.27) and (2.28) in evaluation of displacements in the elastic half-space is limited to the case of surface loading. The vertical displacement of a point within the half-space (having coordinates x, y, z) due to a point load applied at a depth D below the surface (Figure 2.15) (i.e. internal loading) is given by the following equation (Mindlin, 1936):

$$\zeta = \frac{Q(1 + v)}{8\pi E_v(1 - v)}\left\{\frac{3 - 4v}{R_1} + \frac{5 - 12v + 8v^2}{R_2} + \frac{(z - D)^2}{R_1^3}\right.$$

$$\left. + \frac{(3 - 4v)(z + D)^2 - 2Dz}{R_2^3} + \frac{6Dz(z + D)^2}{R_2^5}\right\} \tag{2.32}$$

where

$$R_1^2 = x^2 + y^2 + (z - D)^2 \quad \text{and} \quad R_2^2 = x^2 + y^2 + (z + D)^2$$

A general solution of Equation (2.32) is difficult but solutions to specific problems have been obtained and the results have been presented in the form of graphs which can readily be used in evaluation of settlement of deep foundations (Fox, 1948; Poulos, 1967).

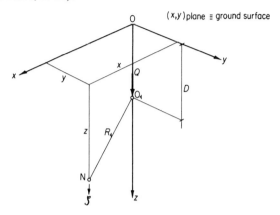

Figure 2.15. Vertical displacement of a point N situated within an elastic, homogeneous, isotropic, semi-infinite body, due to a point load applied at O_1.

From Figure 2.16 one can obtain the ratio α of the mean settlement s_D of a loaded rectangular area of length L and width B situated at a depth D below the surface of the half-space to the mean settlement s_m of the same loaded area at the surface. Using Equation (2.31) and values of ω_m from Table 2.6 a simple expression for settlement s_D is obtained:

$$s_D = \alpha s_m = q\, \frac{B\omega_m(1 - \nu^2)}{E_\nu}\, \alpha \qquad (2.33)$$

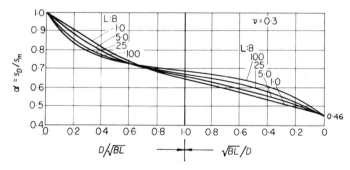

Figure 2.16. Ratio of mean settlement s_D of flexible rectangular footing $B \times L$ at depth D to mean settlement s_m of similar footing at surface.

Similarly from Figure 2.17 one can obtain the ratio α_c of the maximum settlement of a loaded circular area of diameter d situated at a depth D below the surface to the maximum settlement of the same loaded area at the surface.

As before a simple expression for settlement s_D is obtained:

$$s_D = \alpha_c s_{max} = \frac{qd(1 - v^2)}{E_v} \alpha_c \tag{2.34}$$

With acceptable degree of accuracy the above coefficient α_c can be used for evaluation of settlement of a rigid circular foundation in which case Equation (2.34) will be rewritten as follows:

$$s_{Dr} = \frac{0.79\, qd(1 - v^2)}{E_v} \alpha_c \tag{2.35}$$

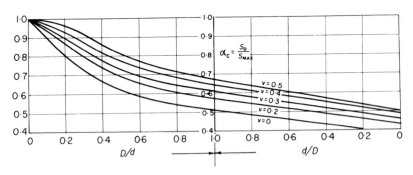

Figure 2.17. Ratio of maximum settlement s_D of flexible circular footing of diameter d situated at depth D below the surface to maximum settlement s_{max} of similar footing at surface.

The above equations are only applicable when continuity of the soil above the foundation base level can be assumed, i.e. when all the sides of the foundation are directly in contact with undisturbed soil or, as in the case of a plate-bearing test inside a borehole, the borehole is lined with rigid casing.

2.11. Coefficient of Subgrade Reaction

The coefficient of proportionality between the applied stress and settlement at the point of loading of an elastic subgrade is referred to as the coefficient of (vertical) subgrade reaction.

$$q = k_z s \tag{2.36}$$

The coefficient of subgrade reaction k_z can also be defined as a stress per unit area that produces a unit settlement at the point of application of the load.

From Equations (2.31) and (2.36)

$$k_z = \frac{E_v}{\omega B(1 - v^2)} \tag{2.37}$$

As can be seen the coefficient k_z cannot be considered as a constant for any soil because it depends on the shape, dimensions, and stiffness of the loaded area.

2.12. Settlement of Eccentrically Loaded Foundations

Tilting or rotation of a shallow rigid strip footing due to eccentric loading can be computed from the equation derived by Jegorov (Vasiljev, 1955):

$$\tan \beta = \frac{16(1 - \nu^2)}{\pi E_\nu B^2} \bar{Q} e \tag{2.38}$$

where B = width of strip foundation in m
        $\bar{Q}$ = loading in kN/m run
        e = eccentricity of loading in m
        E_ν = deformation modulus for laterally unrestrained compression, in kN/m^2
        ν = Poisson's ratio

Tilting of a flexible circular foundation of radius R can be computed from equation (Tettinek and Matt, 1953):

$$s_1 = -s_2 = \frac{16(1 - \nu^2)\,\omega}{3\pi^2 E_\nu R^2} M \tag{2.39}$$

where s_1 = maximum settlement at the perimeter relative to the centre in m
       R = radius of foundation in m
       M = moment applied at foundation base level in kN m
       ω = coefficient from Table 2.6
E_ν and ν = as defined in Equation (2.38)

2.13. Rate of Settlement of Foundations During and After Completion of Construction

The above equations for the evaluation of settlement refer to the total final settlements which are reached on completion of the consolidation of the soil and do not take into account the rate of settlement which mainly depends on the permeability of the soil under consideration. For the majority of the straightforward foundation problems there is no need for evaluation of the rate of settlement and it is sufficient to keep in mind the observations stated in the following paragraphs.

On the basis of recommendations of the Russian Standard N and TU 127-55 and from observations carried out in Poland by ITB (Wiłun and Rogozinski, 1953) the following directives can be formulated with regard to the rates of settlement of foundations on different types of soils.

The settlement of foundations on cohesive soils of very hard consistency and on cohesionless soils takes place almost immediately on application of the loading and 70 to 100% of the settlement is completed by the end of the construction period.

Foundations on cohesive soils of stiff and firm consistency settle proportionally to the increase in the applied loading and it can be assumed that at the time of completion of construction 50 to 70% of the calculated final settlement has taken place.

For foundations on soft cohesive soils and on organic soils it can be assumed that at the time of completion of construction the settlements are of the order of 30 to 50% of the final calculated values.

In special cases where, for example, a building is founded on different soils, greater differential settlements between individual foundations may occur during its construction than after a prolonged period of its utilization.

It is recommended in connection with the above, that, for structures sensitive to differential settlement and founded on variable soils, the differential settlements should be checked for the end of construction condition as well as for the final settlement condition. This can be done using either the one-dimensional theory of consolidation (given in Volume 1, Chapter 5), or, for the case of uniform stress distribution, the empirical method given below. Both methods are subject to the same limitations because both are based on the oedometer test results.

2.14. Determination of the Rate of Progress of Settlement

On the basis of laboratory tests the relationship between settlement time and thickness of layers of the same soil can be presented in the following form:

$$\frac{t_1}{t_2} = \left(\frac{h_1}{h_2}\right)^n \qquad (2.40)$$

where t_1 and t_2 = times of settlement of two layers of different thickness
  h_1 and h_2 = thickness of layers
    n = power index equal to 1·5 to 2·0; the value of n should be determined from oedometer test on several samples of different thickness

If the consolidating stratum overlies an impermeable formation (e.g. bedrock), then the thickness of that stratum should be doubled to allow for the one directional drainage of water during consolidation:

$$\frac{t_1}{t_2} = \left(\frac{2h_1}{h_2}\right)^n \qquad (2.40a)$$

The rate of progress of consolidation with respect to time can be illustrated by a consolidation curve (Figure 2.18(a)) which should be constructed for every increment of load in the oedometer test.

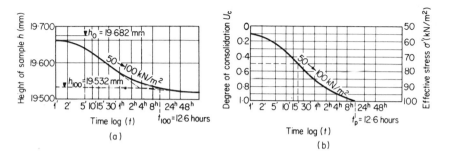

(a)

(b)

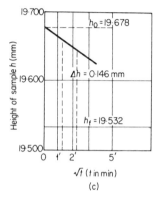

(c)

Figure 2.18. Relationship between degree of consolidation, time, and effective stresses: (a) consolidation curve (rate of settlement with respect to time); (b) degree of consolidation–time relationship; (c) determination of initial height of sample for given load increment.

For the purpose of calculation of the rate of settlement of a layer of soil below a foundation (or embankment) the consolidation curve for the sample (in oedometer) is replotted, in the form shown in Figure 2.18(b), with the ratio of the settlement in a given time to the total settlement of the sample under the given load increment superimposed on it.

The ratio of settlement of the soil at a given time during consolidation to the final settlement on completion of consolidation under the given loading is known as the degree of consolidation:

$$U_c = \frac{s_t}{s_f} \tag{2.41}$$

where U_c = degree of consolidation (dimensionless)

s_t = settlement of soil at time t after the increase in loading

s_f = total final settlement at that loading

The initial height of the sample at the instant of loading is determined according to the construction shown in Figure 2.18(c), where $\sqrt{t}$ (in minutes) is plotted on the horizontal axis and the height of the sample on the vertical axis. The intersection of a straight line through the experimental points with the vertical axis is taken as the initial height of the sample for that particular loading.

The consolidation curve plotted in a semilogarithmic scale (Figure 2.18(a)) is usually convex upwards in the initial stages of the consolidation, concave in the latter stages, and finally changes to a straight line slightly inclined to the horizontal axis. By plotting two tangents to this curve, one at the point of contraflexure and the other to the final straight part of the curve, a point of intersection is obtained which is taken as the end of the primary (due to expulsion of water) consolidation (Lambé, 1951).

The subsequent consolidation is referred to as the secondary consolidation (Volume 1, Chapter 5) and with the exception of organic soils is disregarded in practical considerations of the rates of settlement.

With the knowledge of the initial and final heights of the soil sample the consolidation curve can be plotted in a more useful form by assuming the moment of application of the new load increment $t_0 = 0$ as the beginning of the consolidation and time t_{100} (end of expulsion of free water) as the end.

At time $t = t_0 = 0$ the degree of consolidation $U_c = 0$, and at time $t = t_{100}$ the degree of consolidation $U_c = 1 \cdot 0$. The time t_{100} is obtained from intersection of the horizontal $U_c = 1 \cdot 00$ and the consolidation curve; in Figure 2.18(a) time $t_{100} = 12 \cdot 6$ hours. Intermediate times of consolidation are also obtained from the intersection of horizontal line U_c with the consolidation curve, e.g. time corresponding to $U_c = 0 \cdot 5$ (Figure 2.18(b)) is $t_{50} = 21$ min.

Simultaneously with the change in the degree of consolidation of the sample the effective stresses in the soil must obviously be changing.

If a saturated cohesive soil has been previously consolidated to a certain stress σ_i, then at the moment of application of the new stress increment $\Delta\sigma_i$ the effective stress in the soil σ_i' is equal to σ_i and the stress increment is wholly resisted by the pore water in which the pressure increases by $\Delta u_i = \Delta\sigma_i$. On completion of the consolidation the effective stress increases to $\sigma_{i+1}' = \sigma_i' + \Delta\sigma_i$ and the pore water pressure decreases to $u_{i+1} = 0$ (or u_i).

It can be, therefore, considered that the effective stress increases in parallel with the consolidation time:

$$\sigma_{it}' = \sigma_i' + U_c\Delta\sigma_i \tag{2.42}$$

It follows that the consolidation curve can be used for the determination of the effective stress at any time in the soil as well as for the determination of the degree of consolidation.

Having obtained the relationship between the consolidation time of the sample and that of the soil layer beneath a foundation or embankment

(Equation (2.41)), it is possible to determine, according to Equation (2.42), the settlement s_t of the given layer of soil at any time after the commencement of construction, i.e. loading.

Because the actual loading during construction of a structure increases gradually and not suddenly, as is the case in loading of the soil sample in the oedometer, it should be considered that the consolidation of the *in situ* layer of soil starts in the middle of the period of application of the continuous loading. In cases when loading is applied in several stages then it should be considered that each consolidation stage starts in the middle of the corresponding loading period.

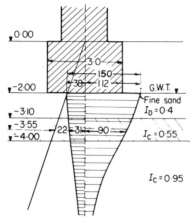

Figure 2.19. Details of soil strata and stress distribution below a pier foundation.

Obviously the above principles, which refer to the consolidation of soils, can also be applied to the problems of predicting the rate of heave (expansion) of soil.

Simultaneously with determination of the rate of heave or settlement it is possible to evaluate the changes in the effective stresses in soils. The knowledge of the effective stresses enables the proper investigation to be made of the changes in their shear strength. Obviously in these circumstances the laboratory shear strength tests should be executed also with the consideration of the degree of consolidation (or expansion) of the soil and with pore water pressure measurements (for the determination of the effective stresses).

The method of evaluation of the rate of settlement and the corresponding changes in the effective stresses is illustrated in the following example in which both the expansion (heave) and consolidation of the soil during the process of construction of a bridge pier are considered.

Example. The details of soil strata and stress distribution are shown in Figure 2.19. The expansion and consolidation curves for the clayey silt are shown in Figure 2.20; the power exponent in Equation (2.41) $n = 2.0$; construction programme: excavation from 2 May to 6 May, concreting of foundation from 15 May to 19 May, concreting of pier from 1 June to 15 June, erection of deck and completion from 15 July to 1 October.

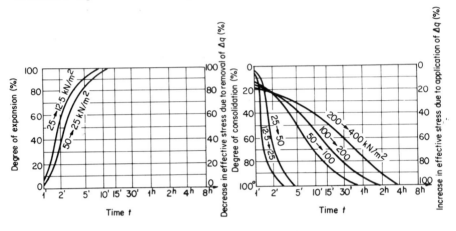

Figure 2.20. Expansion and consolidation curves for clayey silt.

The changes during construction in stresses at the foundation base level and at mid-height of the clayey silt layer are shown in Figures 2.21(a) and 2.21(b).

It is required to determine the progress of expansion and consolidation of the clayey silt layer, during and after the construction of the bridge, together with the changes in the effective stresses.

As can be seen in Figure 2.19 the effective overburden stress in the clayey silt, at a depth of $z = 1.55$ m below the foundation base level, is equal to $\sigma'_{oz} = 53$ kN/m², the minimum stress $\sigma_{oz\ min} = \sigma'_{oz} - \Delta\sigma_{rz} = 53 - 31 = 22$ kN/m², the reloading stress increment $\Delta\sigma_{rz} = 31$ kN/m², additional stress increment $\Delta\sigma_{az} = 90$ kN/m².

In order to evaluate the progress of expansion of the clayey silt the expansion curve for the stress change from 50 to 25 kN/m² should be used as the closest to the change from σ'_{oz} to $\sigma_{oz\ min}$ (from 53 to 22 kN/m²).

In determination of the progress of consolidation in the reloading range, i.e. from $\sigma_{oz\ min}$ to σ'_{oz} (from 22 to 53 kN/m²), the reloading consolidation curve for the stress change from 25 to 50 kN/m² should be used; in the first loading range from σ'_{oz} to $\sigma'_{oz} + \Delta\sigma_{az}$, i.e. from 53 to 143 kN/m², two consolidation curves should be used: from 50 to 100 kN/m² and from 100 to 200 kN/m².

In evaluation of the settlement of the clayey silt layer according to Equation (2.41), it should be considered that the drainage can only take place upwards because the thick stratum of the boulder clay (clayey sand) has a very low permeability. Therefore Equation (2.41) will become

$$t_{oed} = t_1 \frac{h_{oed}^2}{4h_1^2} = t_2 \frac{20^2}{4 \times 900^2} = \frac{t_1}{8100} \qquad (2.43)$$

where t_{oed} = time of consolidation of soil in oedometer in min
   t_1 = time of consolidation of *in situ* layer in min
   h_{oed} = thickness of oedometer sample in mm
   h_1 = thickness of *in situ* layer in mm

The progress of deformation of the layer of clayey silt (both in the case of

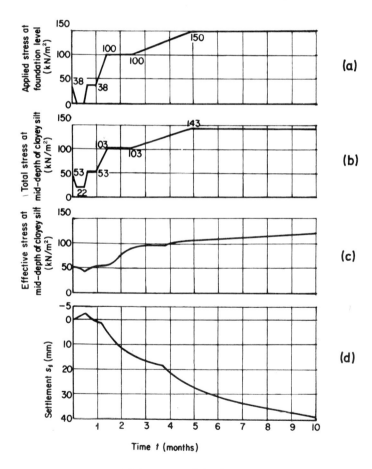

Figure 2.21. Stress changes and deformation of the clayey silt layer: (a) stresses at foundation base level; (b) stresses at mid-height of the layer; (c) effective stresses at mid-height of the layer; (d) deformation.

Table 2.8. Determination of settleme

Changes in stresses	Details				Time fr			
		0	$\frac{2}{30}$	$\frac{4}{30}$	$\frac{7}{30}$	$\frac{14}{30}$	$\frac{16}{30}$	$\frac{18}{30}$
1	2	3	4	5	6	7	8	9
I stage: excavation Total expansion $s_{ei} = -\dfrac{\Delta\sigma_{rz} \times h_1}{E''}$ $= \dfrac{31 \times 900}{6000} = 4.2$ mm $t_{oed} = t_1 \dfrac{h^2_{oed}}{4h^2_1} = \dfrac{t_1}{8100}$	time from commencement of unloading t_1 (months)	–	0	$\frac{2}{30}$	$\frac{5}{30}$	$\frac{12}{30}$	$\frac{14}{30}$	$\frac{16}{30}$
	as above but for oedometer t_{oed} (min)	–	0	0.4	0.9	2.1	2.5	2.8
	U_e	–	0	0.07	0.18	0.44	0.54	0.58
	$\Delta\sigma'_{it}$ (kN/m²)	–	0	–2	–6	–14	–17	–18
	s_t (mm)	–	0	–0.3	–0.8	–1.9	–2.3	–2.7
II stage: concreting of foundation. Total settlement within the reloading range 22 to 53 kN/m² $s_{fi} = \dfrac{\Delta\sigma_{rz} \times h_1}{E''} = \dfrac{31 \times 900}{5000}$ $= 5.6$ mm	time from commencement of loading t_1 (months)	–	–	–	–	–	0	$\frac{2}{30}$
	as above but for oedometer t_{oed} (min)	–	–	–	–	–	0	0.4
	U_c	–	–	–	–	–	0	0.14
	$\Delta\sigma'_{it}$ (kN/m²)	–	–	–	–	–	0	4
	s_t (mm)	–	–	–	–	–	0	0.8
III stage: construction of the pier. Total settlement within stress range 53 to 103 kN/m² $s_{fi} = \dfrac{\Delta\sigma_{az} \times h_1}{E'} = \dfrac{50 \times 900}{2000}$ $= 21.2$ mm	t_1 (months)	–	–	–	–	–	–	–
	t_{oed} (min)	–	–	–	–	–	–	–
	U_c	–	–	–	–	–	–	–
	$\Delta\sigma'_{it}$ (kN/m²)	–	–	–	–	–	–	–
	s_t (mm)	–	–	–	–	–	–	–
IV stage: erection of superstructure. Total settlement within stress range 103 to 143 kN/m² $s_{fi} = \dfrac{40 \times 900}{2000} = 18.0$ mm	t_1 (months)	–	–	–	–	–	–	–
	t_{oed} (min)	–	–	–	–	–	–	–
	U_c	–	–	–	–	–	–	–
	$\Delta\sigma'_{it}$ (kN/m²)	–	–	–	–	–	–	–
	s_t (mm)	–	–	–	–	–	–	–
increase in effective stress	$\Sigma\Delta\sigma'_i$ (kN/m²)	0	0	–2	–6	–14	–17	–14
effective stress	$\sigma'_{i+1} = \sigma'_i + \Sigma\Delta\sigma'_i$	53	53	51	47	39	36	39
settlement	s_t (mm)	0	0	–0.3	–0.8	–1.9	–2.3	–1.6

d effective stresses in clayey silt stratum

mencement of construction (in months)

$\frac{1}{4}$	2	$2\frac{1}{2}$	3	$3\frac{3}{4}$	4	5	6	7	8	9	10	Remarks
1	12	13	14	15	16	17	18	19	20	21	22	23
$\frac{5}{0}$	$1\frac{28}{30}$	$2\frac{13}{30}$	$2\frac{28}{30}$	$3\frac{20}{30}$	$3\frac{28}{30}$	$4\frac{28}{30}$	$5\frac{28}{30}$	$6\frac{28}{30}$	$7\frac{28}{30}$	$8\frac{28}{30}$	$9\frac{28}{30}$	$\Delta\sigma_{rz} = 31$ kN/m²
2	10.3	13.0	15.6	19.5	21.0	26.4	31.6	37.1	42.4	47.6	53.1	
91	0.98	1.0	1.0	1.0	1.0	1.0	1.0	1.0	1.0	1.0	1.0	$\Delta\sigma'_i = U_c\Delta\sigma_{rz}$
28	−30	−31	−31	−31	−31	−31	−31	−31	−31	−31	−31	$s_t = U_c s_{fi}$
.9	−4.1	−4.2	−4.2	−4.2	−4.2	−4.2	−4.2	−4.2	−4.2	−4.2	−4.2	
$\frac{1}{0}$	$1\frac{14}{30}$	$1\frac{29}{30}$	$2\frac{14}{30}$	$3\frac{6}{30}$	$3\frac{14}{30}$	$4\frac{14}{30}$	$5\frac{14}{30}$	$6\frac{14}{30}$	$7\frac{14}{30}$	$8\frac{14}{30}$	$9\frac{14}{30}$	
7	7.8	10.5	13.2	17.1	18.5	24.1	29.1	33.4	39.8	45.1	50.4	
97	1.0	1.0	1.0	1.0	1.0	1.0	1.0	1.0	1.0	1.0	1.0	
0	31	31	31	31	31	31	31	31	31	31	31	
4	5.6	5.6	5.6	5.6	5.6	5.6	5.6	5.6	5.6	5.6	5.6	
▪	$\frac{22}{30}$	$1\frac{1}{4}$	$1\frac{3}{4}$	$2\frac{1}{2}$	$2\frac{3}{4}$	$3\frac{3}{4}$	$4\frac{3}{4}$	$5\frac{3}{4}$	$6\frac{3}{4}$	$7\frac{3}{4}$	$8\frac{3}{4}$	
▪	3.9	6.6	9.2	13.3	14.6	19.9	25.3	30.6	35.9	41.2	46.5	
▪	0.42	0.60	0.71	0.79	0.81	0.88	0.92	0.94	0.97	0.98	0.99	
▪	21	30	36	40	41	44	46	47	48	49	49	
▪	8.9	12.7	15.1	16.8	17.2	18.7	19.5	19.9	20.6	20.8	21.0	
	−	−	−	0	$\frac{7}{30}$	$1\frac{7}{30}$	$2\frac{7}{30}$	$3\frac{7}{30}$	$4\frac{7}{30}$	$5\frac{7}{30}$	$6\frac{7}{30}$	
	−	−	−	0	1.2	6.6	11.9	17.2	22.6	27.9	33.2	
	−	−	−	0	0.18	0.42	0.55	0.68	0.74	0.79	0.84	
	−	−	−	0	7	17	22	27	30	32	34	
	−	−	−	0	3.2	7.6	9.9	12.2	13.3	14.2	15.1	
	22	30	36	40	48	61	68	74	78	81	83	
	75	83	89	93	101	114	121	127	131	134	136	
	10.4	14.1	16.5	18.2	21.8	27.7	30.8	33.5	35.3	36.4	37.5	

expansion during excavation and consolidation during construction and loading of the pier) is evaluated by the following steps.

(1) Determination of the magnitude of the total final settlement of the layer s_{fi} according to Equation (2.24) or (2.31b) under the given stress increment (Table 2.8).

(2) Determination of t_{oed}, i.e. the time taken for the expansion or consolidation of the sample according to Equation (2.43).

(3) Determination from Figure 2.20 of the degree of expansion U_e or degree of consolidation U_c corresponding to the time t_{oed}.

(4) Determination of the increase in the effective stress $\Delta\sigma'_{it}$ from $\Delta\sigma'_{it} = U_c\Delta\sigma_i$.

(5) Determination of the change in thickness of the *in situ* layer in time t_1 for the given U_e and U_c according to $s_t = U_c s_{fi}$.

(6) Summation of stress increments and construction of graph in Figure 2.21(c).

(7) Summation of settlement increments and construction of graph in Figure 2.21(d).

2.15. Allowable Total and Differential Settlements

In most publications and standards the quoted allowable total and differential settlements refer to the calculated values. It is suggested by the authors that in evaluation of settlements to compare with the guide figures given in Table 2.9, the stiffness of the structure is neglected by assuming that the foundations are independent of each other. In practice, the stiffness of the structure undoubtedly will tend to even out the settlements of its foundations and thus will reduce the differential settlements and bring the magnitude of the maximum settlements in line with the average calculated values; this will be accompanied, of course, by increases in stresses in some members of the structure.

Therefore, the most important consideration in proper functioning of a given structure is not the magnitude of the settlements but their uniformity. The limitation of the magnitude of the settlements is, however, very relevant because the smaller the settlements, the lesser are their differences and hence the lesser are the differential movements that have to be absorbed by the structure in the form of additional work.

It is recommended that in consideration of the differential settlement Equation (2.3) should be used for evaluation of the magnitude of angular distortion α. This involves consideration of three collinear adjoining points or foundations of a given structure, situated within the zone of occurrence of the worst differential movements.

A negative value of α indicates that the bottom part of the structure is in tension whereas a positive value indicates tension in its upper parts; if necessary the structure should be strengthened to resist these additional forces.

Table 2.9. Allowable total and differential settlements (angular distortion) of foundations calculated without consideration of the stiffness of the structure

Class of building and structure	Type of building or structure	Maximum allowable final settlement s_{all} (mm)	Maximum allowable angular distortion calculated for three, collinear, adjoining points or foundations of a structure α_{all}
1	massive structures of considerable rigidity about horizontal axes founded on rigid mass concrete foundations or cellular or rigid reinforced concrete rafts	150–200 (6 in–8 in)	maximum differences of settlements at various points of the structure should not cause tilting of the foundation greater than $1/100 \div 1/200$ of the ratio of the smallest dimension of the foundation in plan to the height of the structure
2	statically determinate structures with actual pin joints (three pinned arches, single-span steel trusses, etc.) and timber structures	100–150 (4 in–6 in)	$\dfrac{1}{100} - \dfrac{1}{200}$
3	statically indeterminate steel structures and load-bearing brickwork construction with reinforced concrete ring beams at every floor level, with longitudinally reinforced concrete strip foundations and with cross walls of at least 250 mm (9 in) thickness and spaced at not more than 6 m($\sim$20 ft) centres and reinforced concrete frame — structures with columns at less than 6 m centres and founded on strip or raft foundations	80–100 (3½ in–4 in)	$\dfrac{1}{200} - \dfrac{1}{300}$
4	structures of class 3 but not satisfying one of the stated conditions and reinforced concrete structures founded on isolated footings	60–80 (2½ in–3½ in)	$\dfrac{1}{300} - \dfrac{1}{500}$
5	prefabricated structures consisting of large slab or block elements	50–60 (2 in–2½ in)	$\dfrac{1}{500} - \dfrac{1}{700}$

(1) Smaller values quoted relate to public buildings, dwellings, or buildings with structural members or finishes particularly sensitive to differential settlement; larger values relate to taller buildings of considerable rigidity about horizontal axes or to structures which can accept such movements.

(2) In special cases (such as gantry beams, high-pressure boilers, special storage tanks, silos under differential loading, etc.) allowable maximum or differential settlements or both should be taken as specified by service or mechanical engineers or by manufacturers.

Allowable settlement figures quoted by other authorities are shown in Table 2.10. The values quoted by Skempton and MacDonald (1956) are based on analysis of records of 98 buildings, some of which had suffered damage and some had not. With regard to the differential settlement of load-bearing walls and framed buildings with panel walls they have concluded that as long as $|\Delta s/l|$ is less than 1/300 there will be no settlement damage.

Terzaghi and Peck (1967) suggests that settlements of 25 mm (1 in) for isolated footings and 50 mm (2 in) for rafts on sands are acceptable and quotes 18 mm ($\frac{3}{4}$ in) as the maximum allowable difference in settlements of two adjoining footings without specifying the distance between them.

In every case the magnitude of the allowable settlements and their differences should be related to all the stages of construction of a given structure, and to its type and sensitivity to differential settlements, as well as to the conditions imposed on it during its utilization, e.g. limitation in deformation of gantry beams or some production machinery, etc.

Table 2.10(a). Damage limits for load-bearing walls or for the panels in traditional-type frame buildings (after Skempton and MacDonald, 1956; by permission of the Council of the I.C.E.)

Criterion		Isolated foundations	Raft
Angular distortion $\left|\dfrac{\Delta s}{l}\right|$		$<\dfrac{1}{300}$	
Greatest differential settlements Δs (mm)	clays	43 (1·75 in)	
	sands	31 (1·25 in)	
Maximum total settlements s_f (mm)	clays	76 (3 in)	76−127 (3−5 in)
	sands	51 (2 in)	51−76 (2−3 in)

Table 2.10(b). Allowable total settlements in mm (Polshin and Tokar, 1957)

Brick buildings	Reinforced brickwork	Framed buildings	Heavy reinforced concrete structures
75−100	150	100	300

3

Stability of Slopes and Foundations

3.1. Degradation of Natural and Artificial Slopes

The degradation of natural or artificial slopes (in deep cut excavations or high embankments) is the result of mass movements which occur chiefly owing to the action of gravitational forces, sometimes supplemented by seismic activities. The downward movement of rock or soil masses occurs when the equilibrium is disturbed along a certain plane (within the slope) and the shear stresses along it exceed the available shearing resistance; this can occur as the result of either an increase in the shear stresses or a reduction or deterioration of the shear strength. The manner in which a slope fails is chiefly controlled by the geological, hydrological, topographical, and climatic conditions and by the extent of weathering of the rocks or soils present. This results in a great variety of types of mass movements amongst which the *falls, rotational slides, translational slides,* and *flows* are the most distinguishable (Figure 3.1).

Falls are usually associated with short-term failure of steep slopes (in artificial excavations or river banks) in overconsolidated fissured clays (Figure 3.1(a)). As the lateral support is removed, bulging occurs at the slope foot and tension cracks open behind its crest, usually along the pre-existing fissures. This leads to progressive increase of stresses in the root of the separating mass and to the eventual collapse; the process is frequently accelerated by water entering the tension cracks.

Rotational slides occur characteristically in slopes of fairly uniform clay or shale. The failure surface is curved and usually deep seated. The slipping mass slumps, sinking at the rear and heaving at the toe (Figure 3.1(b)). Approximately circular rotational slips are associated with cut slopes of uniform clays whereas non-circular rotational slips with natural slopes of overconsolidated clays in which weathering has produced non-homogeneity.

Translational slides generally result from the presence of a heterogeneity, in the form of a weak soil layer or structural feature, located at shallow depth

73

beneath the slope. The failure surface is approximately planar and parallel to the ground surface (Figure 3.1(c)). The mass movement is predominantly

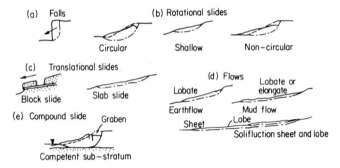

Figure 3.1. Some basic types of mass movement on clay slopes (after Skempton and Hutchinson, 1969; by permission of the Mexican Soil Mechanics Society).

translational. If the plane of weakness is at a moderate depth beneath the slope, a compound slide of partly rotational and partly translational character may occur.

The mass movements in which there are no well-defined failure planes are referred to as *flows* (Figure 3.1(d)). Skempton and Hutchinson (1969) differentiate between earth flows and mud flows; the latter are glacier-like in form whereas the former are considered to be transitional in character between the slides and mud flows.

From the slope stability point of view the most dangerous conditions are encountered in areas where in the past the soils have been deformed and folded by tectonic activities or ice advances or where previous mass movements have taken place. In these circumstances pre-existing slip planes (slickensides) are usually present along which the shear strength is only a fraction of the strength of the intact soil (Volume 1, Section 5.4.6).

The typical features of landslide areas are the following.

(a) The presence of depressions and bulges on natural slopes (Figure 3.2).

(b) The presence of deformed trees with trunks bent in random directions.

(c) The existence of springs on slopes and outcrops of water-bearing strata.

(d) The existence of slickensides and deformed layers of clays (these can be best observed in trial pits or by breaking down undisturbed tube samples).

3.2. Stability of Slopes in Cohesionless Soils

On analysis of the equilibrium conditions of a slope in cohesionless soil (sands, gravels) one comes to the conclusion that the angle of the natural slope is equal to the angle of internal shearing resistance of the soil (Equation (3.1)).

Assuming that W is the weight of element A and that the slope is inclined at an angle β the components of the force Q normal and tangential to the slope are (Figure 3.3)

normal force: $N = W \cos \beta$

tangential force: $B = W \sin \beta$

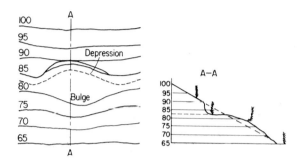

Figure 3.2. Feature of landslide area: plan view and section.

The shearing resistance of cohesionless soil according to Volume 1, Equation (5.39) is

$$T = N \tan \phi$$

The element A will not slide if

$$B \leqslant T$$

In the state of limiting equilibrium (for β_{max})

$$B_{max} = W \sin \beta_{max}$$
$$T_{max} = W \cos \beta_{max} \tan \phi$$
$$B_{max} = T_{max}$$
$$W \sin \beta_{max} = W \cos \beta_{max} \tan \phi$$

hence

$$\tan \beta_{max} = \tan \phi \qquad (3.1)$$

and therefore the maximum angle of a slope (in cohesionless soil) should not exceed the angle of internal friction.

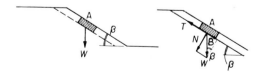

Figure 3.3. Forces acting on element of cohesionless soil in a slope.

In natural conditions sandy slopes are moist and have steeper slopes because of the presence of capillary forces.

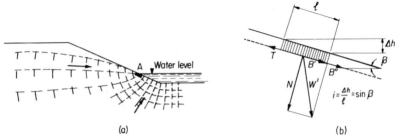

(a)   (b)

Figure 3.4. Forces acting on element of cohesionless soil in a slope in which seepage forces are acting: (a) flow net of seepage through slope; (b) gravitational and seepage forces acting on element.

In the case of action of seepage forces (Figure 3.4) the inclination of the slope must be considerably reduced because in the direction of B an additional force is acting due to the seepage

$$B'' = Vp_s$$
$$B = B' + B'' = W' \sin \beta + Vp_s$$
$$= V\gamma_{sub} \sin \beta + V\gamma_w i$$
$$= V\gamma_{sub} \sin \beta + V\gamma_w \sin \beta$$

The frictional resistance opposing sliding

$$T = W' \cos \beta \tan \phi = V\gamma_{sub} \cos \beta \tan \phi$$

In the conditions of limiting equilibrium

$$B_{max} = T_{max}$$
$$V\gamma_{sub} \sin \beta_{max} + V\gamma_w \sin \beta_{max} = V\gamma_{sub} \cos \beta_{max} \tan \phi$$
$$(\gamma_{sub} + \gamma_w) \sin \beta_{max} = \gamma_{sub} \cos \beta_{max} \tan \phi$$
$$\tan \beta_{max} = \frac{\gamma_{sub}}{\gamma_{sub} + \gamma_w} \tan \phi$$

Assuming $\gamma_{sub} \approx \gamma_w = 9 \cdot 8$ kN/m^3 the following expression is obtained:

$$\tan \beta_{max} = \tfrac{1}{2} \tan \phi$$

For small angles it can be assumed that

$$\beta_{max} = 0 \cdot 5\phi \tag{3.2}$$

and therefore, in the case of action of seepage forces on a cohesionless soil in a slope, the maximum angle of the slope diminishes to half the value of the angle of internal friction.

However, one must also consider the fact that the grains of soil at the point where water emerges on the surface of the slope are under the action of water running down its face which, in addition to the above-mentioned forces, exerts on them a downward drag and thus leads to its erosion. To prevent this, for example in earth dams, toe filters are incorporated which collect the water seeping through the dam and prevent scouring. Without such filters the angle of slope would have to be considerably smaller than 0.5ϕ; it is usually of the order of $6–8°$.

3.3. Stability of Slopes in Cohesive Soils

At present there are two methods of evaluation of the stability of slopes in cohesive soils: the first one is based on the theory of the state of limiting equilibrium of granular media and the second on the hypothesis of the cylindrical slip surfaces (a special case of the upper bound solution of the theory of plasticity) which is generally referred to as the *slip circle method*.

3.3.1. METHOD OF LIMITING EQUILIBRIUM

The first method was chiefly developed by Sokolovsky (1960) and was published in his well-known book entitled *Statics of Granular Media*. In his approach, based on the generalized Prandtl's problem, the stability of slopes is one of the problems of the statics of soil media.

The stability of a slope in a cohesive soil of known strength parameters c and ϕ is considered.

The governing equations are derived from consideration of the static equilibrium and the Coulomb–Mohr failure criterion (Equations (2.10)); the boundary conditions take into consideration any external loading which might be acting on the slope.

For the simplest case of a slope in homogeneous isotropic soil (of unit weight γ and strength parameters c and ϕ) a nomogram was prepared by Sokolovsky (Cytovich, 1963) in terms of dimensionless coordinates x' and z' (Figure 3.5):

$$x' = \frac{\gamma}{c}x \quad \text{and} \quad z' = \frac{\gamma}{c}z$$

where x and z are the actual coordinates defining the profile of the limiting slope.

When c, ϕ, γ, and z are given, the value of z' is evaluated and the corresponding value of x' is read off the nomogram; then

$$x = \frac{c}{\gamma}x'$$

By taking different values of z one can determine the corresponding values of x and hence plot the profile of the limiting slope (with the factor of safety of

$F = 1 \cdot 0$). In order to obtain a factor of safety $F > 1 \cdot 0$ the values of c and ϕ are suitably reduced.

The practical application of the above method encounters considerable difficulties when one has to deal with external loading of slopes, effects of seepage of the ground water, and non-homogeneous soils. Therefore the second method, based on the determination of the most critical cylindrical slip surface, is most frequently used.

There are a number of different versions of the slip circle method (Fellenius, Terzaghi, Krey, Maslov, and others). The differences between them are quite considerable in the actual assumptions as well as in the method of solution.

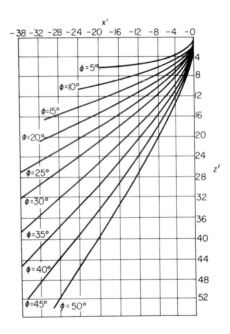

Figure 3.5. Limiting slope profile in dimensionless coordinates x' and z'.

3.3.2. INTRODUCTION TO SLIP CIRCLE METHODS

The failure of a slope in a cohesive soil is commonly in the form of a rotational slide in which sliding of an almost undisturbed mass of soil occurs along a curved surface (Figure 3.6); the failure is usually preceded by the formation of tension cracks behind the upper edge of the slope. For obvious practical reasons it is convenient to replace the real surface of failure, which resembles the arc of an ellipse by an arc of a circle, i.e. by the slip circle. At failure the full shear strength of the soil is mobilized along the slip circle, i.e. the soil along it is in the state of plastic equilibrium.

In the analysis of stability of a slope a quantitative estimate of the factor of safety against failure is obtained by examining the condition of equilibrium when incipient failure is postulated and by comparing the strength necessary to main-

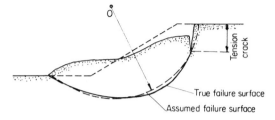

Figure 3.6. True and assumed failure surfaces for rotational slide.

tain limiting equilibrium with the available strength of the soil. The factor of safety F is thus defined as the ratio of the available shear strength to that required to maintain equilibrium. In the most general terms the mobilized shear strength is equal to s, where

$$s = \frac{\tau_f}{F} = \frac{1}{F}(c + \sigma \tan \phi) \qquad (3.3)$$

where c = cohesion of soil
ϕ = angle of internal shearing resistance
σ = stress component normal to slip circle
τ_f = shear strength of soil
F = factor of safety against slope failure

Since for any particular problem a large number of trial surfaces can be assumed, it is necessary to determine the most critical slip circle for which the factor of safety F has the minimum value. This is usually achieved by analysing a sufficiently large number of trial surfaces until the most critical one is found.

It is clear from Equation (3.3) that, in order to examine the equilibrium of the mass of soil above the slip surface, it is necessary to know the value of the normal stress at each point along this surface. For the most general case of soil and ground water conditions, it is convenient to determine the value of the normal stress by using the method of slices (Fellenius, 1936) in which the conditions for the static equilibrium of the slice of soil lying vertically above each element of the slip surface are satisfied. The forces acting on such a slice are shown in Figure 3.7(a) and include the resultants Z_i, Z_{i+1}, X_i, and X_{i+1} of shear and normal stresses along the sides of the slice as well as the resultants T_i and N_i of the shear and normal stresses acting along the failure surface; the polygon of forces is shown in Figure 3.7(b). When a slope is divided into n thin slices it will be observed that there are $4n - 2$ unknowns and only $3n$ equations of equilibrium to determine them, i.e. the problem is highly statically indeterminate. Hence it is necessary to make further assumptions to remove the extra unknowns. The value of the computed factor of safety will, of course, depend on the validity of the assumptions that are made.

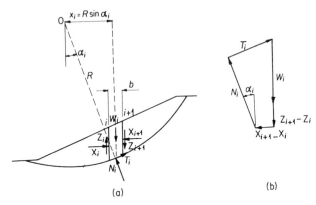

Figure 3.7. Forces acting on a slice: (a) complete system of forces; (b) polygon of forces.

The many existing solutions based on the method of slices usually differ in the assumptions that are made with regard to the forces that act against the sides of the slices. Two such methods which do not fully satisfy the requirements of static equilibrium but have been found to give reasonably correct answers for most problems and are relatively simple in application are presented below.

3.3.3. THE FELLENIUS METHOD*

It is assumed that the resultant of the forces acting upon the sides of any slice is parallel to the failure surface as shown in Figure 3.8(a). With this assumption it is possible to evaluate at all points along the surface of failure the forces normal to it:

$$N_i = W_i \cos \alpha_i \tag{3.4}$$

where W_i = self-weight of slice i
          α_i = angle between surface of failure of slice i and horizontal
             (Figure 3.8(a))

With the knowledge of N_i and of the soil strength parameters c and ϕ it is now possible to determine the available shearing resistance for each slice:

$$T_{i \max} = N_i \tan \phi + cA_i = W_i \cos \alpha_i \tan \phi + cl_i \tag{3.5}$$

where A_i = area of slip surface of element i; for a strip of unit width
          $A_i = l_i \times 1 \cdot 0 = b_i \sec \alpha_i$ (Figure 3.8(a))

* Also known as the *Swedish circle method* or *ordinary method of slices*.

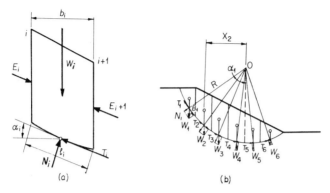

Figure 3.8. Stability of a slope in cohesive soils: (a) forces acting on a slice in the Fellenius method; (b) details of slices and slip circle.

Hence the total maximum moment about the centre of the circle of the forces resisting the slide is given by

$$M_R = \sum_{i=1}^{n} T_{i\,max}\, R = R \sum_{i=1}^{n} (W_i \cos \alpha_i \tan \phi + cb_i \sec \alpha_i) \qquad (3.6)$$

The moment about the centre of the circle of the disturbing forces (the weight of the soil — Figure 3.8(b)) is equal to

$$M_D = \sum_{i=1}^{n} W_i x_i = \sum_{i=1}^{n} W_i R \sin \alpha_i = R \sum_{i=1}^{n} W_i \sin \alpha_i \qquad (3.7)$$

If the same factor of safety F is assumed for all the slices, then it is equal to the ratio of the restoring moment M_R to the disturbing moment M_D:

$$F = \frac{M_R}{M_D} = \frac{\sum\limits_{i=1}^{n} (W_i \cos \alpha_i \tan \phi + cb_i \sec \alpha_i)}{\sum\limits_{i=1}^{n} W_i \sin \alpha_i} \qquad (3.8)$$

By changing the radius of the circle R and the position of its centre, the critical slip circle is obtained for which the value of F is a minimum.

In the case of limiting equilibrium, i.e. when the mobilized shearing resistance along the critical slip surface is equal to the available resistance,

$$F_{min} = 1 \cdot 0$$

The above method can be used for both total and effective stress analyses. In the former case the undrained strength parameters c_u and ϕ_u are used, whereas in the latter case the effective normal force N_i' is used in Equation (3.5) in place of N_i, together with the strength parameters c' and ϕ',

$$N_i' = N_i - u_i A_i = W_i \cos \alpha_i - u_i b_i \sec \alpha_i \qquad (3.9)$$

where u_i = pore water pressure mid-way along slip surface of element i
obtained from flow net

b_i = width of slice i (see Equation (3.5))

The above method is simple in application but because of the initial assumptions the errors involved are quite high although on the safe side (Whitman and Bailey, 1967).

3.3.4. THE SIMPLIFIED BISHOP METHOD

In this method (Bishop, 1955) it is assumed that the resultant of the forces acting upon the sides of any slice is horizontal, i.e. that their resultant in the vertical direction is zero. In the most general case of the effective stress analysis the force N_i' is obtained by considering the vertical equilibrium of the forces shown in Figure 3.9. A value of safety factor is used to express the shear forces T_i, and it is assumed that this factor of safety equals the F defined by Equation (3.8). Then

$$N_i' = \frac{W_i - u_i b_i - c' b_i \tan \alpha_i / F}{\cos \alpha_i (1 + \tan \alpha_i \tan \phi'/F)} \tag{3.10}$$

On evaluation of the total maximum restoring moment M_R and the disturbing moment M_D (Equation (3.7)) the following expression is obtained:

$$F = \frac{\sum_{i=1}^{n} \{c' b_i + (W_i - u_i b_i) \tan \phi'\} \{1/M_i(\alpha)\}}{\sum_{i=1}^{n} W_i \sin \alpha_i} \tag{3.11}$$

where

$$M_i(\alpha) = \{1 + (\tan \phi' \tan \alpha_i)/F\} \cos \alpha_i \tag{3.12}$$

Because the factor of safety F appears on both sides of Equation (3.11) it is determined by a trial and error method; the convergence of trials is very rapid (see Table 3.2). The method lends itself to a tabular method of solution

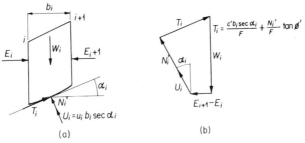

Figure 3.9. Forces considered in the simplified Bishop method of slices: (a) forces acting on a slice; (b) force polygon.

(Table 3.2) and computer programs are readily available. In manual calculations the values of the function $M_i(\alpha)$ can be taken from the nomogram in Figure 3.10.

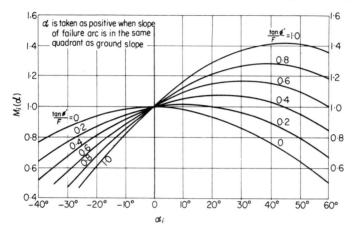

Figure 3.10. Nomogram for determination of $M_i(\alpha)$ (after Janbu *et al.*, 1956; by permission of the Director of the Norwegian Geotechnical Institute).

Because of the initial simplifying assumption the values of N_i and F are not exact. However, numerous examples have shown that the values of F obtained by this method are very close to the solutions determined by the rigorous method (Bishop, 1955). Investigation of cases of actual slope failures for which the strength parameters and the ground water conditions have been accurately established confirm the accuracy of the method. Therefore the simplified Bishop method is recommended for the practical use.

In investigation of the short-term stability of clay slopes the undrained strength parameters c_u and ϕ_u are used and the pore water pressure term in Equation (3.11) is omitted. In the special case of $\phi_u = 0$ Equations (3.8) and (3.11) become identical because the shear strength of the soil is no longer dependent on the normal stress on the slip surface:

$$F = \frac{\displaystyle\sum_{i=1}^{n} c_u b_i \sec \alpha_i}{\displaystyle\sum_{i=1}^{n} W_i \sin \alpha_i} = \frac{\displaystyle\sum_{i=1}^{n} c_u l_i}{\displaystyle\sum_{i=1}^{n} W_i \sin \alpha_i} \qquad (3.13)$$

Because of the necessity of ensuring a reasonable margin of safety the recommended values of the minimum factor of safety $F_{\min}$ are usually taken between 1·1 and 1·5, the choice depending on the importance of the projects (for projects involving buildings $F_{\min} = 1·5$).

In order to reduce the number of trials a graphical method can be used for determination of the line along which the centre of the critical circle lies in the case of homogeneous soils and along which the first trial locations can be taken in the cases of non-homogeneous soils or when seepage is considered (Figure 3.11 and Table 3.1).

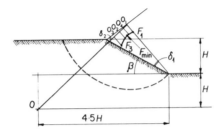

Figure 3.11. Graphical determination of location of centres of critical slip circles.

Table 3.1. Values of angles δ_1 and δ_2
for different slope angles β

β	$1 : m$	δ_1	δ_2
$45°$	$1 : 1$	$28°$	$37°$
$33°41'$	$1 : 1.5$	$26°$	$35°$
$26°34'$	$1 : 2$	$25°$	$35°$
$18°21'$	$1 : 3$	$25°$	$35°$
$11°19'$	$1 : 5$	$25°$	$37°$

For a given slope $(1 : m)$ the required line is constructed by joining points O and O_1, the latter having been determined with the help of angles δ_1 and δ_2 which, for the given slope are obtained from Table 3.1. Values of factors of safety F are evaluated for a series of circles with centres at O_1, O_2, O_3, and O_4. By plotting the values of F at these points the curve $F_1–F_3$ is obtained from which the minimum value of the factor of safety F_{min} is determined. For non-homogeneous soils or, when seepage is considered, factors of safety must also be determined for slip circles with centres outside the line OO_1; F_{min} and the location of the centre of the critical clip circle is then obtained by plotting contours of equal values of F.

3.3.5. DETERMINATION OF PORE WATER PRESSURES

The method of determination of pore water pressures u_i depends on the type of problem under consideration. In some problems the value of the pore water pressure depends either on the ground water level within the embankment or on the seepage pattern of water impounded by it (steady seepage condition), whereas in others the value of the pore water pressure depends on the magnitude of the applied stresses (e.g. rapid draw down or rapid construction of embankment).

In the steady seepage condition the pore water pressure is determined from the flow net, i.e. from the knowledge of the piezometric head at a given point; for stability analysis, points mid-way along the slip surface of each slice element are considered (see example). It is convenient in computer analysis to express the pore water pressure at these points in terms of the pore pressure ratio r_u and the corresponding total vertical stress (Bishop and Morgenstern, 1960):

$$r_u = \frac{\gamma_w h_{wi}}{\gamma h_i} = \frac{u_i}{\gamma h_i} \qquad (3.14)$$

where h_i = height of the slice i
h_{wi} = piezometric head mid-way along slipsurface of the slice i

In the case of a rapid change in the applied stresses the pore water pressure immediately after the change is given by the expression

$$u = u_0 + \Delta u \qquad (3.15)$$

where u_0 = initial value of the pore water pressure before any stress change
Δu = change in the pore water pressure due to the change in the applied stresses

According to Bishop (1954) the ratio of the pore water pressure change Δu to the change in the total major principal stress $\Delta\sigma_1$ can be expressed in terms of an overall pore pressure parameter $\bar{B}$:

$$\frac{\Delta u}{\Delta\sigma_1} = \bar{B} = B\left\{\frac{\Delta\sigma_3}{\Delta\sigma_1} + A\left(1 - \frac{\Delta\sigma_3}{\Delta\sigma_1}\right)\right\} \qquad (3.16)$$

where A and B are the pore pressure parameters defined in Volume 1, Equation (5.48).

Substituting into Equation (3.15) one obtains

$$u = u_0 + \bar{B}\Delta\sigma_1 \qquad (3.17)$$

For most practical purposes the major principal stress can be taken as equal to the weight of the soil (or soil and water) above the point under consideration and hence $\Delta\sigma_1$ can be evaluated simply as the change in that stress. The pore pressure parameter $\bar{B}$ is determined from special triaxial tests (Bishop and Henkel, 1957) in which the sample is subjected to stress changes corresponding to those expected in the field. In stability analysis of the upstream face of an earth dam, under the rapid draw down condition, $\bar{B}$ may be taken as unity.

Example. Using the simplified Bishop method determine the factor of safety F for the slope shown in Figure 3.12. Assume a slip circle of radius $R = 8\cdot5$ m with the centre of rotation O vertically above the point B. Soil properties are given in Figure 3.12.

Table 3.2. Tabulation for the simplified Bishop method
(example: homogeneous soil with steady seepage)

1	2	3	4	5	6	7	8	9	10	11	12	13	14	15	16	17	18
Slice i	Width of slice b_i (m)	Height of slice h_i (m)	$W_i = b_i h_i \gamma$ (kN)	$\sin \alpha_i = x_i/R$ *	α_i (degrees)	$W_i \sin \alpha_i$	Piezometric head at slip surface h_{wi} (m)	$u_i = \gamma_w h_{wi}$	$b_i u_i$	$W_i - u_i b_i$	$(W_i - u_i b_i)\tan \phi'$	$c' b_i$ (kN/m)	$12 + 13$	Assume F on r.h.s. of Equation (3.11), hence $M_i(\alpha)$	14×15	$M_i(\alpha)$ for F_1	14×17
1	0·7	0·35	4·9	−0·16	−9·2	−0·8	0	0	0	4·9	3·0	2·8	5·8	0·86	5·0	0·92	5·4
2	1·0	0·97	19·2	−0·06	−3·4	−0·1	0	0	0	19·2	12·0	4·0	16·0	0·95	15·2	0·97	15·5
3	1·0	1·60	31·7	0·06	3·4	0·2	0·10	1·0	1·0	30·7	19·4	4·0	23·4	1·03	24·0	1·02	23·9

4	1·0	2·20	43·6	0·18	10·2	7·7	1·15	11·3	11·3	32·3	20·2	4·0	24·2	1·10	26·6	1·06	25·6
5	1·0	2·60	51·5	0·29	17·1	15·3	1·60	15·7	15·7	35·8	22·8	4·0	26·8	1·14	30·6	1·07	28·7
6	1·0	3·05	60·5	0·41	24·4	24·9	1·65	16·2	16·2	44·3	27·7	4·0	31·7	1·19	37·8	1·08	34·2
7	1·0	3·04	60·1	0·53	31·9	31·8	1·45	14·2	14·2	45·9	28·6	4·0	32·6	1·19	38·8	1·06	34·5
8	1·0	2·97	58·8	0·65	40·5	38·3	1·05	10·3	10·3	48·5	30·2	4·0	34·0	1·18	40·1	1·02	34·7
9	1·0	2·65	52·4	0·76	49·5	39·8	0·25	2·5	2·5	49·9	31·2	4·0	35·2	1·11	39·1	0·95	33·4
10	1·1	1·43	30·0	0·89	62·8	26·7	0	0	0	30·0	18·9	4·2	23·1	1·02	23·5	0·82	19·0
					$\Sigma 7 = 181\cdot 8$									$\Sigma 16 = 280\cdot 7$		$\Sigma 18 = 254\cdot 9$	

$$F_1 = \frac{\Sigma 16}{\Sigma 7} = 1\cdot 55; \quad F_2 = \frac{\Sigma 18}{\Sigma 7} = 1\cdot 40$$

Remarks

(a) Distance x_i is measured from a vertical line through the centre of the slip circle and is taken as negative on the down-slope side of that line (Figure 3.12).

(b) If the difference between F_2 and F_1 is too large, one or two more iterations may be necessary.

Procedure

(1) Draw the slope and the flow net to 1 : 50 scale, Figure 3.12.

(2) Starting from B, divide the slope into a convenient number of vertical slices, preferably of equal width.

(3) Prepare Table 3.2 and read off the drawing information necessary to complete columns 1, 2, 3, 5, and 8.

(4) Complete columns 4, 6, 7, 9, 10, 11, 12, 13, and 14 and sum up column 7, $\Sigma 7$.

(5) Assume $F = 1.0$ on the right-hand side of Equation (3.11) and read off values of $M_i(\alpha)$ from Figure 3.10, column 15.

(6) Complete column 16 and sum it up, $\Sigma 16$.

(7) Obtain the first approximation to the factor of safety $F_1 = \Sigma 16/\Sigma 7$.

(8) Assume $F = F_1$ on the right-hand side of Equation (3.11) and read off new values of $M_i(\alpha)$, column 17.

(9) Complete column 18 and sum it up, $\Sigma 18$.

(10) Obtain the second approximation to the factor of safety $F_2 = \Sigma 18/\Sigma 7$.

(11) Repeat steps (8), (9), and (10) until the difference $F_{N+1} - F_N \leqslant |0.01|$.

(12) Choose another slip circle and repeat the above procedure until the critical circle is established, i.e. until the minimum factor of safety is obtained.

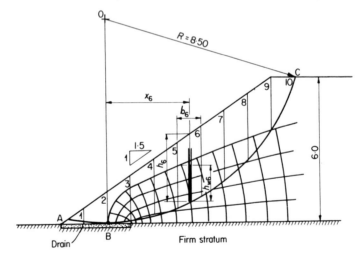

Figure 3.12. Example: details of slope and flow net. Soil properties: $\gamma = 19.8$ kN/m³; $c' = 4$ kN/m²; $\phi' = 32°$.

3.3.6. NOMOGRAMS FOR SLOPES IN HOMOGENEOUS SOILS

In the case of homogeneous soils nomograms can be used with the help of which the factor of safety or other parameters of the slope can easily be determined.

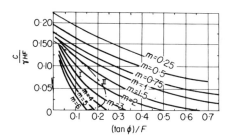

Figure 3.13. Nomogram for determination of slope stability (after Lomize, 1954).

With the help of Lomize's nomogram (Figure 3.13) the following can be determined.

(a) The maximum slope 1 : m for given γ, c, ϕ, H, and factor of safety F.

(b) The maximum height of slope H for given γ, c, ϕ, m, and F.

(c) The factor of safety for given γ, c, ϕ, m, and H.

The dashed line divides the nomogram into two zones: zone 1 refers to the base-slips which are associated with the weak soils of $\phi < 14°$, and zone 2 to the more common toe slip in which the slip surface passes through the toe of the slope.

3.3.7. GENERAL CONSIDERATIONS

According to the authors the initial investigations of stability of slopes associated with important structures should be carried out on the basis of Lomize's nomograms and in the final stages should be checked using the simplified Bishop method.

The strength parameters c and ϕ must be determined under the conditions corresponding to those under which the soil is going to be stressed *in situ*, i.e. for short-term stability of clay slopes c_u and ϕ_u are obtained from undrained tests and for long-term stability c' and ϕ' are obtained from drained tests (or undrained tests with pore water pressure measurements).

In the case of stability of natural or artificial slopes in regions where previous mass movements have taken place or where the soils have been deformed and folded by tectonic activities or ice advances, pre-existing slip planes (slickensides) may be present along which the shear strength parameters are reduced to the residual values of $c_r' \approx 0$ and ϕ_r' ranging between $6°$ and $18°$ (Volume 1, Section 5.4.6).

Long-term stability of artificial slopes in fissured clays, i.e. in most of the very cohesive and heavily overconsolidated clays, should be investigated in terms of the remoulded strength parameters because softening of the soil occurs as water is absorbed through the network of structural discontinuities which tend to open under the action of the induced shear stresses.

Very high locked-in horizontal stresses are usually present in the weathered zones of the very heavily overconsolidated deposits such as shales or Keuper Marls. When the horizontal support is removed by excavation of a trench or a cut, large strains take place which usually result in the damage of structures above the excavation and sometimes culminate in the collapse of the bank. Recent observations of deformations around deep excavations in London Clay indicate that, even if rigid diaphragm walls are used to support the sides, horizontal movements of the order of 60 mm are not uncommon.

Particularly dangerous in the sides of excavations are the zones of bedding planes between clay or silty clay and saturated sand or silt; the excavation results in the decrease of stresses in the soil and with a readily available supply of water the cohesive soil can swell and soften at a fairly rapid rate. If the dip of the bedding plane is steep, a slip may develop in a very short time after the excavation.

3.4. Translational Slides

3.4.1. WEDGE METHOD

In cases when the potential or the actual failure surface consists of several straight or approximately straight-line sections Shahunianc's wedge method (Cytovich, 1963) can be used. The mass of the sliding soil is divided into wedges corresponding to straight-line sections of the failure surface. The weight of each of the wedges W_i is then resolved into normal and tangential components N_i and B_i. The sliding force exerted by wedge 1 is E_1. According to the notation in Figure 3.14

$$E_1 + N_1 \tan \phi + c_1 L_1 - B_1 = 0$$

and on substitution of $N_1 = W_1 \cos \alpha_1$, and $B_1 = W_1 \sin \alpha_1$, one obtains

$$E_1 = W_1 \sin \alpha_1 - W_1 \cos \alpha_1 \tan \phi_1 - c_1 L_1 \qquad (3.14)$$

When considering the next wedge the force E_1 is taken as acting in the opposite direction.

On evaluation of the sliding forces E_i for all the wedges, their values are plotted at individual sections of the sliding mass (Figure 3.14). A retaining wall designed for the appropriate sliding force multiplied by the required factor of safety is usually positioned at the section at which E_i has the minimum value.

3.5. Stability of Embankments on Soft Soils

Considering the shape of the embankment and the soil conditions shown in Figure 3.15 its stability should be checked for the following modes of failure: (a) the displacement of the soft soil from beneath the embankment, (b) a slip failure along the soft layer.

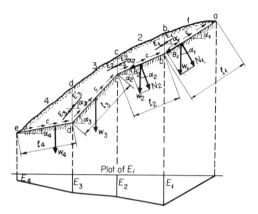

Figure 3.14. Details of forces considered in the wedge method of stability analysis (after Shahunianc, 1945).

The horizontal displacement of the mud from underneath the embankment can take place in connection with the induced difference in the resultant horizontal forces ΔE_m acting on sections AC and BD in the mud layer:

$$\Delta E_m = \int_0^{h_m} (\sigma_{x_1} - \sigma_{x_2})\, dh \qquad (3.15)$$

The displacement is opposed by the cohesive resistance of the mud C_{12} acting along the AB and CD sections of the horizontal planes:

$$C_{12} = 2c_m l_{12} = 2c_m Hm \qquad (3.16)$$

Assuming that the crust of the mud has the same unit weight as the embankment and that the coefficient of lateral stress of the mud $K = 1 \cdot 0$, then

$$\left.\begin{aligned}\sigma_{x_1} &= K\{(H + h_c)\gamma + h\gamma_m\} \\ \sigma_{x_2} &= K(h_c\gamma + h\gamma_m)\end{aligned}\right\} \qquad (3.17)$$

and

$$\Delta E_m = H\gamma h_m \qquad (3.18)$$

For safety the following condition should be satisfied:

$$F = \frac{C_{12}}{\Delta E_m} = \frac{2c_m Hm}{H\gamma h_m} = \frac{2c_m m}{\gamma h_m} \geqslant F_{all} \qquad (3.19)$$

The investigation of the possible sliding of the shoulder of the embankment along the plane AB is based on the comparison of the active thrust E_{aA} in the embankment and the crust, with the cohesive resistance of the mud within the plane AB.

Generally the thickness of the crust h_c is relatively small and it can be assumed that the resultants of stresses in the crust on sections 1A and 2B

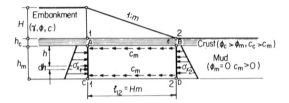

Figure 3.15. Schematic diagram of displacement of mud from beneath an embankment.

cancel out; with this assumption one need only consider the active thrust E_{aA} in the embankment (Equation (4.15)):

$$E_{aA} = \frac{\gamma H^2}{2} \tan^2 \left(45 - \frac{\phi}{2}\right) - 2cH \tan \left(45 - \frac{\phi}{2}\right) + \frac{2c^2}{\gamma}$$

According to Cytovich (1963) the expression for E_{aA} should allow for possible formation of the tension crack and hence includes the term $2c^2/\gamma$.

The cohesive resistance of the mud along AB is

$$C_{AB} = c_m l_{12} = c_m Hm \qquad (3.20)$$

For safety the following condition should be satisfied:

$$F = \frac{C_{AB}}{E_{aA}} \geqslant F_{all} \qquad (3.21)$$

For any given height H of the embankment its stability can be improved, for example, by decreasing its side slopes, i.e. by increasing the value of m or by installation of a reinforced concrete grillage over the entire width of the embankment to prevent the rupture of the crust.

3.6. Additional Factors Affecting Stability of Slopes

Apart from the already considered effects of the self-weight of the soil (and applied loading), the seepage pressure, and the pore water pressure (hydrostatic), the stability of slopes can be considerably affected by other factors such as additional forces or unexpected changes of the ground water conditions.

The slopes of embankments or cuttings in cohesive soils, within a short time of their completion, frequently exhibit vertical cracks above their crest (Figure 3.16). In the authors' opinion the formation of these cracks is due to the desiccation and shrinkage of the soil near the surface of the slope. The cracks form near the crest of the slope where the highest tensile stresses are induced by the combined action of the forces due to the shrinkage and self-weight of the soil. The shrinkage along the surface of the slope can be evaluated approximately from the following expression:

$$\Delta l = \alpha_t l \qquad (3.22)$$

From field observations the coefficient of shrinkage α_t can be the order of 0·005, which, in the case of a slope of length $l = 10$ m, results in shrinkage of approximately 50 mm. The width of the tension cracks depends mainly on the water content of the clay; the higher the water content the greater is the shrinkage on desiccation.

The presence of the tension cracks lowers the stability of the slope owing to the reduction in length of the surface of failure over which the shearing resistance is mobilized and owing to the fact that water can enter the cracks, and, as it is not able to escape, it can exert a hydrostatic pressure on their sides which contributes to the disturbing forces. Because of this, tension cracks should be eliminated, as soon as possible after their first appearance, by opening them up to a depth of 0·5 m and backfilling with well-compacted impermeable soil.

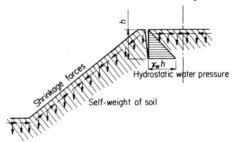

Figure 3.16. Formation of tension cracks near the crest of slope.

The hydrostatic pressure can have a considerable effect on the stability of hill sides in fissured rocks, particularly if the fissures are parallel to the slopes and thus form the potential planes of sliding. According to Wiłun this was the cause of tw) major slides near Zakopane (Poland). In both cases the sliding was taking place in inexplicable circumstances, because according to the conventional methods of analysis the frictional forces were greater than the tangential components of the self-weight of the rock (Śliwa, 1955). However, if one considers the hydrostatic pressure of water in the fissures, the causes of the slides become quite obvious (Figure 3.17). The length of the surface of sliding AB = 300 m. The weight of the sliding mass of rock AEDB $W = 17·7$ MN/m (1800 t/m). The total pressure of water on the surface AB can be as high as 53 MN/m (5400 t/m).

When the fissures forming the surface of sliding AB are filled with water to a piezometric level CD (maximum), the upward hydrostatic pressure along the surface AB reduces the effective weight of the sliding mass of rock, which obviously results in reduction of the frictional resistance along the surface AB and the mass of rock AEDB begins to slide. The fact that the sliding always

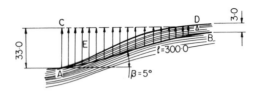

Figure 3.17. The effect of hydrostatic pressure within the sliding plane.

occurred after very heavy rainfalls, when a large quantity of water was available to fill the fissures and to build up a sufficiently high water pressure, confirms this hypothesis.

The phenomenon of the upward pressure on an impermeable stratum can cause translational or rotational slides not only in mountainous areas but also in cuttings in lowlands, when an impermeable soil in the bottom of an excavation is underlain by a permeable stratum with piezometric level of the ground water much higher than the bottom of the excavation.

In the case of very cohesive clays ($w_1 > 50$), interbedded with layers of saturated sand through which water can enter, gradual decrease in the strength of the clay can take place owing to swelling. The swelling of the clay can take place after excavation of the cutting because the clay is unloaded and it can absorb water from the sand over a long period of time. In such cases the sliding takes place after a period of six to twelve months, i.e. after swelling of the clay has taken place.

A high ground water table in slopes in laminated soils may lead to washing out of sand (piping) and hence to swelling of the cohesive soil, which again leads to a decrease in its strength.

3.7. Measures for Improving Stability of Slopes

The stability of slopes in cuts can be improved by the following.

(1) Reduction of the slope angle.

(2) Installation of land drains behind the crest of the slope to cut off the seepage of ground water, or by the installation of deep counterfort type of drains or horizontal shafts to lower the phreatic surface; the lowering of the phreatic surface near the toe of the slope considerably increases the effective stresses in that region thus improving the stability of the slope.

(3) Installation of piles or diaphragm walls parallel to the slope (Bennett, 1971; West et al., 1971) or by construction of heavy retaining walls (Figure 3.18; Zénczykowski, 1949), all of which increase the resistance to sliding. Wiłun (1963) suggests that, if piles are used, they should be capped together with a reinforced concrete grillage installed beneath the surface of the slope.

(4) Restrictions on placing of loads on the slope or above it, which may contribute to the disturbing forces.

(5) Cement grouting — if open joints are observed in the vicinity of the failure surface.

(6) Installation of counterfort type of drains which extend below the surface of failure; such drains when filled with crashed rock also act as counterforts within the slope.

(7) Replacement of the unstable soil from the toe of the slip, to a depth below the failure surface, with a stable material such as sand or quarry-waste. The stability of embankment (fill) slopes can be ensured by (a) the use of appropriate slope angles; (b) not using cohesive soils with liquid limit $w_1 > 50\%$ for embankments higher than 3 metres; for embankments lower than 3 m, clays

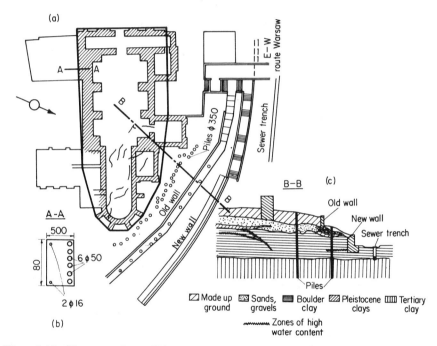

Figure 3.18. Slip area and remedial measures St. Ann's Church by the E–W route in Warsaw: (a) location plan; (b) section through reinforcing ring beam A–A; (c) geological section B–B.

can be used with $w_1 < 65\%$; (c) placing the fill in layers and compacting it properly; care should be taken during the construction to provide adequate falls to prevent excessive softening of the fill by rain water; and (d) sealing of any shrinkage cracks (Section 3.6) through which water can enter the embankment.

In investigation of active slides the causes and the circumstances which lead to their activation should be ascertained as accurately as possible. Inspection of trial pits excavated to the depth of the failure surface can be very informative.

Having established the geometrical shape of the failure surface and the ground water conditions (expressed in the form of a flow net), an approximate analysis of the disturbing and resisting forces can be made by considering the soil to be in the state of limiting equilibrium, i.e. $F = 1.0$.

Once the forces involved have been established it is possible to design remedial measures which will ensure that the factor of safety F has a required higher value.

At the same time the authors wish to stress that the accurate location of areas susceptible to landslides, in long railway or motorway cuttings, is very difficult during the design stages and, if it is not possible to alter the route, then one may have to accept the risk of some landslides actually taking place. In certain cases it is more economic to carry out remedial measures in stabilizing local landslides which may occur on completion of long routes than to carry out extensive and lengthy investigations or to ensure no failures by the use of very conservative slope angle or other expensive measures.

In the case of very important projects the authors suggest that trial cuts should be excavated or trial embankments constructed, at a sufficiently early stage and with slopes steeper than finally envisaged, so that the final factors of safety can be established on the basis of actual failures. The depth of the trial cuts should be so chosen that the resulting slides do not disturb the soil below the final profile of the proposed excavation. Observations of the trial slopes should be carried out over a sufficiently long period of time and, if possible, during the winter—spring period.

3.8. Stability of Foundations

When it is proposed to excavate a cutting close to an existing building or structure it should be ensured that there is an adequate factor of safety against the failure of the loaded slope. The same applies to the construction of new structures close to the crest of existing cuttings or on natural or artificial slopes.

It is suggested that in the case of tall buildings their stability should also be checked when they are founded on level ground and the soil at depths is weaker than that immediately below the foundation. In connection with this it is necessary to know the properties of the soils to a depth at least equal to the width of the building.

The analysis of the stability of buildings on weak soils should be carried out using either the methods developed for the determination of the ultimate bearing capacity (Sections 2.4 to 2.6) or methods outlined in Section 3.3; when the latter are used, which in the context of the theory of plasticity of soils represent another form of the upper bound solution to the same problem (Section 2.4.1), then the shearing resistance forces P_1 and P_2 developed on the sides of the mass of soil perpendicular to the curved surface of failure can be added to the restoring forces (Figure 3.19).

The approximate position of the centre of the critical slip circle can be taken according to Wilson (Reynolds and Protopapadakis, 1946) from Figure 3.20, on the condition that several other slip circles are also investigated.

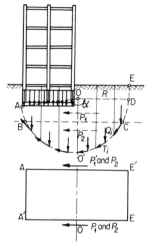

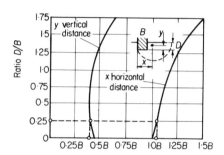

Figure 3.20. Wilson's nomogram for determination of centre of critical slip circle.

Figure 3.19. Stability of a building.

When large horizontal loads are acting on a structure its stability should always be investigated using either the method outlined in Section 2.6 or by considering the possibility of the combined structure–soil rotational slip failure as outlined above.

Whichever method of analysis of the stability of buildings is used, and in the case of important structures both should be carried out, the minimum factor of safety should not be less than two, i.e. $F_{min} = 2$.

4

Earth-retaining Structures

Earth-retaining structures are used when soils have to be retained at slopes steeper than those which they would naturally assume, when for some practical reasons abrupt changes in ground levels have to be introduced or when it is necessary to protect soil banks against destructive agencies. Before these structures can be designed it is necessary to establish the magnitude and distribution of stresses that the soils exert on or transfer to them.

Similar problems arise in the design of structures or foundations which transmit horizontal components of forces to soils and rely upon them to provide the necessary reactions.

The problem of determination of stresses exerted by soils on structures is a very complex one. The magnitude of the total thrust on a retaining wall, for example, depends mainly on the physical and mechanical properties of the retained soils while the distribution of stress depends on the type and mode of deformation of the wall. Because of these difficulties most of the present-day methods of design are still only based on the consideration of the state of limiting equilibrium in soils (Chapter 2) and on semi-empirical knowledge of stress distributions associated with different types of structures. Deformation of the retained soils, which frequently are the main design criteria for retaining structures situated in the vicinity of existing buildings, are not as yet directly taken into consideration.

In the following sections the total thrust on retaining structures will be considered, in general, as consisting of three components.

(1) Thrust due to the self-weight of soil.
(2) Resultant of pore water pressures (if ground water is present).
(3) Thrust due to surcharge loads (if present).

In the case of cohesive soils the first two components may be considered, in certain circumstances, together.

4.1. Stresses Due to the Self-weight of Soil

4.1.1. THE CONCEPT OF ACTIVE AND PASSIVE STATES OF LIMITING EQUILIBRIUM

The stresses which exist in the soil due to the self-weight of the overlying strata are referred to as overburden stresses (Section 1.2). In the case of a horizontal ground surface the vertical and horizontal components of the overburden stresses are also principal stresses and therefore the state of stress at any point M (Figure 4.1(a)) within the soil mass can be simply defined by stress circle PQ (Figure 4.1(b)).

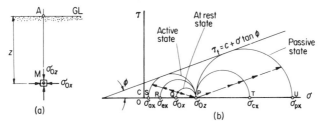

Figure 4.1. Graphical representation of different states of stress at point M.

Unless external loading (surcharge) is applied to the soil or the soil is allowed to deform under the action of internal (body) forces, the stresses within it will remain equal to the overburden stresses. This means that, for example, if the soil to the left of the vertical line AM (Figure 4.1(a)) is replaced with a retaining structure and the soil to the right of that line is not allowed to deform during or after its construction, then the lateral stresses on the structure will remain equal to the lateral overburden stresses σ_{ox}; because these stresses are associated with zero deformations of the soil they are referred to as the *lateral stresses at rest*.

Introducing the concept of the coefficient of lateral stress at rest, K_0, the lateral overburden stresses can be expressed in terms of the vertical stress component, σ_{oz}:

$$\sigma_{ox} = \sigma_{oy} = K_0 \sigma_{oz} \tag{4.1}$$

The coefficient, K_0, refers to the effective overburden stresses and its value depends on the type of soil and on its past history (Section 1.2.2).

Let us now consider a case in which during or after the construction of a smooth retaining structure to the left of line AM the soil at M is allowed to expand laterally under the action of the body forces (i.e. vertical overburden stresses σ_{oz}). The lateral expansion of the soil against a smooth wall does not affect the vertical stress at M but leads to a decrease in the lateral stress σ_{ox} to some new value σ_{ex}; the new state of stress at M is now defined by stress circle

PR. If the expansion is allowed to proceed further, a state of stress is reached eventually which is represented by a stress circle tangential to the Coulomb–Mohr envelope (circle PS). This implies that the soil at M is now in the state of limiting equilibrium (Volume 1, Section 5.4.7) and further lateral expansion takes place at a constant lateral stress σ_{ax}. Because this stress is associated with continuous (active) deformation of the soil it is referred to as the *active lateral stress*; it represents the minimum lateral stress on the wall at M. Utilizing Equation (5.59) of Volume 1 we obtain

$$\sigma_{ax} = \sigma_{oz} \tan^2 \left(45 - \frac{\phi}{2}\right) - 2c \tan \left(45 - \frac{\phi}{2}\right) \tag{4.2}$$

Introducing the coefficient of lateral active stress $K_a = \tan^2 (45 - \phi/2)$ we obtain the following simplified expression:

$$\sigma_{ax} = \sigma_{oz} K_a - 2c \sqrt{K_a} \tag{4.2a}$$

In the case of cohesionless soils ($c = 0$) the last terms in the above expressions are equal to zero.

If now the line AM is considered to represent the back of a smooth foundation which under the action of external horizontal force is pushed into the soil (i.e. to the right of line AM), then the soil at M is now being compressed laterally. Again, the vertical stress at M is not affected by this compression but the lateral stress σ_{ox} increases to some new value σ_{cx}; the new state of stress is now defined by stress circle PT (Figure 4.1(b)). As before, if the compression is allowed to proceed further a state of stress is reached, eventually, which is represented by circle PU tangential to the failure envelope; the soil at M is again in the state of limiting equilibrium and further lateral compression takes place at a constant lateral stress σ_{px}. Because this stress is associated with the passive resistance of the soil it is referred to as the *passive lateral stress*; it represents the maximum resistance of the soil that the foundation will encounter at M. Utilizing Equation (5.59) of Volume 1 we obtain

$$\sigma_{px} = \sigma_{oz} \tan^2 \left(45 + \frac{\phi}{2}\right) + 2c \tan \left(45 + \frac{\phi}{2}\right) \tag{4.3}$$

and introducing the coefficient of lateral passive stress $K_p = \tan^2 (45 + \phi/2)$ we obtain the following simplified expression:

$$\sigma_{px} = \sigma_{oz} K_p + 2c \sqrt{K_p} \tag{4.3a}$$

As before, in the case of cohesionless soils the last terms in the above equations are equal to zero.

In the above simple cases the coefficients of lateral active and passive stresses are functions of the angle of internal shearing resistance, ϕ, only (Table 4.3) and are interrelated as follows:

$$K_a = \frac{1}{K_p} \tag{4.4}$$

Jáky (1944) has shown that in the case of normally consolidated cohesionless soils the coefficient of lateral stress at rest can also be considered as a function of ϕ' only; on the basis of experimental evidence he has suggested the following relationship:

$$K_0 = 1 - \sin \phi' \tag{4.5}$$

It can be shown easily that

$$K_p > K_0 > K_a$$

The gradual transition from the 'at rest' state to the fully active and passive conditions is illustrated in Figure 4.2. Experimental and field evidence indicates that in the case of cohesionless soils the active condition is attained when the top of the wall moves outwards by less than 0·5% of the wall height. On the other hand, to obtain the totally passive condition inward lateral deformations of the order of 4% have to be generated. In the case of heavily preconsolidated cohesive soils the situation is almost reversed, i.e. the lateral stresses at rest are very close to the passive and not active condition and large outward lateral deformations are necessary to attain the active state (Figure 4.2).

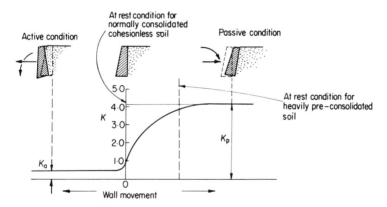

Figure 4.2. Transition from 'at rest' state to fully active and passive conditions.

4.1.2. LIMITING EQUILIBRIUM METHODS

The above simple cases of limiting equilibrium are often referred to as Rankine's active and passive states of stress. They represent, in fact, solutions of special plane strain boundary problems of the general theory of plastic equilibrium of soil media based on the Coulomb–Mohr failure criterion. Rigorous solutions of more complicated boundary problems which include, for example, wall friction and surcharge effects, were presented by Sokolovsky (1960). In the case of plane strain problems they reduce to the solution of simultaneous partial differential equations (2.10) which can be presented in the form of slip surfaces and distribution of direction and magnitude of principal stresses along them. In general, slip surfaces within the plastic zones are curved (Figure 4.3(c)) and only

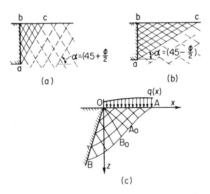

Figure 4.3. Plastic equilibrium zones and slip surfaces: (a) Rankine's active state; (b) Rankine's passive state; (c) general case of an inclined rough wall and surcharge.

in special cases can be expressed in closed mathematical equations (straight lines, circular arcs, or logarithmic spiral arcs).

In practice, apart from the simple cases of Rankine's active and passive states of plastic equilibrium the rigorous theoretical solutions are not frequently used. However, some of the theoretical slip surface patterns are often employed in practice in construction of stress fields and failure mechanisms used in approximate lower and upper bound solutions (Section 2.4.1).

4.1.2.1. General Case of Active and Passive Thrust in Cohesionless Soils

Using theoretical slip surface patterns (Figure 4.4) Sokolovsky (1960) has obtained approximate values of coefficients of active and passive stress for the case of a rough inclined wall with horizontal ground surface — Tables 4.1 and 4.2 respectively.

These coefficients can be used in evaluation of active and passive thrusts from the following simple equations:

$$E_a = \tfrac{1}{2} K_a \frac{\gamma H^2}{\sin^2 \alpha} \tag{4.6}$$

and

$$E_p = \tfrac{1}{2} K_p \frac{\gamma H^2}{\sin^2 \alpha} \tag{4.7}$$

where γ = unit weight of the retained soil
        δ = angle of friction between the soil and wall
        α = inclination of the back of the wall as shown in Figure 4.4

Note that in the case of a smooth ($\delta = 0°$) vertical wall ($\alpha = 90°$) the values
of K_a and K_p are the same as obtained from Rankine's solution (Table 4.3).

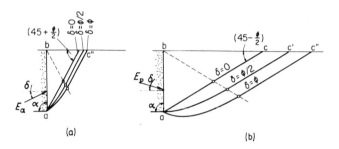

Figure 4.4. Slip surfaces for Sokolovsky's approximate solution: (a) active state;
(b) passive state.

Table 4.1. Values of coefficient of active stress K_a for
rough inclined wall with horizontal ground surface

α	ϕ	10°			20°			30°			40°		
	δ	0°	5°	10°	0°	10°	20°	0°	15°	30°	0°	20°	40°
120°		0·49	0·45	0·44	0·27	0·24	0·23	0·13	0·12	0·12	0·06	0·05	0·05
110°		0·58	0·54	0·52	0·35	0·32	0·30	0·20	0·18	0·17	0·11	0·10	0·09
100°		0·65	0·61	0·59	0·42	0·39	0·37	0·26	0·24	0·24	0·16	0·14	0·15
90°	K_a	0·70	0·66	0·65	0·49	0·45	0·44	0·33	0·30	0·31	0·22	0·20	0·22
80°		0·72	0·70	0·68	0·54	0·51	0·50	0·40	0·37	0·38	0·29	0·27	0·28
70°		0·73	0·70	0·70	0·57	0·54	0·54	0·46	0·44	0·45	0·35	0·34	0·38
60°		0·72	0·69	0·69	0·60	0·57	0·56	0·50	0·48	0·50	0·42	0·41	0·47

The distribution of stress in both active and passive cases is linear with depth and
and the stress components normal and tangential to the wall can be determined
from the following expressions:

$$\sigma_n = K\gamma z \frac{\cos \delta}{\sin \alpha} \tag{4.8}$$

$$\tau_n = \sigma_n \tan \delta \tag{4.9}$$

where K = coefficient K_a or K_p from Tables 4.1 and 4.2

Table 4.2. Values of coefficient of passive stress K_p for rough inclined wall with horizontal ground surface

α	ϕ	10°			20°			30°			40°		
	δ	0°	5°	10°	0°	10°	20°	0°	15°	30°	0°	20°	40°
120°		1·52	1·71	1·91	2·76	3·67	4·51	5·28	9·07	13·5	11·3	28·4	56·6
110°		1·53	1·69	1·83	2·53	3·31	4·04	4·42	7·38	10·8	8·34	19·5	39·0
100°		1·49	1·64	1·77	2·30	2·93	4·53	3·65	5·83	8·43	6·16	13·8	26·6
90°	K_p	1·42	1·55	1·66	2·04	2·55	3·04	3·00	4·62	6·56	4·60	9·69	18·2
80°		1·31	1·43	1·52	1·77	2·19	2·57	2·39	3·62	5·02	3·37	6·77	12·3
70°		1·18	1·28	1·35	1·51	1·83	2·13	1·90	2·80	3·80	2·50	4·70	8·22
60°		1·04	1·10	1·17	1·26	1·48	1·72	1·49	2·08	2·79	1·86	3·17	5·43

Example. Find the resultant active and passive thrusts per lineal metre of a retaining wall with sloping back, having a vertical height of 6·0 m and retaining a cohesionless soil with a horizontal surface.

Data: $\gamma = 16·0$ kN/m^3; $\phi = 30°$; $\delta = 20°$; $\alpha = 80°$

Active thrust
Interpolating from Table 4.1, $K_a = 0·38$ and therefore

$$E_a = \frac{0·38 \times 16·0 \times (6·0)^2}{2 \times (0·9848)^2} = 112·7 \text{ kN/m}$$

Passive thrust
Interpolating from Table 4.2, $K_p = 4·10$ and therefore

$$E_p = \frac{4·10 \times 16·0 \times 36}{2 \times (0·9848)^2} = 1215 \text{ kN/m}$$

For directions of action of E_a and E_p see Figure 4.4.

4.1.2.2. Rankine's Solution for Cohesionless Soils

By putting $c = 0$, Equations (4.2a) and (4.3a) can be used directly for evaluation of the lateral stresses in the case of smooth vertical walls retaining cohesionless soils with horizontal ground surface:

$$\sigma_{ax} = \sigma_{oz} K_a$$

and

$$\sigma_{px} = \sigma_{oz} K_p$$

The values of coefficients K_a and K_p are given in Table 4.3.

In the case of homogeneous soil of unit weight γ the vertical overburden stress is equal to γz and therefore

$$\sigma_{ax} = \gamma z K_a \tag{4.10}$$

and

$$\sigma_{px} = \gamma z K_p \tag{4.11}$$

The resultant thrusts are obtained by simple summation of the stresses over the height of the wall H:

$$E_a = \tfrac{1}{2} K_a \gamma H^2 \tag{4.12}$$

and

$$E_p = \tfrac{1}{2} K_p \gamma H^2 \tag{4.13}$$

Table 4.3. Values of coefficients of active and passive lateral stress for the case of smooth vertical wall with horizontal ground

ϕ (degrees)	K_a $= \tan^2 \left(45 - \dfrac{\phi}{2} \right)$	$\sqrt{K_a}$ $= \tan \left(45 - \dfrac{\phi}{2} \right)$	K_p $= \tan^2 \left(45 + \dfrac{\phi}{2} \right)$	$\sqrt{K_p}$ $= \tan \left(45 + \dfrac{\phi}{2} \right)$
5	0·8396	0·9163	1·1900	1·0913
10	0·7041	0·8391	1·4204	1·1918
15	0·5887	0·7673	1·6983	1·3032
20	0·4903	0·7002	2·0395	1·4281
25	0·4059	0·6371	2·4640	1·5697
30	0·3333	0·5774	3·0000	1·7321
35	0·2710	0·5206	3·6902	1·9210
40	0·2174	0·4663	4·5989	2·1445
45	0·1716	0·4142	5·8274	2·4142

4.1.2.3. Modified Rankine's Solution for Cohesive Soils

It can be seen from Equation (4.2a), which defines the active lateral stress on a smooth vertical wall with horizontal ground surface, that down to a certain depth the lateral stresses are negative.

This is due to the presence of cohesion and surface tension, i.e. due to the existence of compressive forces between the soil particles (Volume 1, Chapter 2), which enable the soil to resist a certain amount of tension. To find the depth of the tension zone, within which the soil is obviously able to stand unsupported, we equate the left-hand side of Equation (4.2a) to zero:

$$0 = K_a \sigma_{oz} - 2c \sqrt{K_a}$$

or

$$\sigma_{oz} = \frac{2c}{\sqrt{K_a}}$$

In homogeneous soils with no surcharge on the surface $\sigma_{oz} = \gamma z$ and hence solving for z

$$z_0 = \frac{2c}{\gamma \sqrt{K_a}} \qquad (4.14)$$

Where a uniformly distributed surcharge, q, is present on the ground surface, the depth z_0 must be measured from a height $h_s = q/\gamma$ above it. The value of h_s greater than z_0 implies that the tension zone has been suppressed by the surcharge and the soil exerts pressure on the wall over its entire height.

Equation (4.14) can also be used for approximate determination of the critical height of vertical slopes in cohesive soils with horizontal ground surface. In practice the critical height is greater than z_0 (Terzaghi, 1943). It should be kept in mind, however, that if such a slope is left unsupported for a long time then changes in the effective stresses will tend to soften the soil and hence decrease its strength parameters c and ϕ. Therefore, with sufficient degree of accuracy for practical purposes and with an increased margin of safety Equation (4.14) can be used for determination of the critical height H_c of unsupported vertical slopes.

As far as the active thrust on the wall is concerned the tensile stresses within the tension zone can be ignored. Therefore the distribution of lateral active stresses on the wall is obtained from Equation (4.2a) and the magnitude of the resultant thrust as given by the following equation:

$$E_a = \tfrac{1}{2} K_a \gamma H^2 - 2cH\sqrt{K_a} + \frac{2c^2}{\gamma} \qquad (4.15)$$

The last term in Equation (4.15) allows for the neglected tensile stresses. The point of application of E_a is as shown in Figure 4.5(a).

Water pressure on the wall in the tension zone should be taken into consideration regardless of the actual ground water conditions because rain water can accumulate in it.

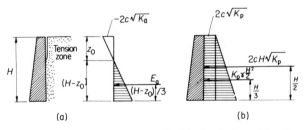

Figure 4.5. Active and passive lateral stresses, Rankine's solution: (a) active case; (b) passive case.

Example. Find the resultant active thrust per lineal metre of a smooth vertical 6·0 m high wall-retaining cohesive soil with a horizontal surface.

Data: $\gamma = 20 \cdot 0 \text{ kN/m}^3$; $\phi = 20°$; $c = 15 \text{ kN/m}^2$

From Table 4.3, $K_a = 0 \cdot 49$ and $\sqrt{K_a} = 0 \cdot 70$. Depth of the tension zone is obtained from Equation (4.14):

$$z_0 = \frac{2 \times 15}{20 \times 0 \cdot 70} = 2 \cdot 14 \text{ m}$$

and

$$H - z_0 = 6 \cdot 0 - 2 \cdot 14 = 3 \cdot 86 \text{ m}$$

The distribution of the active stress with depth is obtained from Equation (4.2a) by putting $\sigma_{oz} = \gamma z = 20z$:

$$\sigma_{ax} = 20 \times z \times 0 \cdot 49 - 2 \times 15 \times 0 \cdot 70 = (9 \cdot 8z - 21 \cdot 0) \text{ kN/m}^2$$

At $z = 0$

$$\sigma_{ax} = 0 - 21 \cdot 0 = -21 \cdot 0 \text{ kN/m}^2$$

and at $z = 6 \cdot 0$

$$\sigma_{ax} = 58 \cdot 8 - 21 = 37 \cdot 8 \text{ kN/m}^2$$

The resultant thrust is obtained from Equation (4.15):

$$E_a = \frac{0 \cdot 49 \times 20 \times 36}{2} - 2 \times 15 \times 6 \times 0 \cdot 70 + \frac{2 \times 15^2}{20}$$

$$= 176 \cdot 4 - 126 \cdot 1 + 22 \cdot 5 = 72 \cdot 8 \text{ kN/m}$$

From integration of the stress diagram

$$E_a = \frac{\sigma_{ax(6)}(H - z_0)}{2} = \frac{37 \cdot 8 \times 3 \cdot 86}{2} = 73 \cdot 0 \text{ kN/m}$$

Water pressure in the tension zone (rain water) is

$$E_w = \tfrac{1}{2} \gamma z_0^2 = \frac{9 \cdot 81 \times 2 \cdot 14^2}{2} = 22 \cdot 5 \text{ kN/m}$$

Therefore the resultant active thrust is

$$E_{ar} = 73 \cdot 0 + 22 \cdot 5 = 95 \cdot 5 \text{ kN/m}$$

The passive resistance of cohesive soil in the case of a smooth vertical wall (foundation) with horizontal ground surface is obtained directly from integration of Equation (4.3a):

$$E_p = \tfrac{1}{2} K_p \gamma H^2 + 2cH \sqrt{K_p} \qquad (4.16)$$

The point of application of E_p is obtained from consideration of the stress diagram in Figure 4.5(b).

4.1.2.4. Approximate Allowance for Soil–Wall Friction in Rankine's Solutions

Rankine's solutions for both cohesionless and cohesive soils can be modified to allow for the friction between the soil and wall simply by substitution in Equations (4.10) to (4.16) of values of coefficients K_a and K_p from Tables 4.1 and 4.2 or 4.5 and 4.7 corresponding to the given value of δ. Because of the approximate nature of this approach the last term in Equation (4.15) is usually neglected.

This approximate method is particularly useful when dealing with layered soils (Section 4.1.5). Note that the resultant thrusts E_a and E_p are now inclined at an angle δ to a line normal to the wall.

4.1.3. COULOMB'S WEDGE METHOD

As far back as 1773 Coulomb has postulated in his treaties on 'the use of maximum and minimum principle in problems of building statics' that the thrust exerted on a retaining wall was due to the weight of a wedge of soil sliding along a certain slip surface. Such a surface, along which the soil shear strength is mobilized, can be either curved or plane and can obviously have different locations. This problem, therefore, was reduced to finding a surface which corresponds to the maximum thrust on a retaining wall or minimum reaction to penetration of a foundation into the soil mass. Before going any further, he assumed that for the limiting conditions the slip surface must be a plane—this led to considerable simplifications in the evaluation of forces acting on the wedge.

In the light of recent developments in the field of theory of plasticity of soils one would consider Coulomb's approach as an indirect application of the upper bound theorem (Section 2.4.1). In the case of a smooth vertical wall with horizontal ground surface Coulomb's wedge method gives the same results as Rankine's solution in the preceding section. This means that for this particular case the lower and upper bound solutions coincide and therefore a theoretically correct solution is obtained. In all other cases the method yields approximate (upper bound) results, the reliability of which must be confirmed individually. This, of course, has already been done for a large number of practical cases (Civil Engineering Code of Practice No. 2, 1951) and the method is generally acceptable for the determination of active thrusts in all cases of gravity- and cantilever-retaining walls and passive thrusts in cases when $\delta \leqslant \phi/3$.

4.1.3.1. General Case of Active Thrust in Cohesionless Soils

In the general case of a rough retaining wall with irregular ground surface the active thrust is found by the graphical procedure shown in Figure 4.6.

A slip plane is chosen and the area of the wedge is determined. The magnitude of the vertical force W can then be evaluated from the knowledge of the density of soil within the wedge. Directions of the thrust on the wall E_a and resultant of the shearing resistance R are determined from geometry of the problems and from the knowledge of the angle of friction between the soil and wall, δ, and

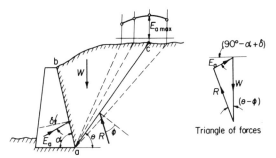

Figure 4.6. Graphical determination of active thrust for cohesionless soils.

angle of internal shearing resistance of the soil, ϕ. The magnitude of the thrust on the wall is then determined from a triangle of forces. The procedure is repeated with other slip planes until sufficient values have been obtained to enable the maximum thrust to be found by graphical interpolation. Not less than three planes should be used. The point of application of E_a can be taken as the point of intersection with the back of the wall of a line drawn through the centre of gravity of the wedge parallel to the slip plane of the wedge.

4.1.3.2. Special Cases of Active Thrust in Cohesionless Soils

In the case of a rough retaining wall with inclined or horizontal regular ground surface (Figure 4.7) the maximum active thrust E_a can be computed analytically from the following equation:

$$E_a = \frac{1}{2} \frac{K_a \gamma H^2}{\sin \alpha \cos \delta} \tag{4.17}$$

where

$$K_a = \frac{\sin^2 (\alpha + \phi) \cos \delta}{\sin \alpha \sin (\alpha - \delta) \left[1 + \sqrt{\frac{\sin (\phi + \delta) \sin (\phi - \beta)}{\sin (\alpha - \delta) \sin (\alpha + \beta)}} \right]^2} \tag{4.18}$$

For specific values of angles ϕ, δ, α, and β, the values of K_a may be obtained from Tables 4.4 and 4.5.

For the special case of a smooth ($\delta = 0$) vertical wall ($\alpha = 90°$) with horizontal ground surface ($\beta = 0$) Equation (4.18) reduces to

$$K_a = \frac{\cos^2 \phi}{(1 + \sin \phi)^2} = \frac{1 - \sin \phi}{1 + \sin \phi} = \tan^2 \left(45 - \frac{\phi}{2}\right)$$

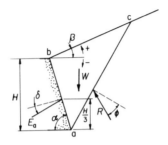

Figure 4.7. Notation for analytical determination of active thrust for cohesionless soils by Coulomb's wedge method.

i.e. K_a obtained from the Coulomb's wedge method is in this particular case identical with that obtained by considering the state of limiting equilibrium of soil, Equation (4.2a).

Table 4.4. Values of coefficient K_a for $\delta = 0$

ϕ	α	β				
		$-30°$	$-12°$	0	$+12°$	$+30°$
20°	110°		0·32	0·35	0·40	
	100°		0·38	0·42	0·50	
	90°		0·44	0·49	0·60	
	80°		0·50	0·55	0·68	
	70°		0·57	0·65	0·81	
30°	110°	0·18	0·20	0·21	0·24	0·50
	100°	0·22	0·25	0·27	0·31	0·61
	90°	0·26	0·30	0·33	0·38	0·75
	80°	0·30	0·36	0·41	0·48	0·92
	70°	0·34	0·43	0·50	0·59	1·17
40°	110°	0·10	0·10	0·11	0·12	0·16
	100°	0·13	0·15	0·16	0·17	0·24
	90°	0·18	0·20	0·22	0·24	0·32
	80°	0·22	0·26	0·29	0·32	0·43
	70°	0·27	0·33	0·38	0·43	0·59

Table 4.5. Values of coefficient K_a for $\alpha = 90°$ and $\beta = 0°$

ϕ	$\delta = 0°$	$\delta = \frac{1}{3}\phi$	$\delta = \frac{2}{3}\phi$	$\delta = \phi$
10°	0·70	0·67	0·65	0·64
20°	0·49	0·46	0·44	0·42
30°	0·33	0·30	0·30	0·30
40°	0·22	0·21	0·21	0·21

Example. Find the resultant thrust per lineal metre of a retaining wall with sloping back, having a vertical height of 6·0 m and retaining a cohesionless material with horizontal ground surface.

Data: $\gamma = 16·0 \text{ kN/m}^2$; $\phi = 30°$; $\delta = 20°$; $\alpha = 80°$; $\beta = 0$

K_a is obtained from Equation (4.18):

$$K_a = \frac{\cos^2 30° \times \cos 20°}{\sin 80° \sin 60° \left\{1 + \sqrt{\left(\dfrac{\sin 50° \times \sin 30°}{\sin 60° \times \sin 80°}\right)}\right\}^2}$$

$$= \frac{(0·8660)^2 \times 0·9397}{0·9848 \times 0·8660 \left\{1 + \sqrt{\left(\dfrac{0·7660 \times 0·5}{0·8660 \times 0·9848}\right)}\right\}^2} = \frac{0·827}{1·67^2} = 0·297$$

and E_a from Equation (4.17):

$$E_a = \frac{0·297 \times 16·0 \times 6·0^2}{2 \times 0·9848 \times 0·9397} = 92·4 \text{ kN/m}$$

4.1.3.3. General Case of Active Thrust in Cohesive Soils

In the general case of a rough retaining wall with irregular ground surface the active thrust is found by the same graphical procedure as for cohesionless soils but two additional factors are taken into consideration: (a) the existence of the tension zone of depth z_0, and (b) the existence of adhesion between the soil and

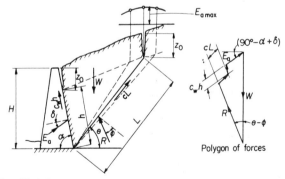

Figure 4.8. Graphical determination of active thrust for cohesionless soils.

wall, c_w (Figure 4.8). The depth of the tension zone is computed from Equation (4.14).

The point of application of E_a can be taken as in the case of cohesionless soils, i.e. as the point of intersection with the back of the wall of a line parallel to the slip plane and passing through the centre of gravity of the wedge.

4.1.3.4. Special Cases of Active Thrust in Cohesive Soils

The active thrust in cohesive soils can be computed analytically for the case of a vertical wall with horizontal ground surface from the following equation (Packshaw, 1946):

$$E_a \cos \delta = \tfrac{1}{2} K_a \gamma (H^2 - z_0^2) - c(H - z_0) K_{ac} \qquad (4.19)$$

where K_a and K_{ac} = coefficients from Table 4.6 depending upon ϕ, δ, and c_w/c ratio

The actual pressure distribution is assumed as shown in Figure 4.9.

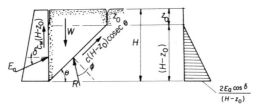

Figure 4.9. Active thrust in cohesive soil, Coulomb's wedge method.

Table 4.6. Values of coefficients K_a and K_{ac} for cohesive soils

K	K_a		K_{ac}			
c_w/c	All values		0	1·0	0·5	1·0
ϕ \ δ	0	ϕ	0	0	ϕ	ϕ
0°	1·00	1·00	2·00	2·83	2·45	2·83
5°	0·85	0·78	1·83	2·60	2·10	2·47
10°	0·70	0·64	1·68	2·38	1·82	2·13
15°	0·59	0·50	1·54	2·16	1·55	1·85
20°	0·48	0·40	1·40	1·96	1·32	1·59
25°	0·40	0·32	1·29	1·76	1·15	1·41

(After the Civil Engineering Code of Practice No. 2, 1951; by permission of Council of the Institution of Structural Engineers.)

4.1.3.5. General Case of Passive Resistance of Cohesionless Soils

In the general case the graphical procedure for determination of the minimum passive thrust in cohesionless soils is basically similar to that used in determination of the maximum active thrust but the directions of the reactive forces are changed (Figure 4.10).

While for practical purposes the accuracy of Coulomb's wedge analysis is sufficient in the active case the passive resistance of soils can be significantly overestimated by this method. This is particularly true for soils with ϕ greater than about $20°$ and δ greater than $\phi/3$. These differences are due to the divergence of the theoretical plane slip surface from the shape of actual slip surfaces which are curved.

4.1.3.6. Special Cases of Passive Resistance of Cohesionless Soils

In the case of a rough wall with inclined or horizontal regular surface (Figure 4.10) the minimum passive thrust E_p can be computed from the following equation:

$$E_p = \frac{1}{2} \frac{K_p \gamma H^2}{\sin \alpha \cos \delta} \qquad (4.20)$$

where

$$K_p = \frac{\sin^2 (\alpha + \phi) \cos \delta}{\sin \alpha \times \sin (\alpha - \delta) \left[1 + \sqrt{\left(\frac{\sin (\phi + \delta) \sin (\phi - \beta)}{\sin (\alpha - \delta) \sin (\alpha + \beta)} \right)} \right]^2} \qquad (4.21)$$

For $\beta = 0$ and $\alpha = 90°$ the values of K_p may be obtained from Table 4.7.

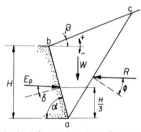

Figure 4.10. Notation for analytical determination of passive thrust for cohesionless soils by Coulomb's wedge method.

Table 4.7. Values of coefficient K_p for $\alpha = 90°$ and $\beta = 0°$

ϕ	$\delta = 0°$	$\delta = \frac{1}{3}\phi$	$\delta = \frac{2}{3}\phi$	$\delta = \phi$
$10°$	1·42	1·51	1·61	1·73
$20°$	2·04	2·38	2·80	(3·32)
$30°$	3·00	4·08	(5·74)	(8·74)
$40°$	4·60	7·94	(16·7)	(70·9)

Note. Values in brackets are high on the unsafe side and in these cases the use of values in Table 4.2 is recommended.

4.1.3.7. Passive Resistance of Cohesive Soils

The use of Coulomb's wedge method is not recommended for determination of the passive resistance of cohesive soils. The actual slip surface in these soils is markedly curved and cannot be approximated by a plane surface.

4.1.4. OTHER METHODS OF DETERMINATION OF PASSIVE RESISTANCE

For more accurate determination of the passive resistance of both cohesionless and cohesive soils by the wedge method it is necessary to introduce a curved slip surface which should, as closely as possible, correspond to the shape of actual surfaces of failure. The two most common of such methods are (a) the logarithmic spiral method (Ohde, 1938) and (b) friction or ϕ-circle method (Krey, 1936); both involve laborious graphical determination of the minimum passive thrust.

For determination of the passive thrust E_p of cohesive soils in the special case of the vertical wall with horizontal ground surface the Civil Engineering Code of Practice No. 2 (1951) suggests the following equation based on the ϕ-circle method (Packshaw, 1946):

$$E_p \cos \delta = \tfrac{1}{2} K_p \gamma H^2 + cHK_{pc} \tag{4.22}$$

where K_p and K_{pc} = coefficients from Table 4.8 depending upon ϕ, δ, and c_w/c ratio

Table 4.8. Values of coefficients K_p and K_{pc} cohesive soils

K	K_p		K_{pc}				
c_w/c	All values		0	0·5	1·0	0·5	1·0
ϕ δ	0	ϕ	0	0	0	ϕ	ϕ
$0°$	1·0	1·0	2·0	2·4	2·6	2·4	2·6
$5°$	1·2	1·3	2·2	2·6	2·9	2·8	2·9
$10°$	1·4	1·6	2·4	2·9	3·2	3·3	3·4
$15°$	1·7	2·2	2·6	3·2	3·6	3·8	3·9
$20°$	2·1	2·9	2·8	3·5	4·0	4·5	4·7
$25°$	2·5	3·9	3·1	3·8	4·4	5·5	5·7

(After the Civil Engineering Code of Practice No. 2, 1951; by permission of Council of the Institution of Structural Engineers.)

The point of application of E_p is obtained from consideration of the stress diagram which is similar to that in Figure 4.5(b).

4.1.5. LAYERED SOILS AND UNIFORM SURCHARGE LOADING

In the general case the determination of active and passive thrusts in layered soils can only be satisfactorily carried out using Coulomb's wedge method. However, in the most important case from the practical point of view, i.e. in the case of a vertical wall with horizontal ground surface, Rankine's solutions can conveniently be used.

The presence of uniform surcharge on the ground surface does not present any problems in the wedge analysis and is simply allowed for in the weight of the wedge.

In Rankine's general solution (Equations (4.2a) and (4.3a)) surcharge, q, is added to the vertical overburden stress, i.e.

$$\sigma_{oz} = q + \gamma z$$

The basic stress Equations (4.2a) and (4.3a) can now be rewritten in a new form

$$\sigma_{ax} = \gamma(h_s + z)K_a - 2c \sqrt{K_a} \tag{4.23}$$

and

$$\sigma_{px} = \gamma(h_s + z)K_p + 2c \sqrt{K_p} \tag{4.24}$$

where z = depth measured from the ground surface
h_s = equivalent height of surcharge of unit weight γ, i.e. $h_s = q/\gamma$

As mentioned in the preceding section the presence of surcharge affects the depth of the tension zone.

Example. Determine the total horizontal active thrust per lineal metre of the vertical strutted sheet piling shown in Figure 4.11.

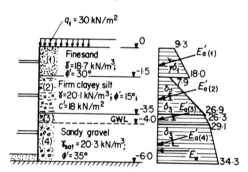

Figure 4.11. Determination of active thrust in layered soil.

Assume the angle of friction between wall and soil in each layer to be equal to $2\phi/3$ and neglect adhesion in layer (2). Approximate Rankine's solution is used together with Table 4.1.

Layer (1) $\begin{cases} q_1 = 30 \text{ kN/m}^2 \\ \\ h_s = \dfrac{30}{18\cdot7} = 1\cdot60 \text{ m} \end{cases}$

Lateral active stresses in layer (1) are obtained from Equation (4.23). From

Table 4.1, for $\phi' = 30°$ and $\delta = 20°$, $K_a = 0.31$; therefore at level 0·0

$$\sigma_a' = 18.7 \times 1.6 \times 0.31 = 9.27 \text{ kN/m}^2$$

and at level −1·5

$$\sigma_a' = 18.7 \times (1.6 + 1.5) \, 0.31 = 18.0 \text{ kN/m}^2$$

From stress diagram

$$E_{a(1)}' = \frac{9.30 + 18.0}{2} \times 1.5 = 20.5 \text{ kN/m}$$

Layer (2)
$$\begin{cases} q_2 = 30 + 1.5 \times 18.7 = 58.1 \text{ kN/m}^2 \\ h_s = \dfrac{58.1}{20.1} = 2.85 \text{ m} \end{cases}$$

From Table 4.1, for $\phi' = 15°$ and $\delta = 10°$, by interpolation $K_a = 0.55$. Depth of tension zone is obtained from Equation (4.14) and is measured from a height $h_s = 2.85$ m above the surface (level −1·5):

$$z_0 = \frac{2 \times 18}{20.1 \sqrt{0.55}} = 2.43 \text{ m}$$

Note that $h_s > z_0$, i.e. the tension zone is suppressed. As before, active stresses in layer (2) are determined from Equation (4·23). The stress at level −1·5 is

$$\sigma_a' = 20.1 \times 2.85 \times 0.55 - 2 \times 18 \sqrt{0.55} = 34.6 - 26.7 = 7.9 \text{ kN/m}^2$$

and at level −3·5

$$\sigma_a' = 20.1 \times (2.85 + 2.0) \times 0.55 - 26.7 = 53.6 - 26.7 = 26.9 \text{ kN/m}^2$$

From stress diagram

$$E_{a(2)}' = \frac{7.9 + 26.9}{2} \times 2.0 = 34.8 \text{ kN/m}$$

Layer (3)
$$\begin{cases} q_3 = q_2 + 2.0 \times 20.1 = 57.2 + 40.2 = 97.4 \text{ kN/m}^2 \\ h_s = \dfrac{97.4}{20.3} = 4.8 \text{ m} \end{cases}$$

From Table 4.1, for $\phi' = 35°$ and $\delta = 23°20'$, $K_a = 0.27$. Therefore the stress at level −3·5 is

$$\sigma_a' = 20.3 \times 4.80 \times 0.27 = 26.3 \text{ kN/m}^2$$

and at level −4·0

$$\sigma_a' = 20.3 \times 5.30 \times 0.27 = 29.1 \text{ kN/m}^2$$

Active thrust:

$$E'_{a(3)} = \frac{26\cdot3 + 29\cdot1}{2} \times 0\cdot5 = 13\cdot9 \text{ kN/m}$$

Layer (4) $\begin{cases} q_4 = q_3 + 0\cdot5 \times 20\cdot3 = 97\cdot4 + 10\cdot2 = 107\cdot6 \text{ kN/m}^2 \\ h_s = \dfrac{107\cdot6}{20\cdot3} = 5\cdot30 \text{ m} \end{cases}$

For calculation of the effective thrust submerged unit weight of soil in this layer is used:

$$\gamma_{sub} = \gamma_{sat} - \gamma_w = 20\cdot3 - 9\cdot8 = 10\cdot5 \text{ kN/m}^3$$

As in layer (3), $K_a = 0\cdot27$. The stress at level $-4\cdot0$ is

$$\sigma'_a = 20\cdot3 \times 5\cdot30 \times 0\cdot27 = 29\cdot1 \text{ kN/m}^2 \text{ (as in layer (2))}$$

and at level $-6\cdot0$

$$\sigma'_a = 29\cdot1 + 10\cdot5 \times 2\cdot0 \times 0\cdot27 = 29\cdot1 + 5\cdot4 = 34\cdot3 \text{ kN/m}^2$$

Effective active thrust:

$$E'_{a(4)} = \frac{29\cdot1 + 34\cdot3}{2} \times 2\cdot0 = 63\cdot4 \text{ kN/m}$$

The resultant of pore water pressure:

$$E_w = \frac{9\cdot8 \times 2\cdot0}{2} = 9\cdot8 \text{ kN/m}$$

To determine the total horizontal thrust the above individual components of the effective active thrusts and the water force are added vectorially in the horizontal direction:

$$E_{ah} = \sum_1^n \cos \delta_n E'_{a(n)} + E_w$$
$$= \cos 20° \times 20\cdot6 + \cos 10° \times 34\cdot8 + \cos(23°20')(13\cdot9 + 63\cdot4) + 9\cdot8$$
$$= 0\cdot940 \times 20\cdot6 + 0\cdot985 \times 34\cdot8 + 0\cdot918 \times 77\cdot3 + 9\cdot8$$
$$= 19\cdot4 + 34\cdot3 + 70\cdot9 + 9\cdot8 = 134\cdot4 \text{ kN/m}$$

Note that the actual stress distribution on the back of the wall would be continuous, defined by some curve, and would not contain discontinuities as shown in Figure 4.11.

4.1.6. EFFECTS OF WALL DEFORMATION ON STRESS DISTRIBUTION

In order to develop completely the state of plastic equilibrium or Coulomb's type of failure mechanism in a retained soil, the movement or deformation of the wall must have certain characteristics and must be of sufficient magnitude. For example, to develop Rankine's state of stress or Coulomb's type of failure it is theoretically necessary for the wall to rotate bodily so that its displacement increases linearly from the bottom (Figure 4.12(a)) and exceeds a certain minimum value at the top (Figure 4.2).

If the movement or deformation of the wall is inadequate, the soil mass remains wholly or partly in the state of elastic equilibrium, and the distribution and magnitude of stresses on the wall are substantially different from those predicted by consideration of the soil in the state of plastic equilibrium; three such cases of insufficient deformation are illustrated in Figure 4.12(b), (c), and (d) for a cohesionless soil.

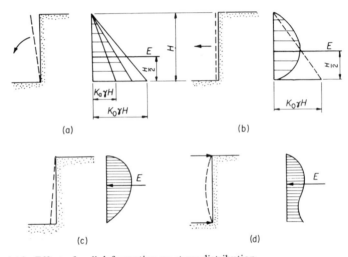

Figure 4.12. Effect of wall deformation on stress distribution.

A series of large-scale tests by Terzaghi (1934) and many subsequent tests and *in situ* measurements by him and other researchers (Kjaernsli, 1958; Di Biago and Kjaernsli, 1961; Terzaghi and Peck, 1967) have clearly demonstrated the importance of wall movement on the stress distribution and have helped in the development of empirical rules which facilitate the extension of both the limiting equilibrium and Coulomb's wedge methods to a wide range of engineering problems for which theoretical solutions do not exist at present or are cumbersome.

4.1.6.1. Gravity- and Cantilever-retaining Walls

For these walls deformations are of the type necessary to develop the state of limiting equilibrium or Coulomb's type of failure in the retained soil and therefore the stress distributions are taken as predicted from these theories.

4.1.6.2. Strutted Excavations

The nature of the deformation in a strutted excavation as shown in Figure 4.13 is an excellent example of limited deformation. Construction begins with the driving of the sheet piles. Usually the first row of struts is placed near the top of the excavation immediately after a small cut, i.e. before any appreciable movement occurs (Figure 4.13(a)). The subsequent rows of struts, however, are placed after a considerable amount of soil has been removed and some deformation in the lower part of the excavation takes place (Figure 4.13(b)). The final deformed shape of the wall is shown in Figure 4.13(c) and bears no resemblance to that assumed in the limiting equilibrium and Coulomb's wedge theories (Figure 4.12(a)). From *in situ* measurements the distribution of stresses is approximately parabolic (Figure 4.13(d)).

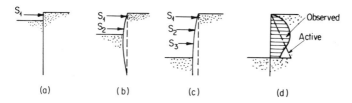

Figure 4.13. Deformation of sheet piles in strutted excavations.

For design purposes trapezoidal stress distributions are assumed (Figures 4.14(a), (b), and (c)). In the method recommended by Civil Engineering Code of Practice No. 2 the design thrust is taken as 44% greater than the active thrust E_a obtained from the Rankine's solution ($\delta = 0$); the corresponding stress intensity is shown in Figure 4.14(c).

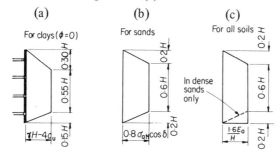

Figure 4.14. Design stress distributions for strutted excavations: (a) and (b) in homogeneous soils (Terzaghi and Peck, 1967); (c) in homogeneous and layered soils (Civil Engineering Code of Practice No. 2, 1951).

Design forces in struts and bending moments in sheet piles are computed assuming a statically determinate system as shown in Figure 4.14(a).

Example. Determine the design stress distribution for a 6 m deep strutted excavation in soil conditions as shown in Figure 4.11.

Using the method recommended by Civil Engineering Code of Practice No. 2, but taking the wall friction into consideration, we can utilize the value of E_{ah} obtained in the previous example:

$$E_{ah} = 134 \cdot 3 \text{ kN/m}$$

Therefore according to Figure 4.14(c) the maximum stress intensity is

$$\sigma_a = \frac{1 \cdot 6 E_{ah}}{H} = \frac{1 \cdot 6 \times 134 \cdot 4}{6 \cdot 0} = 35 \cdot 8 \text{ kN/m}^2$$

The stress diagram is shown in Figure 4.15.

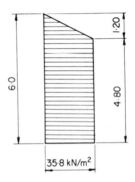

Figure 4.15. Strutted excavation — design stress distribution.

4.1.6.3. *Sheet Pile Cantilever Walls*

The resistance to movement of cantilever sheet piles is provided by the passive resistance of the soil mobilized against the embedded portion of the piles. The movement and deformation of these piles (Figure 4.16(a)) are not appreciably different from those assumed in the limiting equilibrium and Coulomb's wedge theories and therefore the straightforward theoretical stress distributions are acceptable (Figure 4.16(b)). Because of the approximate nature of the problem the simple Rankine solution is generally used and wall friction is ignored ($\delta = 0$).

   In determining the required depth of penetration of the piles it is assumed that at the moment of failure the sheet pile wall rotates about a point O. The resulting system of forces for cohesionless soils is shown in Figure 4.16(b). For design purposes this system is further simplified (Figure 4.16(c)) by assuming E_{p_2} to be a point load with its line of action passing through O. The theoretical depth of penetration, d, is then found by considering the equilibrium of forces, which is conveniently done by taking moments about O. In order to provide a suitable factor of safety and to limit rotation of the wall required to mobilize the

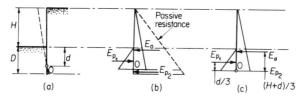

Figure 4.16. Deformation and forces on cantilever sheet pile wall.

passive resistance of the soil only one-half of passive thrust E_{p_1} is considered and the actual depth of penetration, D, is taken as equal to $1\cdot2d$. Thus

$$0\cdot5E_{p_1}\frac{d}{3} = E_a\frac{H+d}{3}$$ (4.25)

and utilizing Rankine's solution for cohesionless soils

$$0\cdot5\frac{K_p\gamma d^2}{2}\frac{d}{3} = \frac{K_a\gamma(H+d)^2}{2}\frac{H+d}{3}$$ (4.26)

which on substitution of $K_p = 1/K_a$ results in a cubic equation

$$d^3 = 2K_a^2(H+d)^3$$ (4.27)

which can easily be solved by trial substitution.

In cohesive soils the presence of the tension zone must be considered, but otherwise the design procedure is the same. In the special case of $\phi = 0$ the coefficients of active and passive stress are equal and, unless $c/\gamma H$ is greater than 0·25, the equilibrium condition cannot be satisfied.

4.1.6.4. Anchored Sheet Piling

The height of sheet pile cantilever walls is generally limited by the large bending moments set up in the wall and excessive depth of penetration which may be necessary to develop fixity at the bottom. It is therefore common in deep excavations to introduce horizontal wallings and tie rods near the top of the wall so that the sheet piling acts in a manner similar to that of a propped cantilever. The tie rods are provided with anchors consisting of concrete blocks or short lengths of sheet piling and situated sufficiently far away from the retaining wall so that their stability is not affected by its movement or deformation.

As in the case of strutted excavations the deformation of anchored sheet pile walls diverges appreciably from that assumed in both theories. In the case of cohesionless soils and unyielding anchor, the actual stress distribution is of the form shown in Figure 4.17(b).

For design purposes the stress distributions in both active and passive zones are assumed to be linear (Figure 4.17(a) and (b)). Again, the simple Rankine solution is used in evaluation of active and passive thrusts and wall friction is ignored ($\delta = 0$). The type of restraint provided by the soil at the bottom end of the wall depends on the depth of penetration, D. If D is small the pile can only mobilize passive resistance on the excavation side (Figure 4.17(a)) and no fixity is provided; this case is referred to as 'free earth support'. If D is large then

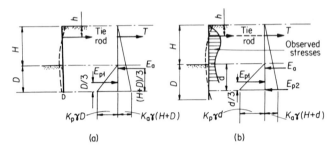

Figure 4.17. Deformation and forces on anchored sheet pile walls: (a) deformation and forces in the case of 'free earth support'; (b) deformation and forces in the case of 'fixed earth support'.

passive resistance is mobilized on both sides of the pile (Figure 4.17(b)) and fixity is achieved; this case is known as 'fixed earth support'. The two corresponding simplified systems of forces used in determination of the depth of penetration, D, are shown on the same diagrams.

In the determination of the tie force T and passive thrusts E_{p_1} and E_{p_2} a factor of safety should be introduced (usually equal to 2) to allow for the large deformations necessary to mobilize passive resistance of the soil.

The calculations are best done by means of assumed depths of penetration and by comparing the sums of the forces and moments, which should balance if the trial depth is chosen correctly.

4.1.6.5. Rigid Earth-retaining Structures

With rigid self-supporting earth-retaining structures, such as monolithic concrete culverts, portal framed bridges, and rigid basements strutted by means of a heavy raft and floor slabs or beams, the deformation is usually insufficient to mobilize active state of stress and stresses will approximate to the earth stresses at rest; in heavily overconsolidated clays this may mean stresses close to the passive condition (Figure 4.2).

4.2. Pore Water Pressure and Seepage Effects

The calculations in the preceding sections did not include the effects of the pore water pressure or seepage. Nor did they distinguish between total stresses and effective stresses. To take the water forces into consideration it is generally necessary to make calculations in terms of effective stresses; this, of course, involves the use of effective strength parameters c' and ϕ'. The principles out-lined in Section 4.1 remain unchanged, except that the water forces are now included in the calculations.

4.2.1. EFFECTS OF WATER PRESSURE IN LIMITING EQUILIBRIUM METHODS

The general theory of plastic equilibrium of soils is limited to homogeneous materials and any inclusion of the effects of pore water pressure or seepage can only be considered as approximate. In the case of the methods in Section 4.1.2 only the effects of a horizontal ground water table can be allowed for.

In the case of Sokolovsky's approximate method the effective stress compo-nents normal and tangential to the wall are computed from Equations (4.8) and (4.9) and in Rankine's solution for cohesionless soils — from Equations (4.10) and (4.11). The hydrostatic water pressure on the wall is then computed and added vectorially to the effective stresses to obtain the total stresses and hence the total thrust on the wall.

Example. Using data from the first example in Section 4.1.2. determine the distribution of stresses and total active thrust per lineal metre of the wall if ground water table is present at 2 m below the ground surface (Figure 4.18).

Data: $\gamma = 16\cdot0 \text{ kN/m}^3$; $\gamma_{sat} = 19\cdot5 \text{ kN/m}^3$; $\phi' = 30°$; $\delta = 20°$; $\alpha = 80°$

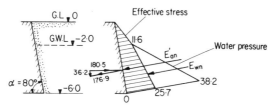

Figure 4.18. Determination of active thrust with ground water present.

Effective stress components normal to the wall are obtained from Equations (4.8) and (4.9):

at $-2\cdot0$ level:

$$\sigma'_{an} = 0\cdot38 \times 16\cdot0 \times 2\cdot0 \times \frac{\cos 20°}{\sin 80°} = \frac{0\cdot38 \times 16 \times 2 \times 0\cdot940}{0\cdot985} = 11\cdot6 \text{ kN/m}^2$$

at $-6\cdot0$ level:

$$\sigma'_{an} = 11\cdot6 + \frac{0\cdot38 \times (19\cdot5 - 9\cdot8) \times 4 \times 0\cdot940}{0\cdot985} = 25\cdot7 \text{ kN/m}^2$$

$$E'_{an} = \frac{11\cdot6 \times 2\cdot0}{0\cdot985} + \frac{11\cdot6 + 25\cdot7}{2} \times \frac{4\cdot0}{0\cdot985} = 23\cdot6 + 75\cdot8 = 99\cdot4 \text{ kN/m}$$

$$T'_{an} = E'_{an} \tan \delta' = 99\cdot4 \times 0\cdot364 = 36\cdot2 \text{ kN/m}$$

Water pressure at $-6\cdot0$ level:

$$\sigma_w = 9\cdot8 \times 4 = 38\cdot2 \text{ kN/m}^2$$

$$E_{wn} = \frac{38\cdot2 \times 4\cdot0}{2 \times 0\cdot985} = 77\cdot5 \text{ kN/m}$$

Total active thrust normal to the wall:

$$E_{an} = E'_{an} + E_w = 176\cdot9 \text{ kN/m}$$

Resultant total active thrust:

$$E_a = \sqrt{\{(36\cdot2)^2 + (176\cdot9)^2\}} = 180\cdot5 \text{ kN/m}$$

In the modified Rankine solution for active thrust in cohesive soils one has to consider two cases: (a) when the ground water table is below the tension zone, and (b) when it is at or above the ground level.

In the first case the procedure is similar to that used above for Rankine's solution for cohesionless soils but additional pressure due to rain water in the tension zone is taken into consideration.

In the second case the depth of the tension zone is determined using the submerged unit weight of soil ($\gamma_{sub} = \gamma_{sat} - \gamma_w$) in Equation (4.14) but otherwise the procedure is the same as for cohesionless soils, i.e. the total thrust is obtained by summation of the effective thrust and the resultant of the pore water pressure.

4.2.2. EFFECTS OF WATER PRESSURE AND SEEPAGE IN COULOMB'S WEDGE METHOD

In consideration of these additional effects the principles of the wedge analysis outlined in Section 4.1.3 remain unchanged except that water forces are now included in consideration of the equilibrium of forces. The method illustrated in Figure 4.19 involves the use of total weight of the wedge, together with boundary water pressures and effective stresses. One can also use an exactly equivalent system of forces involving buoyant weight of the wedge, seepage force, and boundary effective stresses.

4.2.3. REDUCTION OF PORE WATER PRESSURE BY DRAINAGE

It can be seen from the last example that the thrust due to the pore water pressure may be greater than the active thrust exerted on the wall by the soil. Therefore, if possible, it is desirable to reduce or to eliminate the water pressure by provision of drainage. Drainage should also be provided in all cases where there is a likelihood of acummulation of water behind the wall which has not been allowed for in the design. This may be achieved by the provision of a permeable backfill or installation of a special drainage layer placed immediately behind the wall. In both cases a drainage system must be provided along the base of the wall to permit exit of the water (Figure 4.20). Other reasons for

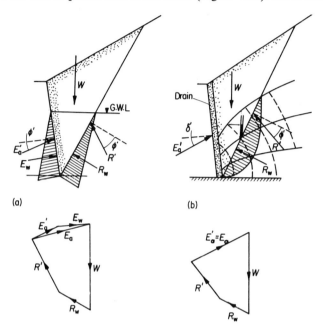

Figure 4.19. Effects of water pressure and seepage in Coulomb's wedge analysis.

provision of drainage are to prevent softening and subsequent loss of strength of cohesive backing material, and to reduce the swelling following ingress of water through fissures formed during hot dry spells.

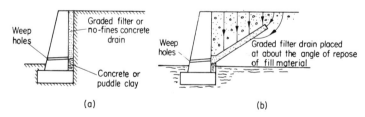

Figure 4.20. Typical drainage details: (a) vertical graded or no fines concrete drain; (b) inclined graded filter drain.

4.2.4. TOTAL STRESS ANALYSIS

In the determination of active or passive stresses in cohesive soils immediately after construction is completed and before any change of water content has taken place the calculations can be carried out in terms of *total stresses* which automatically take into consideration the effects of ground water. In such cases, of course, undrained strength parameters c_u and ϕ_u must be used; in saturated clays ϕ_u is frequently equal to zero and considerable simplifications are introduced in the calculations ($K_a = K_p = 1 \cdot 0$).

4.3. Effects of Surcharge Loads

4.3.1. UNIFORMLY DISTRIBUTED LOADING

The introduction of a distributed surcharge load on the ground surface does not present any problems and can easily be allowed for in both limiting equilibrium and Coulomb's wedge method — see Section 4.1.5.

4.3.2. CONCENTRATED SURCHARGE LINE LOAD

The problem of a concentrated surcharge line load q cannot be solved by any of the limiting equilibrium methods. If the load is small and its influence on the slip surface can be ignored, then Coulomb's method can be used to calculate the resultant lateral thrust. In practice, however, this procedure is cumbersome and the following semi-empirical approach suggested by Terzaghi (1954) and based on Boussinesq's theory is recommended.

The lateral stress on the wall at depth (Figure 4.21(a)) $z = nH$ due to a line load q situated at a distance $x = mH$ from the back face of the wall, where H is its height, can be obtained from the following expression:

for $m > 0 \cdot 4$

$$\sigma_{xn} = \frac{q}{H} \frac{4}{\pi} \frac{m^2 n}{(m^2 + n^2)^2} = \frac{q}{H} K_L \qquad (4.28a)$$

and for $m \leqslant 0 \cdot 4$

$$\sigma_{xn} = \frac{q}{H} \frac{4}{\pi} \frac{0 \cdot 16 n}{(0 \cdot 16 + n^2)^2} = \frac{q}{H} K_L \qquad (4.28b)$$

Values of coefficient K_L can be taken from Table 4.9.

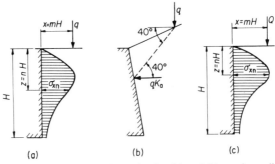

(a)   (b)   (c)

Figure 4.21. Lateral stresses due to surcharge loads: (a) and (b) surcharge line load; (c) surcharge point load.

The Civil Engineering Code of Practice No. 2, suggests the use of a simple graphical procedure for determination of the lateral thrust due to a surcharge line load. The line load, q, per unit length is considered to exert a horizontal force, $K_a q$, per unit length, where K_a is the appropriate coefficient of active stress. The point of application of this force is that of intersection of the back face of the wall with a line drawn from the point of application of the load at an angle $40°$ to the horizontal (Figure 4.21(b)).

Table 4.9. Values of coefficients K_L and K_c for evaluation of lateral stresses due to surcharge loads

0	n	m				
		0·4	0·6	0·8	1·0	1·2
	0·1	0·705	0·335	0·193	0·125	0·087
	0·2	1·020	0·573	0·353	0·235	0·167
	0·3	0·977	0·680	0·459	0·322	0·235
	0·4	0·796	0·678	0·510	0·379	0·287
K_L	0·5	0·606	0·616	0·515	0·408	0·321
	0·6	0·452	0·531	0·490	0·413	0·340
	0·7	0·338	0·444	0·447	0·401	0·345
	0·8	0·255	0·367	0·399	0·379	0·339
	0·9	0·195	0·302	0·349	0·350	0·326
	1·0	0·152	0·248	0·315	0·319	0·308
	0·1	0·576	0·126	0·041	0·018	0·008
	0·2	1·415	0·399	0·144	0·063	0·031
	0·3	1·630	0·629	0·262	0·123	0·064
	0·4	1·382	0·723	0·353	0·181	0·100
K_c	0·5	1·027	0·701	0·401	0·227	0·132
	0·6	0·723	0·615	0·407	0·253	0·157
	0·7	0·505	0·508	0·385	0·262	0·174
	0·8	0·354	0·407	0·345	0·257	0·181
	0·9	0·252	0·322	0·301	0·242	0·181
	1·0	0·181	0·253	0·256	0·221	0·175

4.3.3. CONCENTRATED SURCHARGE POINT LOAD

Since none of the existing theories can adequately account for the stress distributions down the wall due to a concentrated surcharge load, Q, the use of semi-empirical expressions developed from experimental results by Terzaghi (1954) is recommended (Figure 4.21(c)):

for $m > 0.4$

$$\sigma_{xn} = \frac{Q}{H^2} \frac{1·77 m^2 n^2}{(m+n)^3} = \frac{Q}{H^2} K_c \qquad (4.29a)$$

and for $m \leqslant 0.4$

$$\sigma_{xn} = \frac{Q}{H^2} \frac{1 \cdot 77 \times 0 \cdot 16 n^2}{(0 \cdot 16 + n^2)^3} = \frac{Q}{H^2} K_c \tag{4.29b}$$

Values of coefficient K_c can be taken from Table 4.9.

Example. Determine the additional lateral thrust on the sheet pile wall shown in Figure 4.11 due to a surcharge line load of intensity 30 kN/m at a distance of 2·0 m from its back face.

$$m = \frac{x}{H} = \frac{2 \cdot 0}{6 \cdot 0} = 0 \cdot 33 < 0 \cdot 40$$

Because $m < 0.4$ Equation (4.28b) is used in evaluation of lateral stresses σ_{xn}:

$$\sigma_{xn} = \frac{30}{6} K_L = 5 K_L$$

Values of K_L are obtained from Table 4.9 for $m = 0.4$ — distribution of stress is shown in Figure 4.22(a).

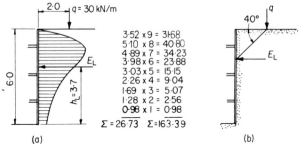

(a)   (b)

Figure 4.22. Lateral stresses and resultant thrust due to surcharge line load: (a) Terzaghi's semi-empirical method; (b) Civil Engineering Code of Practice graphical method.

The resultant thrust can be taken as approximately equal to

$$E_L = \frac{H}{10} \times (\sigma_{x, 0 \cdot 1} + \sigma_{x, 0 \cdot 2} + \dots \sigma_{x, 0 \cdot 9}) \tag{4.30}$$

$$= \frac{6 \cdot 0}{10} \times 26 \cdot 7 = 16 \cdot 0 \text{ kN/m}$$

Its point of application from the bottom of the wall is approximately given by the following expression:

$$h_L = \frac{H}{10} \times \frac{(9 \times \sigma_{x, 0 \cdot 1} + 8 \times \sigma_{x, 0 \cdot 2} + \dots 1 \times \sigma_{x, 0 \cdot 9})}{(\sigma_{x, 0 \cdot 1} + \sigma_{x, 0 \cdot 2} + \dots \sigma_{x, 0 \cdot 9})} \tag{4.31}$$

$$= \frac{6 \cdot 0}{10} \times \frac{163 \cdot 4}{26 \cdot 7} \approx 3 \cdot 7 \text{ m}$$

Using the graphical procedure suggested by the Civil Engineering Code of Practice and taking K_a from Table 4.3 for the uppermost layer of fine sand ($\phi = 30°$). The resultant lateral thrust is

$$E_L = 0.33 \times 30 = 10 \text{ kN/m}$$

and its point of application from the bottom of the wall (Figure 4.22(b)):

$$h_L = 6.0 - 2 \times \tan 40° \approx 4.3 \text{ m}$$

Note that the moment of the resultant about the toe of the wall is 59.2 kN m/m in the case of the semi-empirical Terzaghi's approach and 43 kN/m in the case of the empirical graphical method suggested by the Code; the use of the latter method is only recommended in the case of cantilever-retaining walls.

4.4. General Considerations

4.4.1. STRENGTH PARAMETERS AND WALL FRICTION AND ADHESION

The choice of strength parameters for stability calculations is discussed in detail in Section 3.3.7. In general, the long-term conditions are critical and control the factor of safety of a slope or the thrust for which a retaining wall must be designed. The design thrust for the long-term condition should be evaluated by an effective stress analysis using pore pressures determined by natural ground water conditions. In the case of a temporary excavation which is to remain open for a time that is short compared with that required for dissipation of excess pore water pressures within the soil the stability of the excavation may be analysed in terms of total stresses using undrained strength parameters.

If, for construction purposes, a large space is provided behind a retaining structure which is subsequently backfilled with imported soil or if a wall is specifically designed to retain fill, then the strength parameters of the fill material should be determined according to the principles outlined in Chapter 6 and should correspond to its *in situ* state of compaction. A cohesion-less soil in its loosest state has an angle of internal friction equal to the critical angle of friction; a nominal compaction by a bulldozer will generally increase its state of compaction to medium dense and hence substantially increase its angle of internal friction.

The inclusion of wall friction (defined by angle of friction δ) does not only reduce the active thrust on a wall but also greatly reduces its moment about the toe of the base. Observed values of δ according to Packshaw (1946) vary between $\frac{1}{2}\phi$ to $\frac{3}{4}\phi$ — many authorities recommend the use of $\frac{2}{3}\phi$; in no case can δ exceed ϕ.

The presence of wall adhesion in cohesive soils, in addition to wall friction, has the same beneficial effects. In soft clays the adhesion c_w can be taken as equal to the cohesion c; in harder clays c_w is smaller than c. According to the

Civil Engineering Code of Practice No. 2, c_w should not be taken as greater than 50 kN/m² (1000 lbf/ft²).

In general the presence of wall friction or adhesion increases the calculated passive resistance of the soil. Full advantage of these effects, however, should only be taken into consideration when a wall can settle appreciably in relation to the ground which is providing the support. When such settlement is not certain, values of wall friction or adhesion should be reduced to one-half of the full values, i.e. δ should be taken as equal to $\phi/3$ and c_w as equal to one-half of c or 25 kN/m² (500 lbf/ft²), whichever is the lesser.

It is suggested that because of the large deformations usually required to mobilize fully the passive resistance of soils only one-half of the available passive thrust should be considered in stability calculations.

If there is any possibility of future removal of the ground from in front of a wall, then passive resistance should be ignored in evaluation of its stability.

4.4.2. DESIGN OF RETAINING WALLS

The theories presented in the preceding sections enable us to determine all the forces acting on a wall and hence to design it against all possible modes of failure.

4.4.2.1. Failure by Rotation About the Toe or About the Top

Gravity and reinforced concrete retaining walls may fail by rotation about the toe as shown in Figure 4.23(a) and (b), whereas an anchored sheet pile wall may fail by rotation about the top (Figure 4.23(c)). The Civil Engineering Code of Practice No. 2 recommends a factor of safety against this type of

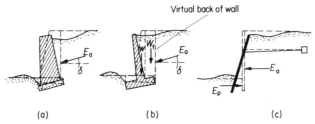

Figure 4.23. Failure of retaining wall by rotation: (a) gravity wall; (b) reinforced concrete cantilever or counterforted wall; (c) anchored sheet pile wall.

failure of at least 3 for gravity walls, i.e. the resultant thrust must be within the middle third of the base, and of at least 2 for all other types of wall. Note that in the case of reinforced concrete cantilever walls active thrust is computed at the virtual back of the wall as shown in Figure 4.23(b). The factor of safety for anchored sheet pile walls, in the case of 'free earth support', should be taken as approximately 2 on the calculated passive resistance of the ground in front of the wall.

4.4.2.2. Failure by Forward Movement

Both gravity and reinforced concrete walls may fail by forward sliding if the base friction and passive resistance of the ground in front of the wall are insufficient; if there is any possibility of removal of the ground from the front of the wall then its passive resistance should not be included in the calculations. For *in situ* concrete foundations on cohesionless soils the angle of friction beneath the base may be taken as equal to the angle of shearing resistance ϕ of the soil; in other cases it should be taken as equal to δ, the angle of wall friction. For foundations on cohesive soils the base friction may be taken as equal to the wall adhesion c_w. The factor of safety against forward sliding should be approximately equal to 2.

4.4.2.3. Bearing Capacity Failure

The maximum stress exerted on the soil beneath the wall base should not exceed the safe bearing capacity of the soil evaluated according to the principles given in Chapter 2, Section 2.7. The factor of safety against bearing capacity failure should be at least 2.

4.4.2.4. Failure by Slip in Surrounding Soil

In cohesive soils only a slope stability type of failure may occur (Figure 4.24). The factor of safety against this type of failure (Chapter 3) should not be less than 1·25 if the strength properties of the soil have been obtained by analysis of a previous failure in the same strata or if the residual strength parameters are used, and it should not be less than 1·5 if the strength properties, other than residual, have been obtained from laboratory tests.

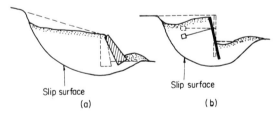

Figure 4.24. Failures by slip of surrounding soil: (a) free standing gravity or cantilever wall; (b) anchored sheet piling.

4.4.3. BACKFILLING

Granular materials are generally used as backfilling because it is easier to control their compaction and because they are not susceptible to frost heave or swelling. Although it is desirable to achieve maximum compaction in the backfill, heavy compaction can induce lateral stresses on the wall well in excess of the active stresses usually used in the design (Sowers *et al.*, 1957). Stresses induced by heavy compaction of a cohesive backfill may, in combination with stresses induced by swelling, lead to failure of retaining structures designed only to resist active stresses. Strength parameters of fill materials should be determined according to the principles outlined in Chapter 6.

5

Effects of Frost on Soils

5.1. Damage due to Frost Heave

It can be observed that as certain soils freeze the surface of the affected ground rises, lifting with it pavements or foundations located above the freezing zone. This phenomenon of the increase in volume of the soil on freezing is known as the *frost heave*. The deformation of pavements or foundations due to frost heave, particularly if of the differential type, can lead to their damage (Figure 5.1). The damaging effects of the frost heave were known to the Romans who, for example, in order to prevent the damage to their roads, built them to a combined thickness (of surfacing and base) of the order of 1·0 m.

In foundation engineering the danger of damage by frost heave is usually eliminated by constructing the foundations below the depth of penetration of the frost in a given locality. However, in some instances the process of the frost heave is so complex that the compliance with the above simple rule does not necessarily completely eliminate the possibility of heaving. In order to be able to cope with these and other cases, such as the design of foundations for cold storage (refrigerated) structures, it is necessary to understand the process of formation of the frost heave and to be able to recognize the soils susceptible to it.

5.2. Frost Heave Process

Towards the end of the last century it was thought that the frost heave was solely due to the increase in volume of water on freezing. It is known that as the water changes to ice the volume increases by approximately 9%. However, observations and calculations have shown that this increase plays only a minor part in the process of frost heave: for example in the case of a clay $w = 40\%$, frozen to a depth of 1·0 m, the heave due to the increase in volume of water (of 9%) is of the order of 50 mm whereas the observed surface movements are many times greater.

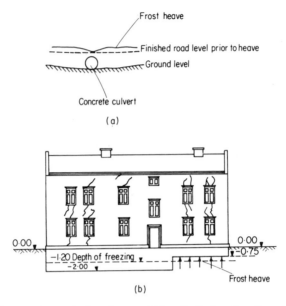

Figure 5.1. Damage due to the frost heave: (a) longitudinal section through a damaged embankment; (b) damage to a building due to inadequate foundation depth.

At the same time it was observed that there is a considerable increase in the water content of the soil in the frozen zone; if prior to freezing the water content was between 20 to 30%, then after heave has occurred the water content of the frozen soil would be two or three times greater.

It is now known that the frost heave occurs owing to the formation of ice lenses (Figure 5.2) which grow as the result of rise of water from the underlying wetter or water-bearing soil. There is no doubt that frost heave occurs only in certain types of soils, particularly in very silty ones, and chalk; these are called frost-susceptible soils.

Generalizing, it can be stated that the frost heave occurs only in the following conditions.

(1) The soil is frost susceptible.

(2) The ground water level is close to the surface or the soil is very wet owing to heavy rainfalls and poor drainage, etc.

(3) The frost is intense and persists over a long enough period.

5.3. Rise of Water into the Freezing Zone

The changes in water contents of the soil that take place during the process of the frost heave can be illustrated graphically as shown in Figure 5.2. Ice lenses form on the boundary of the frozen zone and grow owing to the rise of water. The newly forming ice lenses obviously increase the water content of the frozen soil. The water content of the soil immediately below the frozen zone decreases. This is due to the attraction of water molecules by the ice lenses from their immediate surroundings.

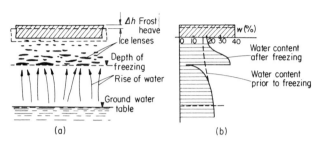

Figure 5.2. Formation of frost heave: (a) rise of water towards frozen zone; (b) change in water content within and in the vicinity of frozen zone.

The attraction of water molecules by the ice crystals is due to the existence of adsorption forces on their surface. Water molecules attracted to the surface of an ice lens supplement the ice crystal, and in turn attract other water molecules from the pores and thus increase the size of the lens.

The attractive forces exist not only on the surface of the ice crystals but also on the surface of the soil particles where the densified adsorbed water is present (Figure 5.3). The adsorption forces are greatest on the surface of the soil particles and decrease quite rapidly away from it. As the result of this the ice crystals attract the water molecules from the free water in the pores in their immediate surroundings and from the outer layers of the adsorbed water of the neighbouring particles. The molecules of the layers closer to the surface of the soil particles do not yield to the attractive forces of the ice crystals; because of this, after a while, an equilibrium is reached between the adsorption forces existing on the ice crystals and on the neighbouring soil particles. It probably corresponds to the water content which is equal to, or slightly greater than, the plastic limit. This can be concluded from observations: pavements constructed on boulder clays of stiff or hard consistency very seldom are subject to frost heave.

The ice lenses in the first place attract water from the pores and adsorbed layers of particles of the soil situated immediately below the frozen zone. The result of this is that the water content of the soil in that region decreases and suction is created which draws water from the underlying wetter soils.

The problem of the rise of water was investigated by many researchers. On the basis of Beskow's (1935) and Dücker's (1939) work, Rückli (1950) has determined the suction forces as a function of the coefficient of permeability (Figure 5.4).

Rückli has also carried out a series of tests, using special apparatus, in which

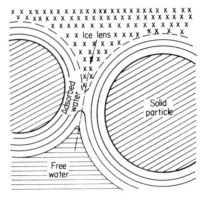

Figure 5.3. Schematic illustration of growth of ice lenses by attraction of water molecules from surface of soil particles.

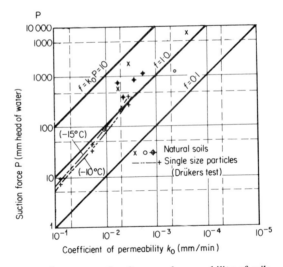

Figure 5.4. Relationship between suction forces and permeability of soils.

the suction forces were measured directly. The difference between the theoretical and the measured suction forces was in the region of 58%. Rückli has attributed this discrepancy to the fact that the experiments were carried out too rapidly (10 min) which prevented the development of the full suction forces.

Rückli does not consider that the changes in temperature have a very marked effect on the magnitude of the suction forces which induce the rise of water in soil. Discussing Dücker's results of freezing of a very fine sand (Figure 5.5), he attributes the marked influence of the temperature on the growth of the frost heave also to the fact that the freezing was too rapid (10 to 20 min).

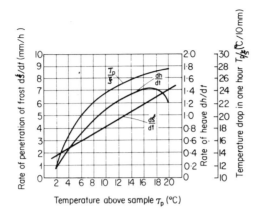

Figure 5.5. Relationship between rate of freezing, growth of frost heave and temperature: ξ, depth to boundary of frozen zone; h, height of frost heave; t, time of freezing.

At the same time Rückli emphasizes the great influence of the interparticle (effective) stresses in the soil on the growth of the frost heave, and hence on the suction forces which induce the rise of water (Figure 5.6).

As can be seen, the rate of growth of frost heave decreases with an increase in the effective stress and becomes equal to zero at a certain value which Rückli refers to as the heaving stress. For slightly cohesive soils the magnitude of the heaving stress is relatively low. This points to the possibility of cessation in the process of formation of frost heave when the frost penetration front reaches a depth at which the effective overburden stress is equal to the heaving stress.

According to Wïtun the suction induced in the freezing soil depends not only on the effective stress but also on the water content of the soil and on the temperature of the air.

The suction force which induces the rise of water into the freezing zone of the soil should be defined as the difference in suction S_1, immediately below the freezing zone, and suction S_2 at a lower level (Figure 5.7); then

$$P = S_1 - S_2 \tag{5.1}$$

Obviously the water content of the soil in the freezing zone depends on the intensity of the frost. The sharper the frost, the quicker the soil freezes and the smaller the amount of water (per unit depth) which is drawn into the freezing zone. The resulting changes in water contents are small and hence the suction force P is small.

The suction force in the unfrozen soil does not depend only on the effective stress, as suggested by Rückli, but to a large extent on the intensity of the frost and on the rate of freezing. It can be assumed that, if the rate of freezing is constant, then the rate of growth of frost heave will depend on the temperature of the air, as confirmed by Dücker's work (Figure 5.5), and also on the depth of the frost penetration and the distance below it to the ground water table.

5.4. Depth of Frost Penetration

All the existing theoretical methods of determination of the depth of frost penetration and rate of freezing of soils (Stefan, Newman, Rückli) either give

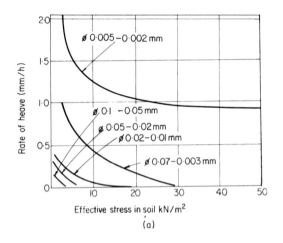

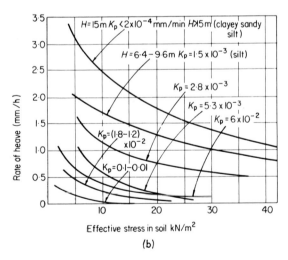

Figure 5.6. Relationship between the rate of growth of frost heave and effective stresses and type of soil: (a) soils of selected particle ranges; (b) soils of capillarity H and coefficient of permeability.

approximate solutions or are based on assumptions which do not take into consideration all the physical phenomena that occur during the freezing of soil media (Rückli, 1950).

Apart from theoretical methods there are several empirical methods of

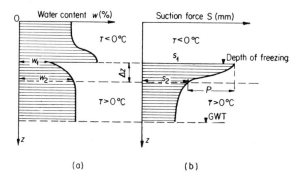

(a)   (b)

Figure 5.7. Distribution of water content and suction in a freezing soil: (a) distribution of water content above and below the freezing zone; (b) distribution of suction forces below the freezing zone.

determination of the depth of frost penetration in soils which are based on actual observations in the field.

In U.S.A. an empirical method developed by the U.S. Corps of Engineers in 1954 (Moos, 1956) has been adopted. The depth of frost penetration in granular soils (gravels and sands) is determined on the basis of the freezing index (Figure 5.8). The freezing index is determined from a cumulative plot of average

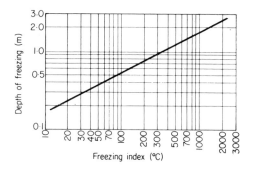

Figure 5.8. Relationship between depth of frost penetration and freezing index for well-drained non-frost-susceptible soils beneath pavements clear of snow.

daily temperatures (degrees Celsius days), as the difference between the maximum and minimum points on the plot, e.g. for a typical winter period in Cracow the freezing index is $89{\cdot}4 + 81{\cdot}5 = 170{\cdot}9\,^{\circ}C$ (Figure 5.9).

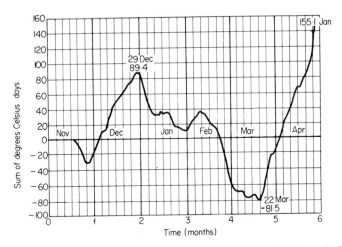

Figure 5.9. Cumulative plot of average daily temperatures for a typical winter in Cracow.

Lapkin's empirical expression (Shahunianc, 1953) is also of interest:

$$\zeta = \frac{k_f}{100}\,(0{\cdot}09\,I_f + 70) \tag{5.2}$$

where ζ = depth of frost penetration in m

      k_f = empirical coefficient; for slightly cohesive soils and cohesive soils of water content less than 30% and clear of snow cover $k_f = 0{\cdot}75$; for gravels and coarse-grained soils $k_f = 1{\cdot}33$

      I_f = freezing index in degrees

According to the Russian Standard N and TU127-55 the depth of frost penetration in sandy/silty clays and clays should be determined from the following formula:

$$\zeta = 0{\cdot}23\,\sqrt{(S_f + 2)} \tag{5.3}$$

where ζ = depth of frost penetration in m

      S_f = sum of average negative (below zero) monthly temperatures according to records accumulated over many years; value of S_f is taken as positive

The above expression is also used in the case of sands or slightly cohesive soils in which case the evaluated value of ζ is increased by 20%.

5.5. Criteria of Frost-Susceptible Soils

It is well known that granular soils which do not contain silt and clay fraction are not subject to frost heave even in the state of complete saturation. Experimental evidence has shown that the forming ice expels the excess water downwards so that on freezing the amount of water contained in the pores is smaller than before freezing. On the other hand, cohesive soils are frost susceptible and the finer is their silt and clay fraction, and the higher the water content, the greater is the amount of heave.

Before discussing the existing criteria of frost-susceptible soils it is necessary to consider the influence of the granular composition of soils on their frost susceptibility. So far this problem has not been clearly explained. According to the authors its explanation may be as follows.

In coarse-grained soils the specific surface of the grains is relatively small; the finer the particles the greater is the specific surface and consequently the greater is the chemical activity of the soil and the quantity of water adsorbed to the surface of the particles. It follows that in granular soils the proportion of the adsorbed water to the free water in the pores is relatively small. In cohesive soils, on the other hand, the adsorbed water forms the larger proportion of the total water contained in the pores.

The adsorbed water behaves in a different manner from the free water. Its freezing temperature is generally slightly lower than 0 °C and decreases further with the decreasing particle size and decreasing distance from the particle face.

Apart from that it should be considered that the ice crystals which form in the free water of granular soils can grow in all directions (Figure 5.10), whereas the ice crystals which form in the small pores of the fine-grained soils, adjacent to the adsorbed water, can only grow by drawing water molecules away from the surface of the particles.

The adsorbed water molecules near the surface of the particles are oriented and arranged in a certain manner; the molecules in the ice crystal are probably arranged in a similar manner. As the result of this, there should be a mutual repulsion between the water molecules on the surface of the particles and of the ice crystals.

Therefore the ice which forms in the pores of the fine-grained soil cannot displace water downwards, as in the pores of the coarse-grained soils, but pushing away from the underlying particles draws more water from the lower regions to form ice lenses and hence to cause the frost heave (Figure 5.10(b)).

The finer the particles in a given soil the smaller are the dimensions of the pores and the greater the proportion of them which are filled with adsorbed water and hence the more favourable are the conditions for the formation of ice lenses and for frost heave.

It follows from the above considerations that basically it is the size of the pores that influences the frost susceptibility of soils and not the size of the grains. The criteria based on the granular composition of the soils are used, however, because in practical terms the determination of the pore sizes is impossible. There are a number of criteria for determination of the frost susceptibility of soils based on the granular composition. The best known one is Casagrande's criterion in which the soils are divided into frost-susceptible

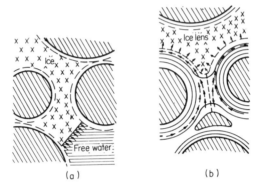

Figure 5.10. Freezing of water in soils: (a) in granular soil; (b) in cohesive soil (clay).

and non-frost-susceptible soils. Other criteria are based on the division of soils into several groups of different degree of susceptibility, e.g. Schaibles' (1954) criterion. In other criteria, in addition to the granular composition, the capillarity of soils is also considered, e.g. Beskow's criterion.

It is beyond the scope of this book to discuss the different criteria in detail. Extensive study of the existing criteria together with supplementary experimental work was carried out by Wiłun in 1957–8 and has lead to the following general recommendations.

The criteria of frost susceptibility should consider not only the granular composition of the soil but also their adsorption and capillarity characteristics. These are not only dependent on the size of the pores but also on mineralogical composition of the soil. The passive capillarity can be considered as such a representative characteristic which can easily be measured even in the field.

To justify the above viewpoint the following are quoted.

(a) Beskow's criterion does not only consider the granular composition of the soil but also the passive capillarity as determined at a water content equal to the liquid limit of the soil.

(b) Investigations carried out by Chaily and Kaplar (Highway Research Board, 1952) have indicated that the magnitude of the heave does not only depend on the granular composition of the soil but also on the mineralogical constituents.

(c) Investigations carried out by Wiłun have shown that there is a fairly clear relationship between the passive capillarity and the content of the fine fraction in soils (Figure 5.11).

The soils can be divided into three groups.

Group A. Non-frost-susceptible soils with passive capillarity < 1·0 m, safe for any ground water and climatic conditions; these are the soils containing less than 20% of particles smaller than 0·05 mm and less than 3% of particles smaller than 0·02 mm.

Group B. Soils, which may be frost-susceptible with passive capillarity between 1·0 to 1·3 m; these are the soils containing 20–30% of particles smaller than 0·02 mm.

Group C. Frost-susceptible soils with passive capillarity greater than 1·3 m; these are the soils containing more than 30% of particles smaller than 0·05 mm and more than 10% of particles smaller than 0·02 mm.

The above criterion is undoubtedly on the safe side; a less conservative approach could only be justified by field tests.

The above grouping takes into consideration the adsorption and capillarity characteristics of the soils and at the same time is easy to apply in practice with the help of the previously described macroscopic analysis (description) of soils and a simple field method of determination of the capillarity.

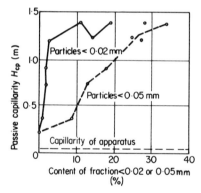

Figure 5.11. Relationship between passive capillarity and content of particles smaller than 0·05 and 0·02 mm.

Group A contains the non-frost-susceptible soils such as clean gravels, hoggins, and sands. These soils can easily be identified because when dry they do not form lumps.

Group B contains soils which may be frost-susceptible, such as very fine sands, silty sands, and organic sands, which on drying form weakly cemented lumps which can be picked up between one's fingers but which disintegrate under slight pressure.

Group C contains all the frost-susceptible cohesive soils and organic muds. These soils exhibit frost heave, unless they are situated high above the ground water table or when their water content is low, i.e. when their consistency is hard or very hard; stiff cohesive soils exhibit only slight heaving, which if uniform is not dangerous.

Although the division of the frost-susceptible soils according to the above criteria is fairly clear-cut, it does not completely exhaust the subject. The final solution to this problem should be sought through the science of pedology and in conjunction with detailed study of the ground water conditions.

5.6. Damage to Road Surfaces and Preventive Measures

In Britain the winter climate is not usually severe enough to cause extensive damage to road surfaces by frost heave, but in countries with a continental type of climate this can be a very serious problem.

In the design and construction of new roads the damage by frost heave can be eliminated by the use of a sufficiently thick sub-base (replacement of frost-susceptible by non-frost-susceptible soil), by increasing the height of embankments, by lowering of the ground water table, or by cutting off the inflow of water by installation of longitudinal drains or by cement stabilization of sub-grade soils.

Embankments constructed in frost-susceptible soils should be compacted in layers consisting of uniform materials and it should be ensured that the water content of frost-susceptible fill materials is not increased during the construction. Each layer should be compacted to a fall from the centre line of the embankment of approximately 4%. Soils containing organic matter or top-soils should not be used as fill material nor should they be left as subgrade at formation level; this frequently happens at the point of transition between cutting and embankment or beneath shallow embankments and leads to differential frost heave and damage of the pavement. In reconstruction of old roads the lowering of the ground water table or introduction of a non-frost-susceptible sub-base are the usual and the most successful preventive measures.

Transition from a frost-susceptible to a non-frost-susceptible section of the subgrade should be gradual with the sub-base feathering out at 1 : 10 to 1 : 20 to the formation level.

In widening of roads the underside of a new construction should be taken down to the same formation level as the existing one in order to minimize the possibilities of differential heaving.

Regardless of whether it is for the purpose of the design and construction of a new road or for the rebuilding of an old one, the underlying soils should be investigated, the ground water table (existing and, if possible, the highest) should be established and laboratory tests should be carried out on soils within the depth of 1·0 m (and particularly within the top 0·5 m) below the formation level.

In every case the subgrade and the shoulders should be protected against ingress of water by (i) provision of appropriate transverse falls in surfacing, formation, and shoulders ($\geqslant 4\%$), (ii) waterproofing of road surfaces and shoulders, (iii) provision of appropriate longitudinal falls in side ditches ($\geqslant 0.2\%$), and (iv) proper drainage of the sub-base to the sides of the road.

5.7. Protection of Building Foundations Against Frost Heave

If the foundations of a structure have not been taken below the depth of penetration of the frost, or if inadequate insulation has been provided beneath cold storage buildings, and the ground beneath them is frost susceptible then

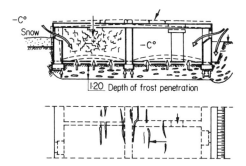

Figure 5.12. Damage of building due to frost heave beneath foundations.

frost heave may occur and may result in damage to the foundations and the structure.

Experimental evidence indicates that frost heave takes place in clayey soils when the existing effective stress is less than approximately 1500 kN/m^2 ($30\,600 \text{ lbf/ft}^2$, 15 kgf/cm^2) and in silty soils and slightly cohesive sands when the stress is less than 200 kN/m^2 (4100 lbf/ft, 2 kgf/cm^2). As the result of the frost heave below shallow foundations cracking of finishes and of structural members may take place (Figure 5.12).

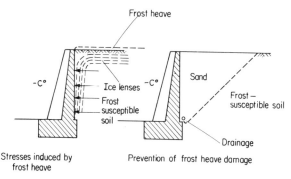

Figure 5.13. Frost heave behind retaining walls.

Frost heave can also occur behind retaining walls if penetration of the frost is deep enough and the backfill consists of frost-susceptible soils (Figure 5.13). The high stresses induced by the frost heave exceed the earth pressures (for which the wall has been designed) and the wall undergoes extensive tilting or cracking.

In a similar manner frost heave can take place behind trench timbering left exposed during the winter; on thawing of the soil in the spring, timbering may fall down leading to the collapse of the sides of excavation. To prevent this, the timbering, walings, and struts must be properly connected together and kept in contact by wedges driven between them.

Damage can occur to freshly concreted bridge or culvert decks if the centring is founded on frost-susceptible soils and heaving takes place (Figure 5.14).

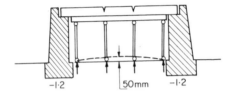

Figure 5.14. Frost heave beneath centring.

Floors or even foundations of cold storage buildings can be damaged in a similar manner (Figure 5.15).

Measures taken to prevent damage to structures founded on frost-susceptible soils should be based on the following.

(a) Foundations of buildings resting on frost-susceptible soils of plastic consistency should be taken down below the depth of frost penetration in a given

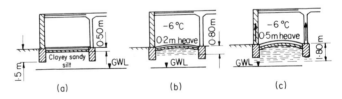

Figure 5.15. Effects of frost heaving beneath cold storage building: (a) initial conditions; (b) after 3 to 4 years; (c) after 10 years.

locality; on soils of stiff, hard, and very hard consistency it is generally sufficient to take the foundation to a depth between 0·6 to 0·8 m below the finished ground level, but only on the condition that the soil is well protected from an ingress of water; pipe lines and sewers should be founded at depths of not less than approximately 1·33 times the depth of penetration of frost in a given locality.

(b) Frost-susceptible soils can be replaced (to previously mentioned depths) with well-compacted clean sands and gravels.

(c) Backfills behind retaining walls should consist of permeable non-frost-susceptible soils.

(d) External insulation (mats, sand, etc.) should be provided to the frost-susceptible soils beneath centring or shallow foundation or the former should be founded on sand pads.

(e) Good insulation should be provided beneath the ground floor of cold storage buildings (Figure 5.16); air space forms the most effective thermal insulation.

5.8. Degeneration of Cutting and Embankment Slopes During Thawing

The formation of ice lenses can also occur in cutting and embankment slopes if these are in frost-susceptible soils and if there is a readily available supply of

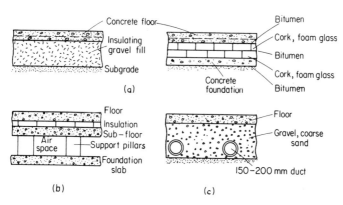

Figure 5.16. Typical detail of insulations beneath ground floors of cold storage buildings: (a) floor insulation systems; (b) insulation with air space; (c) heat ducts.

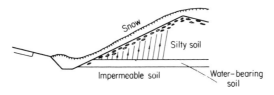

Figure 5.17. Softening of the soil in a slope due to formation of ice lenses.

free water (Figure 5.17). The resulting increase in the water content of the soil in the frozen zone leads, on thawing, to a decrease in its shearing resistance which frequently results in mud flows.

The most effective preventive measure in such cases is an installation of drainage in the water-bearing stratum which at the same time provides an additional support to the slope. Alternatively, the slopes of cuttings and embankments can be reduced to ensure their stability even in the conditions of complete saturation (softening) of the soil.

6

Compaction of Soils

6.1. General Considerations

The introduction of large mechanical excavators has considerably influenced the methods of construction of foundations. Present-day foundations are frequently constructed in large open excavations and the spaces between and around them are backfilled with compacted soil on which ground floor slabs and machine or partition wall foundations are constructed. A badly compacted fill may lead to the damage of walls and floor slabs; this can be particularly severe when, for example, owing to a rise of ground water table the soil is flooded and additional large settlements occur.

The same requirements of good compaction apply to construction of road or railway embankments and in particular to earth dams where water contents always increase owing to seepage and capillary rise.

Therefore, there is a need not only for proper compaction of fill materials and control of such operations but also for the knowledge of their physico-mechanical properties so that the settlement and stability of earthworks can be investigated on scientific bases.

6.2. Compaction of Soils

Soil compaction is the process whereby soil particles are mechanically constrained to pack closely together through a reduction in the air voids. Compaction is measured quantitively in terms of the dry density of the soil ρ_d. The increase in the dry density of soil produced by compaction depends on the type of soil, on its water content, and on the amount and manner of application of the compacting energy.

In the field, soil is compacted with various types of compaction plant which can be listed according to the manner in which they apply the compaction energy to the soil: rammers (dropping weight, frog rammer) which produce compaction by impact, rollers (smooth-wheel, sheepsfoot, or pneumatic-tyred) which utilize

149

high static pressure for compaction, and vibrators (plate or roller type) which utilize the combined effect of pressure and vibration. The plant in the first group can be used for compaction of any soil, that in the second group for cohesive soils, and that in the third predominantly for granular soils, although heavy vibrator rollers give very good results when used for compaction of stony cohesive soils.

The laboratory investigations of compaction of soils are usually carried out using apparatus in which the compaction energy is applied dynamically (by ramming).

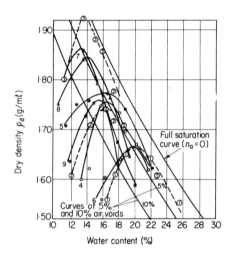

Figure 6.1. Dry density—water content curves for a silty clay illustrating the effects of different laboratory and field methods of compaction. Laboratory tests: 1, standard (Proctor) test; 2, compaction in 2 in (51 mm) cylinder; 3, modified A.A.S.H.O. test. Field tests: 4, smooth-wheel roller 2·75 t; 5, roller 8 t; 6, rubber-covered roller; 7, club-foot roller; 8, taper-foot roller; 9, frog rammer.

The laboratory testing basically involves compaction of soils, at different water contents, in a standardized manner. The values of dry density ρ_d so obtained are plotted against water content w (Figure 6.1).

The water content corresponding to the maximum value of the dry density $\rho_{d\,max}$ is referred to as the optimum water content w_{opt}.

The characteristic property of the compaction curves for any given soil is that, as the amount of the compaction energy is increased, the curves shift upwards and to the left so that as the maximum dry density increases the corresponding optimum water content decreases (Figures 6.1 and 6.2). In addition, the right-hand branches of the compaction curves are close and almost parallel to the maximum compaction (full saturation) curve.

The maximum compaction curves are determined analytically by assuming that the soil is fully saturated, i.e. that the pores are completely filled with water; in such a case, the higher the water content w, the lower is the dry density ρ_d. Obviously, neither in the field nor in the laboratory is it possible to expel all

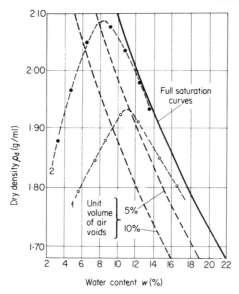

Figure 6.2. Compaction curves for slightly clayey sand (G_s = 2·65): 1, B.S. test, E = 580 kN m/m³; 2, modified A.A.S.H.O. test, E = 2650 kN m/m³.

the air from the pores of the compacted soil and therefore the actual values of $\rho_{d\,max}$ are always smaller than the theoretical $\rho_{d\,max}$.

The relationship between ρ_d, water content w, unit volume of air n_a, and density of solids ρ_s can be evaluated starting with the following equation:

$$V = V_s + V_w + V_a \qquad (6.1)$$

where V = total volume of soil
V_s = volume of solids
V_w = volume of water
V_a = volume of air

Dividing both sides of Equation (6.1) by V one obtains

$$1 = n_s + n_w + n_a$$

The volume of solids n_s contained in a unit volume of soil is

$$n_s = \frac{\rho_d}{\rho_s}$$

and similarly

$$n_w = \frac{\rho_d w}{\rho_w \, 100}$$

and therefore on substitution

$$1 = \frac{\rho_d}{\rho_s} + \frac{\rho_d w}{100 \, \rho_w} + n_a$$

Solving for ρ_d

$$\rho_d = \frac{100(1 - n_a)\rho_s \rho_w}{100 \rho_w + w\rho_s} = \frac{100(1 - n_a)G_s \rho_w}{100 + wG_s} \tag{6.2}$$

and in the case of full saturation, i.e. for $n_a = 0$,

$$\rho_d = \frac{100 G_s \rho_w}{100 + wG_s} \tag{6.3}$$

where G_s = specific gravity of solids (dimensionless)

The results of compaction tests, apart from showing the compaction curves for different levels of compaction energy, should contain the plots of $\rho_d = f(w, G_s, n_a)$ for $n_a = 0$, 5%, and 10%; this enables one to check if the tests have been properly carried out (e.g. if a compaction curve is partly situated outside the $n_a = 0$ curve, then a mistake must have been made in testing or in evaluation of results).

The compaction energy E is evaluated as the kinetic energy supplied per unit volume of compacted soil.

In compaction of soil of volume V, a drop-hammer of weight Q has fallen N times from height H.

The kinetic energy of a free falling body is equal to the change in its potential energy:

$$E_k = \Delta E_p = QH$$

Therefore the compaction energy per unit volume of soil is

$$E = E_k \frac{N}{V} = QH \frac{N}{V} \tag{6.4}$$

For the same soil different compaction curves can be obtained, not only by changing the compaction energy but also by changing the unit momentum of a blow M (per unit volume).

The unit momentum M is evaluated by considering the total momentum corresponding to N blows of the drop-hammer in compaction of soil of volume V:

$$M = M_{blow} \frac{N}{V} = mv\frac{N}{V} = mgt\frac{N}{V} = Q\sqrt{\left(\frac{2H}{g}\right)} \times \frac{N}{V} \qquad (6.5)$$

the quantities M and E are related

$$M = E\sqrt{\left(\frac{2}{gH}\right)} \qquad (6.6)$$

As can be seen from the above any change in the apparatus will involve changes in N and H, and possibly in E, if it is required to maintain $\rho_{d\ max}$ and w_{opt} constant.

6.3. Laboratory Soil Compaction Tests

The three most common laboratory methods of determination of the dry density—water content relationship are: the standard compaction method (also known as Proctor method), the modified (A.A.S.H.O.)* method, and the vibrating hammer method (for granular soils).

The standard compaction method was introduced by Proctor in 1933 and has since become the most widely used method of compaction in the world (British Standard 1377, 1967, Test 11).

A representative sample (approximately 15 kg) of air-dried soil passing the $\frac{3}{4}$ in (20 mm) B.S. test sieve is obtained and is subdivided into five or six 2·5 kg samples.

Each sample is then thoroughly mixed with different amounts of water to obtain a suitable range of water contents; the difference between them should be of the order of 1·5 to 2%. The soil is then compacted into a special mould (Figure 6.3) with an extension attached, in three layers of approximately equal weight, each layer being given 25 blows from the 2·5 kg (5·5 lb) rammer dropped from a height of 305 mm (12 in) above the soil; after each blow the rammer is moved through approximately $\frac{1}{5}$ of the circumference of the mould.

The surface of each layer should be roughened to obtain a better bond between them. The amount of soil used should be sufficient to fill the mould, leaving not more than about 5—10 mm ($\frac{1}{4}$ in) to be struck off when the extension is removed. On removal of the surplus soil the mould and soil (without the base) are weighed and a representative sample of the specimen is taken for determination of water content. From the knowledge of natural density ρ and water content w the dry density is evaluated according to the equation

$$\rho_d = \frac{\rho}{100 + w} \times 100 \qquad (6.7)$$

* American Association of State Highway Officials.

The same procedure is repeated with the remaining samples and the evaluated values of ρ_d are plotted against water content w (Figure 6.2).

The optimum water content is determined graphically: it is the water content of the soil at which ρ_d has the highest value.

Example. Soil—slightly clayey sand of specific gravity $G_s = 2.65$. Determine $\rho_{d\,max}$ and w_{opt} on the basis of results obtained from a standard compaction test (Figure 6.2).

From curve 1 in Figure 6.2,

$$\rho_{d\,max} = 1.94 \text{ g/ml}, \quad w_{opt} = 11.3\%$$

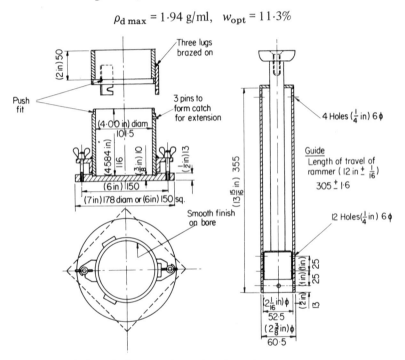

Figure 6.3. Typical standard compaction test equipment.

The modified (A.A.S.H.O.) method (British Standard 1377, 1967, Test 12). This method was developed to give a higher standard of compaction for airfield construction. The apparatus is basically the same as that used in the standard compaction test, except that the weight of the rammer is increased to 4·5 kg (10 lb) and the height of its fall on to the soil to 458 mm (18 in). The test procedure differs from the standard compaction test in that the soil is compacted into the mould in five equal layers. Typical results are shown in Figure 6.2, curve 2.

The vibrating hammer method (British Standard 1377, 1967, Test 13). This method has been developed for use with highly permeable soils, such as clean gravels, and uniformly graded and coarse clean sands, for which the previous two methods were not giving reliable results.

In this method the soil is compacted in a cylindrical mould (152 mm (6 in) in diameter and 127 mm (5 in) height) in three layers of approximately equal weight with a 146 mm ($5\frac{3}{4}$ in) diameter tamper attached to a special electric vibrating hammer. The results are interpreted in the same manner as for the standard compaction test.

Average ranges of optimum water contents and maximum dry densities for different types of soils are shown in Table 6.1.

Table 6.1. Average values of w_{opt} and $\rho_{d\,max}$

Type of soil	Method of compaction			
	Standard		Modified	
	w_{opt} (%)	$\rho_{d\,max}$ (g/ml)	w_{opt} (%)	$\rho_{d\,max}$ (g/ml)
gravels and sands	8−12	2·0−1·8	6−8	2·1−1·9
slightly clayey sand sands and clayey sandy silts	9−12	2·0−1·8	7−11	2·1−1·9
silts and clayey silts	12−16	1·9−1·7	11−13	2·0−1·8
sand clays	10−13	1·95−1·8	9−11	2·0−1·9
sand−silt−clays and clays	13−18	1·8−1·7	12−15	1·9−1·75
silt−clays and silty clays	16−22	1·7−1·6	13−17	1·8−1·7

6.4. Determination of Mechanical Properties of Compacted Soils

The methods of testing described in Sections 6.2 and 6.3 enable one to establish a relationship between the physical properties of soils and the compaction energy and momentum. Functions $\rho_d = f(w, E, \text{ and } M)$ are obtained.

For modern methods of design of earthworks it is necessary also to know the mechanical properties of the compacted soils: E_{oed}, ϕ, and c.

The determination of mechanical properties described in the following sections is carried out on samples remoulded to the same ρ_d and w as determined from the standard or modified compaction tests. The size of samples used in this type of testing depends on the size of available equipment, but, generally, the larger the samples the better; the following sections describe testing using the standard laboratory equipment.

6.4.1. COMPRESSIBILITY TESTS

Samples for compressibility tests are compacted directly in an oedometer-confining ring which is placed on the bottom porous disc in the apparatus; each sample is compacted in two layers — the bottom layer through a special rough platten, and the top layer through the proper oedometer platten which is then used in testing, thus eliminating bedding in errors.

For compaction in the oedometer the soil is prepared in the same manner as for the standard compaction test but only the material passing a 2 mm sieve is used. In cases when it is necessary to increase the water content of the soil water is added by spraying while the soil is being mixed; this prevents the formation of lumps which normally takes place when water is added by pouring.

The mass of the compacted soil is so chosen that, on obtaining the required volume, the sample of given water content w attains the required dry density ρ_d (according to the compaction test). The height of the sample is checked between every few blows with a height gauge.

The compressibility tests on compacted soils should be carried out on five samples of the same w and ρ_d. When expansion or consolidation has stopped load increments are added to double or quadruple the stress on the sample; the first load increment is usually taken as $12 \cdot 5$ kN/m² and the subsequent as 25, 50, 100, 200, 400 kN/m² or 50, 200, 800, 3200 kN/m² depending on the height of the proposed embankment. The first of the five samples is flooded and allowed to soak in water at the end of consolidation under the applied stress of $12 \cdot 5$ kN/m², the second after consolidation under 25 or 50 kN/m², the third after consolidation under 50 or 200 kN/m², etc. In this manner swelling and compressibility of the soil in normal and soaked conditions are investigated simultaneously. Before samples are soaked they must be protected against loss of water by evaporation.

On completion of consolidation of all samples under the maximum load (either 400 or 3200 kN/m²), water is drained from the oedometer cells, the apparatus is dismantled and the samples are removed for weighing and drying so that the final values of water content, dry density, voids ratio, and air voids can be determined. At the same time the initial values of the quantities are checked.

Test results are presented in the form of compressibility curves, with deformations due to soaking appearing as vertical lines at corresponding consolidation stresses (Figure 6.4). The dashed line represents an average compressibility curve for the compacted soil under normal conditions, i.e. prior to soaking.

The tests should be repeated on soil samples prepared to different initial water contents and dry densities; it is recommended that these tests should be carried out for samples prepared at w_{opt} and $\rho_{d\,max}$ and at two other water contents which are within the range of the water contents at which the soil will be compacted in the field; most frequently, these will be the water contents of the fill material in its natural state.

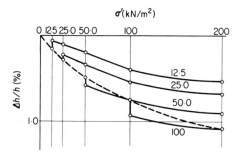

Figure 6.4. Compressibility curves for samples of compacted sandy clayey silt; stresses at which samples were soaked are indicated above each compressibility curve.

Example. From a standard compaction test $w_{opt} = 17\%$ and $\rho_{d\,max} = 1.76\,g/ml$; from a modified test $w_{opt} = 15\%$ and $\rho_{d\,max} = 1.86\,g/ml$; water content of the proposed fill material in its natural state varied between 18.2 and 20.1%. It is proposed to use this soil for construction of a central core within a 20 m high earth dam; use of light compaction plant is anticipated. It can be assumed, on the basis of the above data, that the results of the standard compaction test are applicable in this case, and it is therefore suggested that mechanical properties of the fill material should be determined at $w_{opt} = 17\%$ and at $w_1 = 18.5\%$ and $w_2 = 20\%$.

6.4.2. SHEAR STRENGTH TESTS

The samples for investigation of shear strength in triaxial apparatus are prepared in the same manner as for the oedometer test but are compacted in sections in a small cylindrical mould of 38 mm ($1\frac{1}{2}$ in) diameter and 19 mm high (approximately quarter of the final height of the sample); four such discs of compacted soil are used to make up a 76 mm high sample which is then assembled in a triaxial cell in the usual manner and is bedded in prior to testing by a brief application of the cell pressure.

Samples can also be formed in full height split moulds by compressing the soil to the required density.

The samples are then tested in the consolidated undrained manner with pore water pressure measurements so that effective strength parameters ϕ' and c' can be determined (Volume 1, Section 5.4.5).

If such facilities are not available, then the tests can be carried out without pore water pressure measurements but under conditions of consolidation and shearing similar to those expected *in situ*.

The lowest values of ϕ and c are obtained in the case of shearing of the compacted soil without consolidation; for each combination of w and ρ_d (as obtained from the compaction curve) two samples are sheared at cell pressure $\sigma_3 = 20$ kN/m^2 and two at $\sigma_3 = 400$ kN/m^2.

On completion of shearing small samples of soil are taken from the shear plane for determination of water content.

6.4.3. GRAPHICAL SUMMARY OF RESULTS

Results of the different tests on compacted soils can be conveniently summarized in a graphical manner as shown in Figure 6.5.

This type of graphical summary (Figure 6.5) enables one to determine, by interpolation, mechanical properties of soils with intermediate values of parameters w and ρ_d.

The relationships obtained between mechanical and physical properties are utilized in the design of embankments or earth dams and in the analysis of their behaviour during different stages of their construction and utilization.

To illustrate this let us consider changes that occur in the properties of a soil of initial parameters w and ρ_d, as indicated by the point A on the left-hand branch of the compaction curve (Figure 6.6) due to an increase in loading $\Delta\sigma$ and due to soaking. The soil under consideration has a relatively low water content and high percentage of air voids ($n_a = 12\%$).

With the known stress increment $\Delta\sigma$ the change in the voids ratio can be obtained from the compressibility curve and hence new parameters ρ_d, w, and n_a can be evaluated — the soil will now be described by the point B.

In the case of soaking a further volumetric change takes place. The effects can be evaluated quantitatively from the observed compression or swelling of the soil during soaking in oedometer tests. It will be assumed that only slight swelling but considerable reduction in air voids have taken place; the state of the soil can now be represented graphically by the point C corresponding to the new parameters ρ_d, w, and n_a.

The effects of these changes on the mechanical properties can be easily established by projecting the point C onto ϕ and c curves. As can be seen considerable reductions have taken place in the values of both strength parameters ϕ and c.

A different sequence is followed by the changes of mechanical properties of soil D which is situated on the right-hand branch of the compaction curve. An increase in loading (increase of height of embankment) results in a decrease of the water content w of the soil due to consolidation and, therefore, in an increase in its dry density ρ_d; the state of the soil is now described by the point E; soaking of the soil does not lead to an increase in its water content. It follows, therefore, that the soil D which initially possessed much lower strength parameters ϕ and c has now become stronger than soil A. The above analysis of the

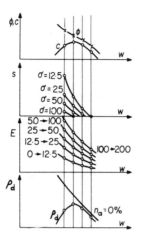

Figure 6.5. Graphical summary of results of compressibility, swelling, and shear strength tests with reference to the relationship between w and ρ_d.

changes in properties of these two soils indicates that even at the design stage it is possible to select proper and economic technological processes for construction of embankments.

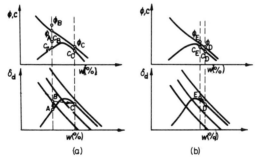

Figure 6.6. Changes in strength parameter ϕ and c in compacted soils: (a) at $w < w_{opt}$; (b) at $w > w_{opt}$.

6.5. Criterion of Minimum Index of Compaction

In the past, most of the embankments were constructed with little initial compaction other than that due to the construction traffic; obviously with certain soils such compaction was not very effective and the embankments were settling under their own weight over very long periods of time. This method of construction is only acceptable in cases when it is possible to allow the embankments to settle under their own weight before they are put into use and when during their utilization it is possible to repair them, e.g. re-levelling of railway lines with ballast.

Artificial compaction of fill is necessary, however, when the embankments are to be utilized within a very short time of their completion and when additional settlements may lead to damage of pavements and fatal accidents or when cohesive soils of high liquid limit are used which swell on soaking in an uncompacted state and may lead to stability failure.

The degree of compaction of fill materials can be defined using the index of compaction I_{comp}:

$$I_{comp} = \frac{\rho_{d\ in\ situ}}{\rho_{d\ max}} \qquad (6.7)$$

Minimum acceptable values of the index of compaction are given in Table 6.2 (Department of Scientific and Industrial Research, 1956). For cohesive soils additional criterion, according to Table 6.3, is used.

Table 6.2. Minimum index of compaction

Values of $\rho_{d\ max}$ obtained from standard compaction test (g/ml)	Minimum compaction index
1·42–1·60	1·00
1·60–1·73	0·95
1·73–1·92	0·95
1·92–2·06	0·90
2·06	0·90

Table 6.3. Additional criterion for cohesive soils

Average values of		$\rho_{d\ max}$ as obtained from standard compaction test (g/ml)	Suitability of soil for construction of embankments
liquid limit	plastic limit		
>65	>22	<1·60	not suitable to very poor
65–50	22–19	1·60–1·73	poor
50–32	19–16	1·73–1·92	fair
32–24	16–14	1·92–2·06	good
<24	<14	>2·06	excellent

According to the authors the criterion of the minimum index of compaction is not sufficient on its own, particularly with reference to subgrades (i.e. the soil within 0·3 to 0·5 m of the formation level), fill materials beneath floor slabs and earth dams. Experimental evidence indicates that, for example, the strength of cohesive soils compacted to the required densities at water contents lower than optimum may deteriorate considerably on soaking (points A and B and points A' and B' in Figure 6.7). Furthermore, the index of compaction should not be specified without reference to the individual characteristics of the soil under consideration nor without the knowledge of the type of construction and conditions in which the soil is going to be used. In connection with the above, the tabulated values should only be treated as the minimum requirements, and, in cases of doubt, design values of I_{comp} should be established on the basis of individual tests relating, for example, the California bearing ratio* values with water contents and compaction as shown in Figure 6.7.

It can be seen in Figure 6.7 that soils compacted at water contents lower than optimum should attain higher dry densities than soils compacted at water contents higher that optimum, because on soaking their strength does not decrease as much as those in the first group.

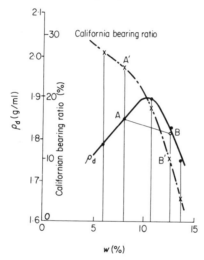

Figure 6.7. Effects of soaking on dry density and strength of soil: A and A', dry density and California bearing ratio value prior to saturation; B and B', the above properties after saturation.

In the design of important structures a complete analysis of settlements and bearing capacities of the compacted soils should be carried out and the effects of soaking or freezing should be considered.

6.6. Field Compaction of Soils

Placement of fill or construction of embankments involves two activities: preparation of soil prior to compaction and the actual compaction.

According to the preceding considerations the soil should be compacted at a water content close to the optimum. Frequently, however, the water content of the fill material in its natural state is either lower or higher than that.

* The California bearing ratio value is the result of an empirical penetration test used in the design of pavements and developed by the California Highways Department (Road Research Laboratory, 1955).

In the case of water content being lower than optimum, the soil can be wetted to increase it, or heavier compaction plant can be used to obtain higher density. The water content can be increased either by watering the soil *in situ*, prior to excavation, or by wetting it during loading and transportation.

If the soil is on the wet side of the optimum, then the water content can be reduced by spreading it out and allowing it to dry prior to compaction; in certain instances the soil can be dried out prior to excavation by leaving it exposed to the drying action of the sun and wind.

In any case, the usefulness of a soil as a fill material should be decided on the basis of the results of compaction tests, which for major works may involve construction of trial embankments.

If wheel type plant is used for transportation and spreading of the soil, then the surface should be continually levelled with scrapers or bulldozers to obliterate wheel tracks and to prevent vehicles from following them. If the soil is deposited in sufficiently thin layers (0·2 to 0·3 m), and at a water content close to the optimum, then the movement of track and wheel type plant produces good compaction. Very good results can be obtained using large dumper tracks; the kinetic energy of soil falling from a great height gives it the initial compaction and the track wheels compact it further, particularly near the surface. In the case of sands and gravels good compaction is obtained with layers of up to 1 m in thickness.

The use of scrapers and bulldozers is absolutely essential in connection with shaping of the top surfaces of embankments to provide adequate falls (3–4%) towards the edges in order to facilitate run-off and to prevent wetting of cohesive soils.

In cases when compaction by construction plant is not adequate, special compaction plant must be used. In these cases field trials should be made to determine the optimum thickness of layers, water content, and number of passes of different types of plant that are necessary to obtain the required degree of compaction.

When it is necessary to compact fill on waterlogged ground which deforms under the weight of the compaction plant, the ground should first be covered with a thin layer (0·10 to 0·15 m) of cement-stabilized soil (60–100 kg/m^3) to form a crust which will provide a sufficiently rigid base for proper compaction of the remainder of the fill.

Construction of embankments using frozen soil presents considerable problems and generally is not recommended.

6.7. Control of Compaction

One of the essential requirements in proper construction of embankments is a very close control of the quality of earth-works which involves the keeping of detailed records of the type of material used, thickness of layers, type of compaction plant, and number of passes and of the results of compaction tests.

Such a close control enables one: (a) to select proper fill materials and to improve compaction by increasing or decreasing their water contents, and (b) to select economic methods of compaction which utilize the construction traffic and special compaction plant.

The control of compaction can be carried out using the following methods.

(1) Detailed laboratory tests.

(2) Visual (macroscopic) control spot-checks.

(3) Penetrometer tests.

(4) Nuclear control tests.

Detailed laboratory tests involve extraction of samples of the compacted soils and determination of water content, density, and degree of saturation, and also the optimum water content, maximum dry density, and index of compaction.

Samples of cohesive soils are extracted with a 101 mm (4 in) diameter 127 mm long core-cutter (British Standard 1377, 1967, Test 14D). The cutter is rammed into the soil, using a 25 mm long ring dolly to prevent burring the edges of the cutter, until the dolly is just proud of the surface. The cutter containing the soil is then dug out of the ground. Any soil extruding from its ends is trimmed off so that the volume and mass of the soil contained in the cutter can be determined. The resistance to penetration in well-compacted soils can be considerable and it may be necessary to remove the soil from around the cutter to ease it.

The most general method which can be used in any type of soil involves excavation of a cylindrical hole of about 100 mm in diameter to the depth of the layer being tested. The soil removed is weight and its water content is determined while the volume of the hole is measured using the sand-replacement method (British Standard 1377, 1967, Tests 14A, B, and C) or the rubber balloon method; the volume can also be determined by pouring plaster of Paris into the hole and measuring the volume of the resulting solid.

It is very important to select the correct depth for sampling; samples should be taken from the middle of the compacted layer and not from the top. In cases when it is difficult to determine the extent of compacted layers, samples should extend from the surface to a depth of at least 0·8 of the thickness of the uncompacted layers.

For each density test two representative samples of at least 50 g mass are taken for determination of water contents of the soil.

For each different type of soil being compacted at least one complete laboratory compaction test should be carried out per day to determine $\rho_{d\,max}$ and w_{opt}. The compaction index I_{comp} is evaluated from Equation (6.7) using the values of ρ and w obtained from the control tests.

If the compaction is to be controlled by density measurements, the control should not be based on the result of any one test. A number of tests should be made and the results should be analysed by a statistical method (Volume 1,

Section 6.4.3) to determine the standard deviation and the 90% confidence limits.

The number of tests to any area will of course depend on the nature of the work, and on the degree of accuracy of the results required but, as the basis of the statistical analysis, at least ten density determinations should be made for each 1000 m^2 of compacted area.

For most classes of work standard deviations of 80 kg/m^3 (5 lb/ft^3) for fine-grained soils and 160 kg/m^3 (10 lb/ft^3) for coarse-grained soils are permissible, and the significant representative dry densi.. should be equal to, or exceed, the specified density.

Visual control spot-checks are based on determination of the type of the soil and of its consistency using the thread-rolling method (Volume 1, Chapter 3). Soils which can be rolled into a thread more than once are too wet. The visual control spot-checks should be made on soils before their compaction; doubtful materials should be improved (by drying or wetting). On compaction of doubtful materials their index of compaction should be checked with the penetrometer; if the results are not satisfactory, detailed laboratory tests should be carried out.

Penetrometer tests (see Volume 1, Section 6.3) involve counting the number of blows per each 100 mm of penetration of a 50 mm diameter conical penetrometer, driven with blows from 20 kg mass falling through 250 mm (Figure 6.8). The conical penetrometer is held in a vertical position by a tubular guide fixed to a 300 mm diameter plate which should be loaded with the weight of the operator.

The standard number of blows should be established for each typical soil used on the basis of penetration tests carried out in places where the indices of compaction I_{comp} have been accurately established with the detailed laboratory tests.

Nuclear control tests. Over the last twenty years nuclear methods of *in situ* measurements of density and water content of soils have been developed and are now widely used, particularly in the U.S.A., for the control of the compaction of all types of soils.

The two main types of commercial equipment available are (a) 'direct transmission' type, and (b) 'back-scatter' type. The broad principles of the techniques involved in both types of equipment are similar and are fairly simple although the actual physics involved is complex (Meigh and Skipp, 1960).

In the direct transmission apparatus the radio-active source (e.g. caesium-137 or cobalt-60) producing the gamma radiation is contained within a probe which is inserted to a depth of up to 150 mm into the material being measured. A Geiger counter for detection of gamma radiation is contained in a surface unit about 200 mm from the source. The rate of transmission of gamma radiation through the soil is determined by a separate scaler unit which contains the power supplies and counters, and a timing unit which stops the counters automatically after a predetermined interval of time. With the help of calibration curves a reading in terms of counts per minute is translated into the average density of the penetrated mass of soil (some instruments are calibrated to read the density directly). Usually the surface unit also contains another counter (e.g. boron trifluoride proportional counter) used in the measurement of the water content of the soil. This counter only detects slow neutrons scattered after collisions have occurred between the fast neutrons emitted by the source and the nuclei of the hydrogen atoms present in the soil. Again the count rate reading is translated into the average water content of the soil by means of calibration curves.

The time-consuming operation of introduction of the probe into the soil, which is particularly difficult and may lead to considerable errors in the case of

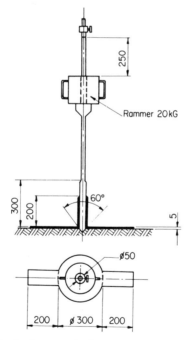

Figure 6.8. Penetrometer for *in situ* control of compaction.

gravelly soils, has led to the development of the back-scatter apparatus in which both the source and detector of radiation are contained in a unit which is placed on the surface of the material under test. The detector is separated from the source by a lead shield. Some of the gamma radiation and slow neutrons are scattered back and are detected by respective counters. A separate scaler unit is used which is of similar design to that described above.

Investigations at the Road Research Laboratory (Lewis, 1965) have shown that the calibration of equipment may be affected by the type of material tested and therefore, if a single calibration curve is used for all materials (which would enable direct readings to be taken), calibration errors in the density reading may be of the order of ± 80 kg/m^3 (5 lb/ft^3). The use of a single calibration curve for determination of water content does not appear to introduce any serious errors.

As in the case of penetrometer tests, nuclear control tests should be spot-checked at regular intervals (for each typical soil used) with detailed laboratory tests.

It can be seen that with sufficient accuracy for practical purposes the above-described methods of control enable one to ensure proper compaction of soils in construction of embankments.

The choice of the most efficient and economic method of compaction and the type of equipment can only be made on the basis of extensive experience but for major projects should be confirmed by trials.

The observations of stability of completed earth structure and records of performance of pavements constructed on embankments should be supplemented with observations of their settlements. For this purpose special bench marks or other means of levelling should be provided (Chapter 7).

The results of such observations form a very important contribution to both science and engineering practice.

7

General Practical Suggestions and Field Observations of Settlements

7.1. Practical Suggestions for Foundation Design Engineers

As can be seen from the content of the preceding chapters, and from the given methods of testing and design, the determination of safe bearing stresses is a very complex problem.

A proper determination of allowable loads is impossible without knowledge of the type and dimensions of the proposed structure; from knowledge of the soil and ground water conditions only, without any information about the proposed structure, one can only calculate approximate values of the allowable bearing stresses. Such approximate values can, in any case, be obtained from Table 2.4.

Therefore only the design engineer who is aware of all the problems associated with a proposed structure and site should evaluate the safe bearing stresses and design foundations.

The design engineer who understands the fundamentals of soil mechanics, and, in particular, the principles associated with the determination of allowable bearing stresses, will produce more rational designs not only of the foundations but also of the structure as a whole; this understanding will also help him in the choice of location of the structure on a given site and in the choice of the type of foundations,

On many occasions the authors have come across violations of the most obvious requirements resulting from the local soil and ground water conditions. For example, a basement to a building was constructed in highly permeable soils when it was possible, without affecting the planning, to locate it in soils of low permeability present within the outlines of the building; this would have considerably simplified the construction of the foundations and waterproofing of the basement and also reduced the cost.

A second example of planning without consideration of foundation problems is in locating the deepest parts of buildings (basements or lift wells) adjacent to

167

shallow foundations of neighbouring structures, when they could well be situated at a distance from them.

Very important is the problem of seepage forces and the associated loosening of soils in the bottom of excavations (the boiling condition). Failure by the design engineer to recongize such conditions usually leads to considerable extra cost: if the danger of loosening is detected during construction, the work has to be stopped while either foundations are redesigned or a dewatering system is installed. If the loosening is not detected, serious damage to the structure may occur later.

The occurrence of these common mistakes must be explained either by the lack of experience on the part of the engineers concerned or by the lack of publications which in a clear and concise manner present the basic principles of determination of safe bearing stresses.

It is impossible in any publication to discuss all combinations of soil and ground water conditions that can be encountered in practice, and to give solutions to all foundation problems; theoretical knowledge of the design engineer in the field of geotechnical engineering (geology, soil mechanics, and foundation engineering) must be supplemented with practical experience and with sound engineering judgement.

The methods of determination of allowable bearing stresses given in Chapter 2 are approximate and will probably remain so for a very long time to come. However, they enable one to determine analytically the values of allowable stresses which for practical purposes are sufficiently accurate.

The following very important rules of geotechnical engineering should always be remembered.

(1) If the results of the geological analysis of a given site are in agreement with the findings of the *in situ* and laboratory tests and together with the design calculation form a complete logical entity, then everything is in order.

(2) If there is no agreement between these findings, then supplementary investigations should be carried out to establish which results are erroneous and should be rejected.

(3) In determination of allowable bearing stresses in kN/m^2 an error in the unit digit is unavoidable; an error in the tens digit should not lead to failure; an error in the hundreds digit will not occur if the principles given in this book are correctly and logically followed.

7.2. Practical Suggestions for Contractors

The bearing capacity and stability of buildings depends, to a large extent, on the manner in which the work was executed. A good ground can be weakened by improper excavation and construction of foundations. Bad organization of site works and wrong sequence of construction of foundations may not only increase the cost of construction but may also lead to damage to the structure.

Practical suggestions are given below to help with proper execution of foundation works in different soil and ground water conditions.

Before preparation of a construction programme and commencement of site works a very thorough study of the site should be made in relation to the available geotechnical documentation (site investigation report) and design of the structure.

One of the most difficult problems in construction of foundations is the presence of a high ground water table. If soil explorations were carried out during a dry period there is a possibility that the ground water table (particularly if it is a perched one) may rise by several metres during a wet period. It is, therefore, advisable to check its position prior to the commencement of site works and to establish, on the basis of geotechnical sections, the direction of seepage of the ground water so that proper dewatering installation can be designed and appropriate equipment ordered.

As the next step one should check if there is a possibility of a build-up of water pressure beneath impermeable soil layers into which excavations are taken.

In cases when organic soils, made-up ground, or rocks are present they must be accurately located during the excavations; this can be achieved with the help of the vane/cone penetrometer (see Volume 1, Section 6.3).

Prior to excavations in metastable soils or calcareous marls surface drains should be constructed around the excavations to prevent flooding with rain water.

In deep excavations the possibility of falls or slides should be investigated.

Completed excavations should be inspected by the design engineer who should check whether the actual soil and ground water conditions agree with the assumption made in the design and who, if everything is in order, should authorize the construction of the foundations.

7.2.1. FOUNDATION WORK BELOW THE GROUND WATER TABLE

In cases when high levels of ground water are encountered the ground conditions should be re-examined carefully and the depths of water-bearing strata should be established.

If the bottom of an excavation is situated in a layer of water-bearing sand, which at shallow depth is underlain by an impermeable soil, then it is sufficient to form trenches in the bottom of the excavation to divert water to sumps from which it can be pumped away (as a rule the excavation should begin at the deepest spot). In these conditions loosening of the soil due to seepage forces is highly unlikely (Figure 7.1).

If with a high ground water table the impermeable soils are situated at considerable depths, then large quantities of water may be expected to enter the excavation and a fairly extensive dewatering installation may be necessary;

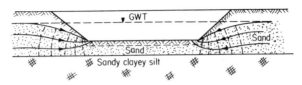

Figure 7.1. Ground conditions which enable dewatering from within the excavation.

if individual wells are used for dewatering, then these should be located in the most permeable sands and should be deep enough to depress the ground water table to the required level.

If the water-bearing stratum is relatively thin (sandwiched between two impermeable layers), and occurs at a shallow depth, then installation of a narrow interceptor drain may be sufficient to stop the flow.

In cases in which the bottoms of excavations in slightly cohesive soils (slightly clayey sands, silts) or varve clays are subject to upward water pressure, the intensity of this pressure should be reduced by depressing the water table by means of deep wells (Figure 7.2).

In more complicated ground conditions various means of exclusion of ground water from the excavations should be considered on an economic basis and with due regard to the bearing capacity of the soils.

In very permeable or weak soils (in which large foundations are required) it may be more economic to use piled foundations and thus avoid expensive excavations.

7.2.2. STABILITY OF SIDES OF EXCAVATIONS

The short- and long-term stability of sides of deep and wide excavations should be considered prior to the commencement of site works. Falls and slides most frequently occur in clays, particularly if these were in the past deformed and folded by glaciers or were subject to previous mass movements, and in which a high ground water table exists. Landslide areas are characterized by the presence of springs or local depressions and bulges on hill sides, which are signs of previous movements. Existing buildings in landslide areas are usually heavily cracked and tree trunks are bent indicating different directions of growth. If such conditions are encountered then precautions must be taken to ensure stability by reduction of slope angles, lowering of water table, installation of piles, etc.

7.2.3. EFFECTS OF MECHANICAL PLANT

The movement of mechanical plant (excavators) over the bottom of excavations in cohesive soils (particularly silty soils) does frequently lead to thixotropic loosening of their structure which exhibits itself by spongy or rubber-like deformation of the soil. In such cases one should allow for hand excavation of the final layer of 0·3—0·5 m in thickness.

7.2.4. PROTECTION OF BASEMENTS AGAINST GROUND WATER

If a basement is to be constructed in medium cohesive soils (clayey sands, clayey sandy silts, clayey silts) and there are even the slightest signs of seepage on the sides of the excavation, then appropriate drainage should be installed or

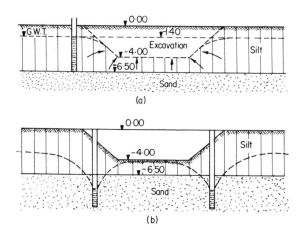

Figure 7.2. Ground water lowering for excavation purposes: (a) dewatering by pumping directly from excavation (may lead to loosening of the soil due to seepage forces); (b) dewatering by means of well points or deep wells (prevents loosening).

the basement should be waterproofed because in these types of soil the excavation may eventually fill up with water. In all basements deeper than 3 m one should include the waterproofing, and also the drainage so that at any later stage the ground water level can be temporarily or permanently lowered.

Protection of concrete foundations against chemical attack. The worst conditions from the point of view of chemical attack occur in permeable soils such as sands where continuous movement (seepage) of the ground water takes place. Concrete foundations should be suitably protected against the action of aggressive water. In the case of medium aggressiveness the foundations can be protected by backfilling around them with well-compacted cohesive soils to a thickness of at least 200 mm. In the case of very severe aggressiveness of the ground water the foundations should be waterproofed or water level should be permanently lowered.

7.2.5. COMPACTION OF SOIL AROUND FOUNDATIONS

To ensure proper behaviour of the foundation—soil system particular attention should be given to the compaction of soil around the foundation.

Fills consisting of cohesionless soils should be generously watered during the compaction.

Fills consisting of cohesive soils should be compacted at optimum water content (see Chapter 6). The thread-rolling method (Volume 1, Section 3.12.2) can be used as a rapid check of the optimum water content of cohesive soils; a soil which can be formed into a ball, but during the first rolling operation the thread crumbles, has water content close to the optimum.

If the soil is too dry, a ball cannot be formed because the soil crumbles, then it should be wetted by soaking it with water a day before excavation, or by spraying it with water during loading or transportation.

If the thread-rolling process has to be repeated several times before the soil crumbles, then the soil is too wet: such soils should be left to dry out prior to compaction; this can be done either by ploughing the face of the borrow pit and leaving the soil to dry there, or by spreading it on the embankment.

The type of plant used for compaction will depend on the extent of the area that has to be filled; for embankments sheepsfoot and smooth-wheel rollers can be used; the former is used first, to compact the deeper layers, and the latter last, to compact the top layer and to provide a smooth finish to it.

7.2.6. FROST-SUSCEPTIBLE SOILS

When shallow foundations or retaining walls are constructed it should be checked whether the soils are frost susceptible. A rapid macroscopic method of finding this out is based on checking whether dried-out lumps of the soil disintegrate on lifting them between fingers. If the lumps do not disintegrate then the soil is frost susceptible. The most dangerous conditions are with silts, slightly clayey sands, and clayey sandy silts of soft and firm consistency or when ground water is present at less than 2·0 m depth.

Frost-susceptible soils beneath foundations or behind retaining walls are usually replaced (to depths of freezing in a given locality) with well-compacted clean sands. If the soil in the bottom of an excavation is waterlogged and deforms during compaction, a layer of lean concrete should be placed over it to facilitate proper compaction of the sand.

In cases when foundation works have started in the autumn (or in the British Isles — during the winter) and the temperature has suddenly dropped below 0 °C, the ground beneath foundations should be protected against freezing by covering it with a thick layer of soil. In cases when concreted structures are going to be left propped during the freezing weather, it should be ensured that the props (or centring) either are founded on non-frost-susceptible soils (sand pads) or are taken below the depth of freezing; lifting of the structure or of its parts can also be prevented by continuous inspection and adjustment of the props.

Excavated trenches should be inspected during the winter (when thawing occurs), and in the spring to ensure that timbering has not fallen in, as this could lead to the collapse of the sides.

7.3. Observation of Settlement of Structures and Surrounding Ground Surface

7.3.1. OBJECT OF FIELD OBSERVATIONS OF SETTLEMENTS

Field observations enable one to control the progress of settlement of structures and to check the correctness of the settlement calculations (if these were necessary).

It is very important to ensure that all parts of a structure settle uniformly, even during the construction period.

Uneven settlement of individual foundations of a building may result in a damage of its structural framework. To prevent such damage temporary construction joints can be introduced in certain elements, e.g. by providing construction gaps during concreting of reinforced concrete beams; these joints are usually concreted in when the observations of settlements show that the movements have ceased.

In the case of heavy structures subject to rapid increases of loading (e.g. grain silos) large settlements may occur owing to displacement of soil from underneath the foundation if the bearing capacity of the soil is exceeded. In such cases settlement of structure is accompanied by heaving of the surrounding ground. If the results of settlement observations are known, it is usually possible to avoid reaching such a dangerous condition by reducing the rate of loading; in cases when the bearing capacity of the soil has been exceeded the movement can sometimes be arrested by placing surcharge over the heaving ground surface.

7.3.2. POSITIONING OF REFERENCE BENCH MARKS

To conduct reliable observations of settlements it is necessary to ensure that reference bench marks are situated sufficiently far away from the considered buildings not to be affected by the settlements and that the observation points within and outside the area of settlement are sufficient in number and are adequately spaced.

It has been observed that large heavy buildings induce settlements of the surrounding ground surface which, at distances equal to half their width, can be of the order of 15 to 20% of their own total settlement; in practical terms this means settlements of the order of 3 to 5 mm in soils of low compressibility and 10 to 20 mm in heavily loaded soils of high compressibility.

It follows, therefore, that any bench marks situated next to newly erected buildings or embankments may be subject to settlement.

Lowering of the ground water table or a sudden rise of water level in an adjoining reservoir may also result in substantial settlement of bench marks.

In connection with the above the following factors should be taken into consideration in selection of location and in design of reference bench marks.

(1) Wherever possible, depending on knowledge of the local geology, the

reference bench marks should be situated in places where rocks or overconsolidated soils (sands, gravels, boulder clays, Keuper Marls, etc.) are close
to the surface in the form of uniform strata of considerable thickness; reference
bench marks should not be situated on made-up ground or on recent soft and
highly compressible soils (e.g. alluvial muds, peats, waterlogged dune sands, etc.),
nor in landslide areas.

(2) They should be situated at reasonable distances away from existing
buildings, regardless of their age; this applies to both surface and underground
structures.

(3) Their foundations should be below the depth of freezing and outside the
zone of agricultural soils, i.e. at a depth of at least 2·0 m below the ground
level.

(4) At chosen locations the ground water table should be below the base of
the bench mark.

(5) The pillar of the bench mark (with the bolt on it) should be suitably
protected from any possible ground surface movements due to, for example,
uneven freezing of the soil or nearby traffic (Figure 7.3).

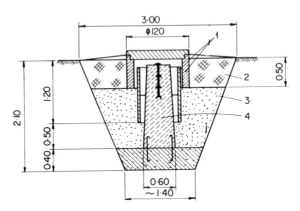

Figure 7.3. Details of a typical reference bench mark: 1, concrete pipes; 2, compacted
medium cohesive soil; 3, recompacted excavated soil; 4, prefabricated bench mark
pillar.

(6) In cohesive soils care should be taken during construction of bench mark
foundations to keep the excavations dry because soaking of these soils may lead
to swelling and hence movement of the completed bench marks.

(7) If great accuracy is required, at least three reference bench marks should
be provided so that they can be checked against each other.

(8) For less important structures settlements can be measured with reference
to existing buildings (at least 5 years old); if possible, three reference bench
marks should be installed.

An alternative method of establishing reference levels for the observation of settlements is to install deep bench marks (in boreholes) which are taken either well below the significantly stressed zone or into bed-rock or a deep stratum of overconsolidated soil.

7.3.3. POSITIONING AND SPACING OF OBSERVATION POINTS AND ACCURACY OF MEASUREMENTS

Settlement observation points for buildings are in the form of bolts set in walls and foundations. In the case of earth structures, such as embankments, an electrical system can be used which is based on location of steel plates embedded in the soil with an induction probe; for very accurate measurements overflow water level settlement gauges can be used.

Wall observation points should be as rigid as possible (Figure 7.4(a)) because during construction they can easily be disturbed by resting heavy objects against them or by accidental blows. The projection of the bolts from the wall should be sufficient (after finishes have been applied) for resting a levelling staff. If a thick cladding is used one should allow for changing of the bolts rather than install very long and unstable ones in the first place.

Removable wall observation points of the type shown in Figure 7.4(b) can also be used.

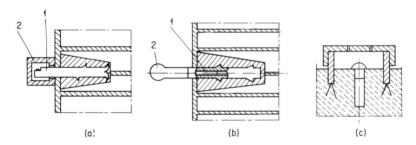

Figure 7.4. Typical settlement observation points for buildings: (a) permanent wall observation point with a cover; (b) removable wall observation point; (c) permanent foundation or floor slab observation point.

Foundation or floor slab observation points (Figure 7.4(c)) are fixed either in outside foundation projections or, in the case of raft foundations, at various positions inside the building.

Observations of settlements (and horizontal displacements) of earth structures can be made using a simple electrical system which is based on location of steel plates embedded in the soil with an induction probe which slides inside a rigid PVC pipe with telescopic joints (Figure 7.5). The probe is lowered into the pipe on the end of a graduated cable. It contains a coil which forms the active arm of a parallel resonance bridge. When the coil passes through each plate the bridge is thrown out of balance and this is observed on a portable recording unit

(Figure 7.6); by taking depth readings at 50% meter needle deflection as it both rises and falls, the steel plate position can be measured to an accuracy of about 1 mm (Figure 7.7).

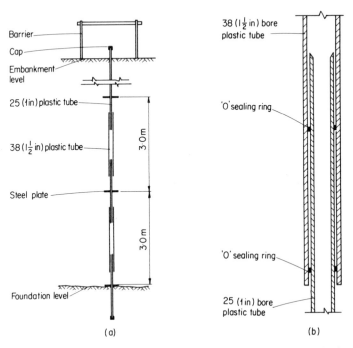

Figure 7.5. Electrical vertical settlement system: (a) general arrangement; (b) detail of tube joint (by courtesy of Soil Instruments Ltd.).

The above system can also be used for measurement of settlements of individual soil layers below or adjacent to foundations. A 150 mm (6 in) borehole is made at the required location and a PVC pipe (with telescopic joints) with special steel expanding devices (Figure 7.8) attached to it at selected levels is lowered into it. The devices are hydraulically keyed into the sides of the borehole as the casing is withdrawn and the space around them is filled with a thick bentonitic slurry; their position is located in the same manner as that of the steel plates.

The accuracy of measurement of vertical settlements has been recently improved to 0·1 mm by introduction of ring magnets instead of the steel expanding devices. The system of measurement is still basically the same but instead of the induction probe a special type of reed switch is used which is activated by the magnetic field within the ring magnets; the installation of these magnets is very simple and does not require extra equipment on site as was the case with the expanding devices.

The installation in embankments or fills of any type of devices which restricts movement of the mechanical plant (e.g. open piezometers or telescopic pipes for settlement observations) is, for obvious reasons, undesirable. Because of this, the overflow water level settlement gauge (Figure 7.9) is now becoming

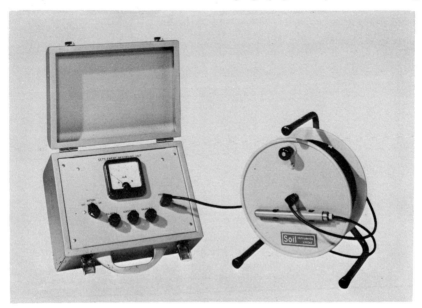

Figure 7.6. Induction probe and recording unit (by courtesy of Soil Instruments Ltd.).

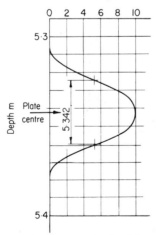

Figure 7.7. Typical curve relating movements of coil to movement of indicating meter needle (after Penman, 1969; by permission of the Director of the Building Research Station).

popular, particularly in earth dams, where it can be operated as an extension of the pore water pressure measuring installation.

Ground surface observation points are similar in detail to the reference bench mark (Figure 7.3) but are not as deep.

Very important is the problem of spacing of observation points in plan, within and outside a given structure, and of the time of commencement and of subsequent frequency of readings.

The number of observation points within and outside a given structure should be sufficiently large to enable one to plot settlement contours. Practical

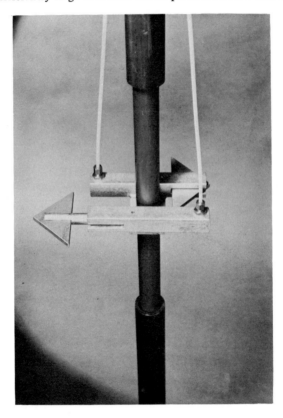

Figure 7.8. Borehole expander used in electric settlement system (by courtesy of Soil Instruments Ltd.).

experience indicates that a large proportion (up to 50%) of the observation points get damaged during construction or become inaccessible. The observation points should be positioned not only on the outside walls but also on foundation projections and on raft foundations inside the buildings. It can be assumed that for a complete coverage observation points should be spaced at distances between 10 and 15 m, in the case of buildings of load-bearing brickwork construction, and between 15 and 20 m in the case of rigid buildings founded on reinforced concrete continuous slab or cellular raft foundations.

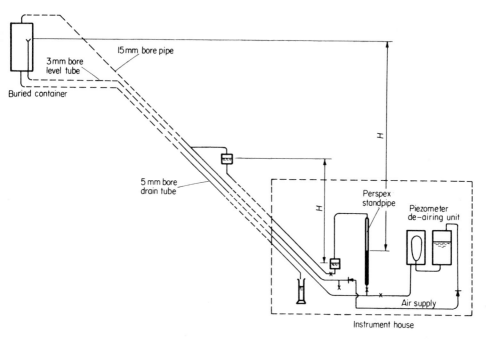

Figure 7.9. Line diagram of an overflow water level settlement gauge using back pressure (after Penman, 1969; by permission of the Director of the Building Research Station).

Very important are observation points along sections of strip foundation where sudden changes in loading occur or on both sides of an expansion joint or in places where dynamic loading is acting (turbo-generator blocks, or large hammer foundations).

Ground surface observation points around a structure should be located along at least eight lines radiating from its centre and passing through the corners and mid-points of the sides; on each line between two and three observation points should be positioned at distances equal to half the width of the structure.

Settlement observations should be commenced soon after the foundations have been completed, i.e. when the bearing stresses do not exceed 20–30 kN/m².

The subsequent readings should be taken at one-month intervals during the construction period and 3, 6, and 12 months after the completion of the structure until it is observed that the settlement in one year is less than 1% of the total settlement observed from the beginning of construction.

A detailed record should be kept of all the readings. Details of excavations and the progress of construction should be recorded at the time of each reading; this information is essential in proper interpretation of the results.

The accuracy of readings undoubtedly depends on the magnitude of the expected settlements. From the figures given in Table 2.9 one can obtain some idea of the magnitude of total settlements and of their allowable differences for individual types of buildings. Assuming the accuracy of measurements to be 1% of the total settlement then the following values are obtained:

for total settlement equal to   20 mm, 0·2 mm

for total settlement equal to 150 mm, 1·5 mm

The above accuracy is considered to be sufficient. If difficulties are encountered in the measurement of settlements inside buildings with optical instruments, then a water balance (Figure 7.10) can be used. To facilitate its use the inside observation points should be approximately at the same level as the outside wall observation points or otherwise appropriate equalizers must be used. The accuracy of the water balance is of the order of 0·5 mm, i.e. similar to that of an ordinary level; the maximum distance between observation points for readings with a water balance should not exceed 20 m.

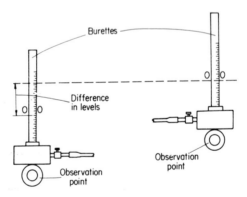

Figure 7.10. Measurement of settlement with water level.

Records of settlement readings should include the following.

(1) A foundation plan showing levels of the underside of all the foundations and of the finished basement floors with original ground contours and positions and absolute levels of all the observation points and reference bench marks.

(2) Complete records of all the measurements.

(3) A graph showing the progress of settlements at all observation points (Figure 7.11).

Floating observation points. It is advisable in the case of evaluation of settlements of very important structures (tower blocks, etc.) to check the

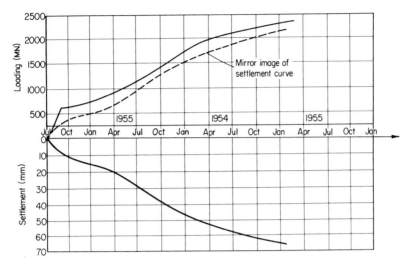

Figure 7.11. Settlement of the Palace of Culture and Science in Warsaw (Wiłun, 1955).

magnitude of the reloading stiffness moduli by comparing them with the expansion moduli obtained from the analysis of heave during excavations.

Before the commencement of excavation, at least nine floating observation points are installed inside 130–350 mm diameter boreholes. When the boring

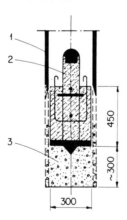

Figure 7.12. Floating observation point: 1, borehole casing (to be withdrawn); 2, prefabricated observation point; 3, semi-liquid concrete.

has reached a depth of 1·2–1·5 m below the proposed excavation level the boreholes are cleaned of all loose soil and semi-liquid concrete is poured; the casing is then partly withdrawn and prefabricated observation points are lowered into position (Figure 7.12). After the concrete has hardened the observation points are accurately levelled (at least twice) using a special steel tape, and the bore-holes are filled with sand of different colour from the local soils; this helps with the location of observation points after excavations have been completed. On completion of excavations the points are exposed again and are levelled (at least twice) and heave is evaluated (Figure 7.13).

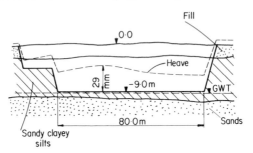

Figure 7.13. Heave of the bottom of excavation for foundations of the Palace of Culture and Science in Warsaw (Wiłun, 1955).

Appendix A. Example of Selection of Type of Foundations for an Industrial Building

The following example has been specially selected to acquaint the reader with a wide range of practical problems and with alternative methods of determination of the allowable bearing stresses: the first method is based on the use of values given in Table 2.4, whereas the second method is based on the use of Equations (2.1), (2.2), and (2.3), i.e. on a detailed evaluation of the ultimate bearing capacity and settlement (as suggested by British Code of Practice CP 2004).

A.1. Soil and Ground Water Conditions

The soil and ground water conditions determined on the basis of borings and *in situ* and laboratory tests are summarized in Figures A.1, A.2, A.4, and A.8.

As can be seen from the geological section in Figure A.2 the ground conditions beneath the proposed foundations are not uniform.

The thickness of the sand bed immediately below the proposed foundation level varies between 0·3 to 1·3 m. Below the sand, two types of soils are present which completely differ in their geotechnical properties (Figures A.1 and A.2). To the left of the frame E (Figure A.2), beneath frames A to D, stiff organic clayey silts are present. Their thickness reaches 2·5 m in places and stiffness moduli are fairly low ($E' = 4$ MN/m^2, $E'' = 7$ MN/m^2). To the right of frame E, beneath frames E to H, stiff clays (preconsolidated during the last glaciation) are present − their reloading stiffness modulus $E'' = 30$ MN/m^2.

The position of the ground water table established during the boring operations is approximately 0·5 m below the proposed foundation level. With such variable ground conditions and with no possibility of relocation of the building it is necessary, when considering spread foundations, to check whether the total and differential settlements of the structure at two points at which the soil conditions differ most are within the acceptable limits and will not lead

183

to harmful deformations of the structure. The bearing capacity of the soil beneath each frame should be checked separately.

The determination of the safe bearing stresses for the foundations of frame E is given in Section A.3 and can be taken to apply to the foundations of frames F, G, and H. In the first instance the safe bearing stresses were obtained from Table 2.4 but, since it was necessary to check differential settlements relative to frame C, detailed analysis based on Equations (2.1) to (2.3) was carried out.

Because of the presence of organic clayey silts beneath frames A, B, C, and D the determination of the safe bearing stresses should be carried out using the detailed analysis. In evaluation of the ultimate bearing capacity and maximum settlement, the foundations of frame C should be considered (Section A.5) because the soil conditions beneath them are the worst on the site (maximum thickness of organic silts).

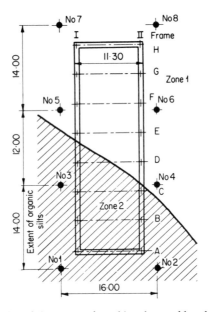

Figure A.1. Location plan of the proposed machine shop and borehole layout.

A.2. Details of the Proposed Structure and Loading

The structure of the proposed machine shop consists of reinforced concrete portal frames spaced at 5·0 m apart (Figure A.3), stiffened with continuous longitudinal beams at roof and window cill levels and with two continuous gantry beams.

The gantry of 9·5 m span and of 300 kN (30 tons) capacity is only used for assembly and dismantling of the machines. The external walls, of 330 mm thick hollow brick construction, form infilling panels between the frames.

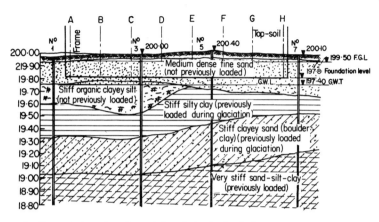

Figure A.2. Geological section through boreholes 1−3−5−7.

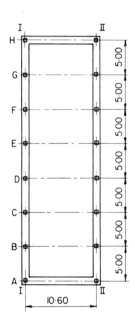

Figure A.3. Structural layout of the machine shop building.

The structure was designed for the basic loading consisting of (a) self-weight, and (b) snow, and for additional loading consisting of (a) vertical and horizontal gantry reactions, and (b) wind loading.

The summary of moments and forces induced by the different systems of loading at the foundation level in the frames (section $\alpha-\alpha$) is given in Table A.1.

Table A.1

Loading details	Loading details	Column 1−2			Column 6−5		
		Bending moment M	Axial force P	Horizontal force H	Bending moment M	Axial force P	Horizontal force H
		(kN m)	(kN)	(kN)	(kN m)	(kN)	(kN)
I	Self-weight and snow loading	−49·1	+720	−9·4	+49·1	+720	+9·4
II	Vertical gantry loading (a)	−12·3	+380	−15·5	+71·7	+140	+15·5
	(b)	−71·7	+140	−15·5	+12·3	+380	+15·5
III	Horizontal gantry loading (a)	−112·6		−19·1	−59·2		−8·5
	(b)	+69·2		+8·5	+112·6		+19·1
IV	Wind loading (a)	+339	−23	+50·7	+259	+23	+31·9
	(b)	−259	+23	−31·9	−339	−23	−50·7
		M_{max} −492	+883	−75·9	M_{max} +492	+883	+75·9
		P_{max} 1123	−433	−70·9	P_{max} 1123	−433	+70·9
		+344	1077	+34·3	−344	1077	−34·3

Note. The gantry is only used for assembly and dismantlement of machines.

Basic loading— case I.

Additional loading—cases II, III, and IV.

Full fixity of the columns was considered in the analysis in order to obtain the worst loading for the design of foundations.

It can be seen from the details in Figures A.1 and A.2 that the soil conditions differ most below the frames E and C and for this reason these two frames are used in the following calculations.

A.3. Computation of Safe Bearing Stress for Soils Beneath Footing EI

In the following calculations the safe bearing stresses are evaluated first and it is then checked that the applied stresses do not exceed the determined safe values.

A.3.1. PRELIMINARY COMPUTATION OF SAFE STRESSES

(a) Allowable bearing stress at the foundation level. The proposed foundations, in the form of isolated footings (Figure A.4), are to be founded in the fine sand stratum at a depth $D = 1 \cdot 6$ m (below the finished ground level) and $H = 2 \cdot 2$ m (below the original ground level).

In order to determine the allowable bearing capacity from Table 2.4 the density index and the degree of saturation of the sand at that depth must be known.

The value of the natural voids ratio e necessary for this purpose was obtained from nomograms given in Volume 1, Chapter 7 using the following data: $w = 18\%$, $\rho = 1 \cdot 95$ g/ml, and $G_s = 2 \cdot 65$ (see Figure A.4).

Using the nomogram for $G_s = 2 \cdot 65$ (Volume 1, Figure 7.2) the following results were obtained:

$$\rho_d = 1 \cdot 65 \text{ g/ml}$$
$$e = 0 \cdot 61$$
$$S_r = 0 \cdot 78$$

The properties could have also been worked out from appropriate equations:

$$\rho_d = \frac{\rho \times 100}{100 + w} = \frac{1 \cdot 95 \times 100}{100 + 18} = 1 \cdot 65 \text{ g/ml}$$

$$e = \frac{G_s \rho_w - \rho_d}{\rho_d} = \frac{2 \cdot 65 - 1 \cdot 65}{1 \cdot 65} = 0 \cdot 607$$

$$S_r = \frac{w G_s}{100 \times e} = \frac{18 \times 2 \cdot 65}{100 \times 0 \cdot 61} = 0 \cdot 78$$

It is now possible with the above results to obtain the density index:

$$I_D = \frac{e_{max} - e}{e_{max} - e_{min}} = \frac{0 \cdot 72 - 0 \cdot 61}{0 \cdot 72 - 0 \cdot 46} = \frac{0 \cdot 11}{0 \cdot 26} = 0 \cdot 43$$

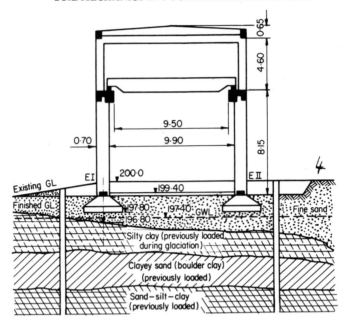

Figure A.4. Soil profile beneath frame E.

Fine sand: $\rho = 1\cdot95$ g/ml; $w = 18\%$; $G_s = 2\cdot65$; $e_{max} = 0\cdot72$; $e_{min} = 0\cdot46$
$E' = 30$ MN/m^2; $E'' = 50$ MN/m^2; $\phi = 30^\circ$

Silty clay: $\rho = 2\cdot05$ g/ml; $w = 21\%$; $G_s = 2\cdot70$; $w_l = 46\%$; $w_p = 14\%$
$E'' = 30$ MN/m^2; $c = 30$ kN/m^2; $\phi = 12^\circ$

Clayey sand: $\rho = 2\cdot15$ g/ml; $w = 12\%$, $G_s = 2\cdot67$; $w_l = 29\%$; $w_p = 10\cdot4\%$
$E'' = 50$ MN/m^2; $c = 17$ kN/m^2; $\phi = 19^\circ$

The soil can now be fully described as moist ($S_r = 0\cdot78$) medium dense fine sand and by interpolation from Table 2.4 the allowable bearing stress q_2 can be determined for $I_D = 0\cdot43$:

$$q_2 = 200 + 80\,\frac{0\cdot10}{0\cdot33} = 224 \text{ kN/m}^2$$

Since $H = 2\cdot2 > 2$ m the actual allowable bearing capacity at the foundation level will be slightly greater.

(b) Safe bearing stress at the foundation level taking into consideration the presence of saturated sand (weaker soil) below the ground water level. In such a case the safe bearing stress should be computed using Equation (2.18) and factor of safety $F = 2\cdot0$. For simplicity and with an increased margin of safety Equation (2.18) is taken as for a strip foundation:

$$q_{ult}^{(a)} = \left\{ cN_c + (\gamma_0 D + \gamma_1 z)N_q - \gamma_1 z + \frac{\gamma_2 B}{2}N_\gamma \right\}\frac{1}{\eta_0} + \gamma_0 D$$

where $D = 1.6$ m, $z = 0.4$ m, $B = 2.5$ m

c = cohesion, is taken as zero for sand

$\gamma_c = g\rho = 9.8 \times 1.95 = 19.1$ kN/m^2

for $z : B = z : b = 0.4 : 2.5 = 0.16$, from Figure 1.16, $\eta = 0.98$

for $\phi = 30°$, from Table 2.2, $N_q = 23.0$, $N_\gamma = 20.0$

$$q_{\text{ult}}^{(a)} = \left\{ (19.1 \times 1.6 + 19.1 \times 0.4)23 - 19.1 \times 0.4 + \frac{10.1 \times 2.5}{2} \times 20 \right\} \frac{1}{0.98} + 1.6 \times 19.1$$

$$= 1187 \text{ kN/m}^2$$

The safe bearing capacity is obtained using Equation (2.22) and $F = 2.0$:

$$q_{\text{safe}}^{(a)} = \frac{q_{\text{ult}}^{(a)} - \gamma_0 D}{F} + \gamma_0 D = \frac{1187 - 31}{2} + 31 = 609 \text{ kN/m}^2$$

and hence is much greater than the already obtained value of $q_2 = 224$ kN/m^2.

(c) Safe bearing stress at the foundation level taking into consideration the presence of stiff silty clay below the sand stratum. In order to determine the allowable bearing capacity of the silty clay from Table 2.4 it is necessary to know its consistency index I_c and to satisfy additional conditions specified in the remarks column of that table. In the case under consideration only two of these conditions are satisfied: the soil has been preconsolidated during previous glaciation and the proposed foundation level is above the ground water table. In such a case intermediate values of q_2 must be taken, i.e., for $I_c = 1.0$, $q_2 = 275$ kN/m^2 and, for $I_c = 0.75$, $q_2 = 175$ kN/m^2.

The consistency index of the clay of natural water content $w = 21\%$, plastic limit $w_p = 14\%$, and liquid limit $w_l = 46\%$ is obtained from equation

$$I_c = \frac{w_l - w}{w_l - w_p} = \frac{46 - 21}{46 - 14} = 0.78$$

Interpolating,

$$q_2 = 175 + \frac{275 - 175}{0.25} \times 0.03 = 187 \text{ kN/m}^2$$

i.e. less than the value of q_2 obtained for the moist medium dense sand ($q = 224$ kN/m^2).

It is therefore also necessary to check the safe bearing capacity at the foundation level using Equation (2.18). In this case

$z = 1.0$ m; $D = 1.6$ m

$c = 30$ kN/m^2; $\gamma_0 = 19.1$ kN/m^3

$\gamma_1 = (19.1 \times 0.4 + 10.1 \times 0.6) = 13.7$ kN/m^3

$\gamma_2 = \gamma_{\text{sub}} = 9.8(2.05 - 1.0) = 10.3$ kN/m^3

for $z : B = 1.0 : 2.5 = 0.40$, from Figure 1.16, $\eta_0 = 0.90$

for $\phi = 12°$, from Table 2.2, $N_c = 10$, $N_q = 3.3$, $N_\gamma = 1.5$

$$q_{ult}^{(b)} = \left\{ 30 \times 10 + (19 \cdot 1 \times 1 \cdot 6 + 13 \cdot 1 \times 1 \cdot 0) \, 3 \cdot 3 - 13 \cdot 7 \times 1 \cdot 0 + \frac{10 \cdot 3 \times 2 \cdot 5 \times 1 \cdot 5}{2} \right\}$$

$$\times \frac{1}{0 \cdot 90} + 19 \cdot 1 \times 1 \cdot 6 = 532 \text{ kN/m}^2$$

The safe bearing capacity is obtained from Equation (2.22):

$$q_{safe}^{(b)} = \frac{532 - 31}{2} + 31 = 282 \text{ kN/m}^2$$

Since the more accurately determined $q_{safe}^{(b)}$ is greater than $q_2 = 224 \text{ kN/m}^2$ its value will be taken as the safe bearing capacity of the soil but it is still necessary to check whether the settlements are within the allowable limits. It will be seen later than these conditions are not quite satisfied.

(d) The maximum stresses under the combined basis and additional loading can (according to British Standard Code of Practice CP 2004) exceed the safe bearing stress by 25%, i.e. $q_{max} = 1 \cdot 25 \times 282 = 353 \text{ kN/m}^2$.

Because the horizontal forces H are acting parallel to the length of the foundations it is not necessary to include them in the computation of the ultimate bearing capacity (see Section 2.6).

A.3.2. COMPUTATION OF ACTUAL STRESSES

(a) The combined basic loads (from Table A.1) and self-weight of footings:

axial column load	720 kN
weight of infilling wall panel	210 kN
self-weight of footing and backfill (estimated)	270 kN
$\Sigma P =$	1200 kN

$$M = 49 \cdot 1 \text{ kN m}; \quad H = 9 \cdot 4 \text{ kN}$$

Moment at the foundation level:

$$\Sigma M = 49 \cdot 1 + 9 \cdot 4 \times 1 \cdot 6 = 49 \cdot 1 + 15 \cdot 0 = 64 \cdot 1 \text{ kN m}$$

$$\sigma_{1, 2} = \frac{\Sigma P}{A} \pm \frac{\Sigma M}{W}$$

Assumed dimensions of footings (Figure A.5) are

$$L = 4 \cdot 0; \; B = 2 \cdot 5 \text{ m}; \; A = 4 \times 2 \cdot 5 = 10 \cdot 0 \text{ m}^2; \; W = \frac{2 \cdot 5 \times 4 \cdot 0^2}{6} = 6 \cdot 7 \text{ m}^3$$

$$\sigma_{max} = \frac{1200}{10} + \frac{64 \cdot 1}{6 \cdot 7} = 120 + 10 = 130 \text{ kN/m}^2$$

$$\sigma_{min} = 120 - 10 = 110 \text{ kN/m}^2$$

The structure is sensitive to differential settlement and since the foundations are resting on a not very compressible soil it is suggested that under the eccentric basic (long-term) loading the ratio $\sigma_{max} : \sigma_{min}$ should be less than 2·0.

This condition is satisfied for the above figures:

$$\frac{\sigma_{max}}{\sigma_{min}} = \frac{130}{110} = 1\cdot18 < 2\cdot0$$

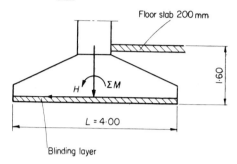

Figure A.5. Details of footing and applied loading.

(b) The combined basic and additional loading (see Table A.1):

axial column load	1123 kN
weight of wall	210 kN
weight of footing and backfill	270 kN
$\Sigma P =$	1603 kN

$$M = 433 \text{ kN m}; \quad H = 70\cdot9 \text{ kN}$$
$$\Sigma M = 433 + 70\cdot9 \times 1\cdot6 = 547 \text{ kN m}$$

$$\sigma_{max} = \frac{1603}{10} + \frac{547}{6\cdot7} = 160 + 82 = 242 < 353 \text{ kN/m}^2$$

i.e. within the value of the safe bearing stress (282 kN/m²) increased for wind loading.

$$\sigma_{min} = 160 - 82 = 78 \text{ kN/m}^2$$

(c) Another combination of the basic and additional loading:

$$\Sigma P = 883 + 210 + 270 = 1363 \text{ kN}$$
$$\Sigma M = 492 + 75\cdot9 \times 1\cdot6 = 492 + 121 = 613 \text{ kN m}$$

$$\sigma_{max} = \frac{1363}{10} + \frac{613}{6\cdot7} = 136 + 91 = 227 \text{ kN/m}^2 < 353 \text{ kN/m}^2$$

$$\sigma_{min} = 136 - 91 = 45 \text{ kN/m}^2$$

$$e = \frac{\Sigma M}{\Sigma P} = \frac{613}{1363} = 0\cdot45 < \frac{L}{6} = \frac{4\cdot0}{6} = 0\cdot67 \text{ m}$$

The point of application of the resultant force for the worst condition of loading is well within the middle third and hence from the bearing capacity point of view the chosen foundation is satisfactory.

A.4. Computation of Settlement of Footing EI

Because of the presence of organic silts beneath the foundations of frames A, B, C, and D it is necessary to evaluate settlements for the two different soil conditions, i.e. for the soils beneath frames E and C (Figures A.4 and A.8).

The settlement is calculated with consideration of the unloading of the soil due to the excavation for the footing EI and with consideration of the neighbouring foundation loads. The effects of unloading due to the general regrading of the site and due to excavations for the neighbouring footings are not considered. The errors involved are small (<2 kN/m^2) and result in a slight increase in the safety margin.

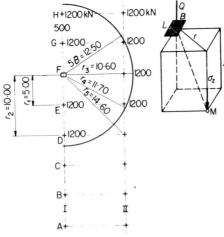

Figure A.6. Loading for evaluation of settlement of a typical footing.

In this example all neighbouring foundations within a distance of 6B were considered; it can be seen in Table A.2 that the neighbouring foundations at distances greater than 5B have very little effect on the distribution of stresses beneath the considered footing.

The stress at depth z below the centre of a footing due to a surface point load Q applied at a distance r away from it (Figure A.6) is evaluated from Equation (1.8):

$$\sigma_z = \frac{Q}{z^2} c_z$$

When the effects of a number of equal loads are considered, then

$$\sigma_z = \sum \frac{Q}{z^2} c_{zi} = \frac{Q}{z^2} \sum c_{zi}$$

Calculation of stresses is given in Table A.2 and the results are plotted in Figure A.7.

Table A.2. Calculation of stresses in soil due to point loads
(neighbouring foundations)

Depth below foundation level z (m)	Ratios of horizontal distance of point load to depth of the considered point $r : z$ (Figure A.6)					Values of coefficients c_i					$\sum_1^5 c_i$
	$r_1 =$ 5·0 m	$r_2 =$ 10 m	$r_3 =$ 10·6 m	$r_4 =$ 11·7 m	$r_5 =$ 14·6 m	c_1	c_2	c_3	c_4	c_5	
1·0	5·0	10·0	10·6	11·7	14·6	0·0001	–	–	–	–	0·0001
2·0	2·5	5·0	5·3	5·9	7·3	0·0034	0·0001	–	–	–	0·0035
3·0	1·70	3·3	3·5	3·9	4·9	0·0160	0·0011	0·0007	0·0004	0·0001	0·0183
4·0	1·25	2·5	2·65	2·9	3·7	0·0454	0·0034	0·0027	0·0017	0·0003	0·0510
5·0	1·00	2·0	2·12	2·3	2·9	0·0844	0·0035	0·0070	0·0048	0·0017	0·1064
6·0	0·83	1·7	1·8	1·95	2·4	0·1288	0·0160	0·0129	0·0095	0·0040	0·1712
7·0	0·71	1·43	1·51	1·67	2·05	0·1721	0·0295	0·0245	0·0171	0·0077	0·2509

For the given system $\sum c_{zi} = (2 \sum_1^5 c_i) - c_3$

$$\sigma_{2,0} = \frac{1200}{4} 0·0035 \times 2 = 2·2 \text{ kN/m}^2$$

$$\sigma_{3,0} = \frac{1200}{9} (0·0183 \times 2 - 0·0007) = 4·8 \text{ kN/m}^2$$

$$\sigma_{4,0} = \frac{1200}{16} (0·0510 \times 2 - 0·0027) = 7·5 \text{ kN/m}^2$$

$$\sigma_{5,0} = \frac{1200}{25} (0·1064 \times 2 - 0·0070) = 9·9 \text{ kN/m}^2$$

$$\sigma_{6,0} = \frac{1200}{36} (0·1712 \times 2 - 0·0129) = 11·0 \text{ kN/m}^2$$

$$\sigma_{7,0} = \frac{1200}{49} (2 \times 0·2509 - 0·0245) = 11·7 \text{ kN/m}^2$$

Calculation of settlements to a depth at which $\Delta\sigma_{rz} + \Delta\sigma_{az} \leqslant 0·2\sigma'_{oz}$ is contained in Table A.3.

A.5. Computation of Safe Bearing Stress for Soils Beneath Footing CI

Because of the presence beneath the foundation of a layer of organic silt of thickness greater than 0·5 m the values of the allowable bearing stresses given in Table 2.4 can only be treated as preliminary and in every case it is necessary to check the safe bearing capacity and settlement of the foundation according to Equations (2.1) to (2.3).

For preliminary evaluation of the size of the foundation an estimated value of $q_2 = 70 \text{ kN/m}^2$ was taken from Table 2.4 (for organic clayey silt $q_2 = 0$ for $I_c = 0$ and $q_2 = 100 \text{ kN/m}^2$ for $I_c = 1·0$; therefore, for $I_c \approx 0·70$, $q_2 \approx 70 \text{ kN/m}^2$).

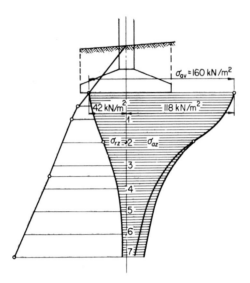

Figure A.7. Distribution of stresses below footing EI.

Because of such a low value of the safe bearing stress it is uneconomic to use isolated footings and therefore a strip foundation was designed under the columns spaced at 5·0 m apart. The width of the strip foundation

$$B = \frac{\Sigma P}{L \times q_2} = \frac{2100}{5 \times 70} = 6·0 \text{ m}$$

A.5.1. PRELIMINARY COMPUTATION OF SAFE BEARING STRESSES

The ultimate bearing capacity is computed according to Equation (2.18), simplified for the case of strip footing:

$$q_{ult}^{(a)} = \left\{ cN_c + (\gamma_0 D + \gamma_1 z)N_q - \gamma_1 z + \frac{\gamma_2 B}{2} N_\gamma \right\} \frac{1}{\eta_0} + \gamma_0 D$$

For the organic clayey silt (weakest soil) at a depth $z = 0·3$ m below the proposed foundation level:

$c = 20 \text{ kN/m}^2$; $\phi = 2°$; $D = 1·60$ m; $z = 0·3$ m; $B = 6·0$ m
for $z : B = 0·3 : 6·0 = 0·05$, from Figure 1.16, $\eta_0 \approx 1·0$
for $\phi = 2°$, from Table 2.2, $N_c = 6$, $N_q = 1·0$, $N_\gamma \approx 0$
$q_{ult}^{(a)} = \{20 \times 6 + (19·1 \times 1·6 + 19·1 \times 0·3)1·01 - 19·1 \times 0·3\} + 19·1 \times 1·6$
$\qquad = 150 + 30 = 180 \text{ kN/m}^2$

The safe bearing stress according to Equation (2.22) and for $F = 2$ is

$$q_{safe}^{(a)} = \frac{180 - 30}{2} + 30 = 75 + 30 \approx 105 \text{ kN/m}^2$$

Table A.3. Calculation of settlement of footing E1

(1) Depth below EGL H (m)	(2) Type of soil, unit weight (kN/m³)	(3) Effective overburden stress (kN/m²)	(4) Depth below foundation level z (m)	(5) z/B (B = 2.5 m)	(6) η_0 for L/B = 1·60	(7) Reloading stress $\Delta\sigma_{rz}$ (kN/m²)	(8) Stress applied by foundation $\Delta\sigma_z = \eta_0\sigma_{av}$ (kN/m²)	(9) Stress due to adjacent foundations (Table A.2) (kN/m²)	(10) Resultant stress 8 + 9 (Figure A.7) (kN/m²)	(11) Additional stress $\Delta\sigma_{az} = 10 - 7$ (kN/m²)	(12) Average stress $\Delta\sigma_{rz}$ (kN/m²)	(13) Average stress $\Delta\sigma_{az}$ (kN/m²)	(14) Layer thickness h_i (m)	(15) Stiffness moduli E' and E'' (MN/m²)	(16) Settlement due to $\Delta\sigma_{rz}$ $S'' = \frac{\Delta\sigma_{rz}}{E''} \times h_i$ (mm)	(17) Settlement due to $\Delta\sigma_{az}$ $S' = \frac{\Delta\sigma_{az}}{E'} \times h_i$ (mm)	(18) Total settlement $S = S' + S''$ (mm)
0·0 EGL	fine sand	0·0															
Foundation level 2·20	$\gamma = 19.1$	42·0	0	0	1·00	42·0	160·0	0·0	160·0	118·0	38·9	109·2	1·0	$E'' = 50$	0·78	3·64	4·42
2·60 GWT ▼	$\gamma_{sub} = 9.9$	49·6	1·0	0·4	0·85	35·7	136·0	0·1	136·1	100·4	30·5	86·7	1·0	$E' = 30$	1·02	2·89	3·91
3·20 silty clay	$\gamma_{sub} = 10.5$	55·5	2·0	0·8	0·60	25·2	96·0	2·2	98·2	73·0	20·2	60·1	1·0	$E'' = E' = 30$	0·67	2·00	2·67
			3·0	1·2	0·36	15·1	57·6	4·8	62·4	47·3	13·7	44·4	0·5		0·23	0·78	1·01
5·70 clayey sand		81·8	3·5	1·4	0·29	12·2	46·4	6·2	52·6	40·4	11·1	38·1	0·5	$E'' = E' = 50$	0·11	0·38	0·49
	$\gamma_{sub} = 11.8$		4·0	1·6	0·24	10·1	38·4	7·5	45·9	35·8	8·4	32·3	1·0		0·17	0·65	0·82
			5·0	2·0	0·16	6·7	25·6	9·9	35·5	28·8	5·9	27·1	1·0		0·12	0·54	0·66
			6·0	2·4	0·12	5·0	19·2	11·0	30·2	25·2	4·4	23·8	1·0		0·09	0·48	0·57
9·30 sand-silt-clay		124·3	7·0	2·8	0·09	3·8	14·4	11·7	26·1	22·3	3·0	20·0	2·0	$E'' = E' = 50$	0·12	0·80	0·92
11·8	$\gamma_{sub} = 11.8$	147·9	9·0	3·6	0·05	2·1	8·0	12·0	20·0	17·9				ΣS	3·31	12·16	15·47

During construction:
settlement of sand will be complete 100% = 4·4 ⎫
settlement of underlying soils will reach 70% of S_{final} 0·7 × 11·1 = 7·8 ⎬ 12·2 mm
After construction:
Final settlement – construction settlement 15·5 – 12·2 ≈ 3 mm

Note. For practical purposes calculations can be rounded off to the nearest 1 kN/m².

196

Table A.4. Calculation of settlement of

Depth below EGL H	Type of soil, unit weight	Effective overburden stress	Depth below foundation level z	z/B ($B = 6{\cdot}0$ m)	η_o for $x/B = 0$	Unloading due to excavation for found. $\Delta\sigma'_{rz}$	η_2 for $\dfrac{x}{B} = \dfrac{10{\cdot}0}{6{\cdot}0} = 1{\cdot}77$	Unloading due to excavation for adjacent found. $\Delta\sigma''_{rz}$	Stress applied by foundation $\Delta\sigma_z$	Stress applied by adjacent foundation $\Delta\sigma'_z$	Resultant stress	Reloading stress $\Delta\sigma_z$
(m)	(kN/m³)	(kN/m²)	(m)			(kN/m²)				(kN/m²)		
		$\sigma'_{oz} = \Sigma h_i\gamma$			Table 6.2	$\sigma'_{oH}\eta_1$	Table 6.2	$\sigma'_{oD}\eta_2$	$\eta_1\sigma_D$	$\eta_2\sigma_D$	10 + 11	7 +
1	2	3	4	5	6	7	8	9	10	11	12	13
0·0	existing ground level											
0·3	finished ground level											
1·90	fine sand ▼ base	36·3	0·0	0·0	1·00	36·3	0·00	0·0	70·0	0·0	70·0	36·?
2·20	$\gamma = 19{\cdot}1$	42·0	0·3	0·05	1·00	36·3	0·00	0·0	70·0	0·0	70·0	36·?
2·40	$\gamma = 16{\cdot}2$ ▼ GWT	45·2	0·5	0·083	0·99	35·9	0·00	0·0	69·3	0·0	69·3	35·?
	organic clayey silt	50·4	1·2	0·200	0·97	35·2	0·00	0·0	67·8	0·0	67·8	35·
		56·3	2·0	0·333	0·92	33·4	0·01	0·4	64·4	0·7	65·1	33·
4·70	$\gamma_{sub} = 7{\cdot}4$	62·2	2·8	0·466	0·85	30·8	0·02	0·7	59·5	1·4	60·9	31·
	silty clay	72·7	3·8	0·634	0·75	27·2	0·03	1·1	52·5	2·1	54·6	28·
6·70	$\gamma_{sub} = 10{\cdot}5$	83·2	4·8	0·800	0·65	23·6	0·04	1·4	45·5	2·8	48·3	25·
	clayey sand	95·0	5·8	0·968	0·58	21·0	0·05	1·8	40·6	3·5	44·1	22·
		106·8	6·8	1·132	0·53	19·2	0·06	2·2	37·1	4·2	41·3	21·
9·70	$\gamma_{sub} = 11{\cdot}8$	118·6	7·8	1·300	0·46	16·7	0·07	2·5	32·2	4·9	37·1	19·
	sand– silt–clay	130·4	8·8	1·467	0·41	14·9	0·08	2·9	28·7	5·6	34·3	17·
		142·2	9·8	1·633	0·37	13·4	0·09	3·3	25·9	6·3	32·2	16·
12·70	$\gamma_{sub} = 11{\cdot}8$	154·0	10·8	1·968	0·32	11·6	0·10	3·6	22·4	7·0	29·4	15·

$0{\cdot}2\sigma'_{oz}$ 30·8

$\Delta\sigma_{rz} + \Delta\sigma_{az} = 29{\cdot}4$

Notes.
(1) For practical purposes calculations can be rounded off to 1 kN/m².
(2) The unloading effects of general regrading of the site were not considered because they were insignificant. In other circumstances they may have to be allowed for.

strip foundation beneath column CI

Additional stress $\Delta\sigma_{az}$	Average stress		Layer thickness h_i	Stiffness modulus		Settlement of layers			Settlement of individual strata	Settlement during construction	
	Reloading $\Delta\sigma_{rz}$	Additional $\Delta\sigma_{az}$		Reloading E''	First loading E'	s''	s'	s''			
	(m)	(MN/m²)	(MN/m²)	(mm)	(mm)	(mm)	(mm)	(%)	(mm)		
12 – 13	Average from 13	Average from 14				$\dfrac{\Delta\sigma_{rz}\times h_i}{E''}$	$\dfrac{\Delta\sigma_{az}\times h_i}{E'}$	20 + 21			23 × 24
14	15	16	17	18	19	20	21	22	23	24	25
33·7											
33·7	36·3	33·7	0·30	50	30	0·22	0·36	0·58	0·58	100	0·58
33·4	36·1	33·6	0·20			1·03	1·68	2·71			
32·6	35·6	33·0	0·70	7	4	3·56	5·78	9·34			
31·3	34·5	31·9	0·80			3·94	6·38	10·32			
29·4	33·7	30·4	0·80			3·85	6·08	9·93	32·95	50	16·46
26·3	29·9	27·9	1·00	30	30	1·00	0·93	1·93			
23·3	26·7	24·8	1·00			0·89	0·83	1·72	3·65	70	2·55
21·3	33·9	22·3	1·00			0·68	0·45	1·13			
19·9	22·1	20·6	1·00	50	50	0·44	0·41	0·85			
17·9	20·3	18·9	1·00			0·41	0·38	0·79	2·77	70	1·94
16·5	18·5	17·2	1·00			0·37	0·34	0·71			
15·5	17·3	16·0	1·00	50	50	0·35	0·32	0·67			
14·2	16·0	14·9	1·00			0·32	0·30	0·62	2·00	100	2·00
			Σs			17·06	24·24	41·30			23·53
			on rounding off			17 mm	24 mm	41 mm			23 mm

settlement during construction 23 mm
settlement after construction 18 mm
final settlement 41 mm

According to British Standard Code of Practice C2004, the maximum bearing stress can be 25% greater than the average: $q_{max} = 1 \cdot 25 q_{safe}^{(a)} \approx 130 \text{ kN/m}^2$.

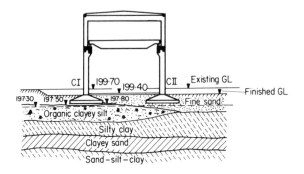

Figure A.8. Soil conditions beneath frame C.
Organic clayey silt: $\rho = 1 \cdot 65 \text{ g/ml}$; $w = 35\%$; $G_s = 2 \cdot 50$; $w_l = 67\%$; $w_p = 22\%$
$E' = 4 \text{ MN/m}^2$; $E'' = 7 \text{ MN/m}^2$; $c = 20 \text{ kN/m}^2$; $\phi = 2$
Other soils as in Figure A.4.

A.5.2. COMPUTATION OF ACTUAL STRESSES

Surface area of the footing corresponding to one column is $A = 5 \cdot 0 \times 6 \cdot 0$ = 30·0 m² and $W = (5 \times 60^2)/6 = 30 \text{ m}^3$.

Basic and additional loading:

axial column load	1123 kN
weight of wall panel	210 kN
weight of foundation and backfill (estimated)	780 kN
	$\sum P = 2113 \text{ kN}$

$M = 433 \text{ kN m}$; $H = 70 \cdot 9 \text{ kN}$

$\sum M = 433 + 70 \cdot 9 \times 1 \cdot 6 = 433 + 113 = 546 \text{ kN m}$

$$\sigma_{1, 2} = \frac{\sum P}{A} \pm \frac{\sum M}{W}$$

$$\sigma_{max} = \frac{2113}{30} + \frac{546}{30} = 71 + 18 = 89 \text{ kN/m}^2 < 124 \text{ kN/m}^2$$

$\sigma_{min} = 71 - 18 = 53 \text{ kN/m}^2$

The resultant force acts within the middle third. Under the other systems of loading the actual stresses are smaller than the above.

The following data are used in consideration of the influence of the neighbouring strip foundation:

$$\sigma_{av} = 70 \text{ kN/m}^2, \quad B = 6 \cdot 0 \text{ m}, \quad x = 10 \cdot 60 \text{ m}$$

$$\frac{x}{B} = \frac{10 \cdot 60}{6 \cdot 0} = 1 \cdot 77$$

A.6. Computation of Settlement of Strip Foundation Beneath Column CI

Settlement of the soil is considered to a depth of $12 \cdot 7$ m. The calculations are given in Table A.4.

A.7. Choice of Type of Foundations

As can be seen from the above calculations, the strip foundation beneath CI may settle approximately 41 mm, whereas the isolated footing foundations of frame E only 15 mm. If, therefore, the evaluated safe bearing stresses for the two soil conditions are adopted, it will be necessary to check whether these settlements, and the resulting angular distortion, are within the acceptable limits. According to Table 2.9 the structure under consideration belongs to class 4; for this class of structures maximum settlement of 60 mm (> 41 mm) and angular distortion of 1 : 300 are acceptable.

In consideration of angular distortion the foundations of three adjoining frames C, D, and E are considered. It is assumed that settlements of the strip footing are the same at CI and DI and are equal to 41 mm; the settlement of foundation EI is 17 mm. Angular distortion α is determined from Equation (2.3):

$$\alpha = \left| -\frac{41 - 17}{5000} \right| = \left| -\frac{24}{5000} \right| \approx \frac{1}{200}$$

which is greater than 1 : 300.

According to the recommendations given in Table 2.9 such an angular distortion is not acceptable in the case of a single-storey monolithic reinforced concrete structure (class 4) with non-structural panel walls and on separate foundations.

With the acceptable angular distortion of 1 : 300 and the distance between the footings CI and EI of 5 m the acceptable differential settlement between the two footings should not exceed 16 mm.

Because with the adopted safe bearing stresses the differential settlement of 24 mm is greater than the acceptable limit of 16 mm, one should try, in the first place, to reduce this difference by increasing the actual stress beneath the footing EI up to the safe bearing value (Section A.3.1); as the result of reduction in the size of the footing this only would increase its settlement by approximately 3 mm. In the second place the possibility of reduction in settlement of strip foundation CI–DI should be considered.

A cursory analysis of the results in Table A.4 indicates that in order to reduce the settlement of the foundation beneath column CI and DI to approximately 30 mm the bearing stress would have to be reduced down to about 50 kN/m^2 which would not be economic because of the resulting large dimensions of the foundation.

With the given soil conditions and the proposed type of construction one should aim to change the location of the building. In the circumstances, a minor shift in plan would avoid the necessity of founding on weak soils such as the organic clayey silts.

If the change in location of the building is out of the question then a cost analysis should be carried out for the following four alternative types of foundations and structures.

(a) Introduction of continuous foundations under all frames; this would stiffen the structure and would place the building in the class 3 (Table 2.9) and hence evaluated settlements would be within the acceptable limits.

(b) The entire building to be founded on piles which would transfer the loads to the deeper and stronger strata; an alternative would be to found the frames A to D on piles and frames E to H on footings, either with or without a 'movement' joint between them; the latter solution is feasible in this case because the differences in settlement between piles and spread footings would be small.

(c) In zone 1 (Figure A.1) the building to be founded on isolated foundations and in zone 2 on strip foundations with a delay in concreting of construction joints in all structural members in which the greatest additional stresses may occur owing to differential movements.

(d) The structure of the building to be changed to steel which is less sensitive to differential settlement of foundations (class 3, Table 2.9).

When the alternative (c) was considered the maximum vertical loads, which only occur during the assembly of the machinery, were used in computation of settlements of footings CI and EI.

As can be seen in Table A.1 the vertical loads during the normal usage of the building do not include the weight of the gantry nor of the transported loads. Instead of the maximum load considered (1123 kN) the vertical load during the normal usage of the building will only be equal to 743 kN (Table A.1) and the average bearing stress will decrease by 380/30 = 12·7 kN/m^2: the value of the additional bearing stress σ_{aD} will decrease by the same amount (see Table A.4, column 16). This will effectively decrease the settlements after construction by at least 12·7/70 x 100 = 18% hence the decrease in the settlement of column CI will be 18 x 18/100 = 3·2 mm and the total settlement of 41 mm will be reduced to 38 mm. The settlement after the completion of construction and assembly of machinery would have been only equal to 15 mm.

The fact that the greater proportion of the settlement will occur during construction and assembly of machines enables one to reduce the damaging effects of the differential settlement by the incorporation of construction joints between frames D and E which would not be concreted until this stage of the work is completed. Settlements should be observed from the beginning of construction of the building by precision levelling of special bench marks incorporated in the columns (Section 7.3). As soon as it is observed that the greater proportion of the settlement due to the self-weight of the structure has taken place, the construction joints can be concreted. Further observations of settlement should be carried out during the installation of the gantry and assembly of the machines.

Table A.5. Summary of settlements

Part of structure	Stresses σ_{ar} (kN/m^2)	Settlement (mm)		
		During construction	After construction	Total
Footing EI	160	12	3	15
Strip foundation at CI	70	23	18 (15)*	41 (38)
		Differential settlement		
		11	15 (12)	26 (21)
		Angular distortion between D and E		
		$\dfrac{11}{5000} = \dfrac{1}{450}$	$\dfrac{1}{335} \left(\dfrac{1}{420}\right)$	$\dfrac{1}{200} \left(\dfrac{1}{220}\right)$

* The figures in brackets were computed by neglecting the effect of the short-term gantry loading.

It follows from the above analysis of settlements and of the behaviour of the structure and their influence on the foundation conditions that, as previously stated, the determination of the allowable bearing stresses is a complex problem, not limited only to the recognition of the type and the state of the soils, but unquestionably involving consideration of the dimensions and the type of the proposed structure.

Volume 2: References

Bell, A. L., 1915, 'The lateral pressure and resistance of clay and the supporting power of clay foundations', *Min. Proc. Inst. Civil Engrs.* (*London*), Paper No. 4131.

Bennett, D. H., 1971, Private Communication, The University of Aston in Birmingham, England.

Beskow, G., 1935, *Tjälbildningen och Tjällyffningen*, Statens Väginstitut, Meddelande 48, Stockholm (English translation, J. O. Osterberg, 1957, Northwestern University, Chicago, Ill.).

Bierezancev, V. G., 1953, *Ossisimmetrichnaya Zadacha Teorii Predelnogo Ravnovesya Sypuchei Sredy*, Gostekhizdat, Moscow.

Biezukhov, M. I., 1953, *Teoria Uprogosti i Plastichnosti*, G.I.T.K., Moscow.

Bishop, A. W., 1954, 'The use of pore pressure coefficients in practice', *Geotechnique*, 4, 148–52.

——1955, 'The use of the slip circle in the stability analysis of slopes', *Geotechnique*, 5, 7–17.

Bishop, A. W., and Henkel, D. J., 1957, *The Measurement of Soil Properties in Triaxial Test*, Edward Arnold, London.

Bishop, A. W., and Morgenstern, N., 1960, 'Stability coefficients for earth slopes', *Geotechnique*, 10, 129–50.

Bogoslavski, N. N., 1947, *Osnovaniya i Fundamenty*, G.I.S.L., Moscow.

Boussinesq, H., 1885, *Applications des Potentiels a l'Etude de l'Equilibre et du Mouvement des Solides Elastique*, Gauthier-Villars, Paris.

British Standard 1377, 1967, *Methods of Testing Soils for Civil Engineering Purposes*, British Standards Institution, London.

British Standard Code of Practice CP 2004, 1971 Draft, *Foundations*, The Council for Codes of Practice, British Standards Institution, London.

Caquot, A. and Kérisel, J., 1949, *Traite de Mechanique des Sols*, Gauthier-Villars Paris.

Civil Engineering Code of Practice No. 2, 1951, *Earth Retaining Structures*, The Institution of Structural Engineers, London.

Cytovich, N. A., 1963, *Mekhanika Gruntov*, G.J.S.A. and S.M., Moscow.

Department of Scientific and Industrial Research, 1956, *Soils, Concretes, and Bituminous Materials*, H.M.S.O., London.

Di Biago, E., and Kjaernsli, B., 1961, 'Struts loads and related measurements on contract 63a of the Oslo subway', *Proc. 5th Intern. Conf. Soil Mech. Found. Eng., Paris*, Vol. 2, pp. 395–401.

Drucker, D. C., and Prager, W., 1952, 'Soil mechanics and plastic analysis or limit design', *Quart. Appl. Math.*, **10**, 157–65.

Dücker, A., 1939, *Neue Erkentrisse auf dem Gebiete der Frostforschung, Bodenmechanik und neuzeitlicher Strassenbau*, Volk und Reich Verlag, Berlin.

Fellenius, W., 1936, 'Calculation of the stability of earth dams', *Trans. 2nd Congr. Large Dams, Wash., D.C.*, Vol. 4, pp. 445–65.

Florin, V. A., 1959, *Osnovy Mekhaniki Gruntov*, G.I.L.S.A. and S.M., Leningrad.

Fox, E. N., 1948, 'The mean elastic settlement of a uniformly loaded area at a depth below the ground surface', *Proc. 2nd Intern. Conf. Soil Mech. Found. Eng., Rotterdam*, Vol. 1, pp. 129–32.

Fröhlich, O. K., 1934, *Druckverteilung im Baugrunde*, Springer-Verlag, Vienna.

Glushkov, G. I., 1954, 'Opredeleniye gorizontalnykh napryazhenii v grunte', *Gidrotekhn. Stroit.*, No. 3.

Grasshof, H., 1955, 'Setjungsberechungen starrar Fundamententen mit Hilfe des Kennzeichnenden Punktes', *Bauingenieur*, No. 2.

Harr, M. E., 1966, *Foundations of Theoretical Soil Mechanics*, McGraw-Hill, New York.

Highway Research Board, 1952, 'Frost action in soils', *Natl. Acad. Sci., Wash., D.C.*, No. 213.

Jáky, J., 1944, 'The coefficient of earth pressure at rest', *J. Soc. Hung. Architects Engrs.*, 355–8.

Janbu, N., Bjerrum, L., and Kjaernsli, B., 1956, 'Veiledning ved løsnig av fundamenterings appgaver', *Norweg. Geotechn. Inst., Oslo, Publ.*, No. 16.

Kjaernsli, B., 1958, 'Test results, Oslo subway', *Proc. Conf. Earth Pressure Problems, Brussels*, Vol. 2, p. 108.

Krey, H., 1936, *Erddruck, Erdwiderstand, und Tragfähigkeit des Baugrundes*, W. Ernst u. Sohn, Berlin.

Lambé, T. W., 1951, *Soil Testing for Engineers*, Wiley, New York.

Lewis, W. A., 1965, 'Nuclear apparatus for density and moisture measurements, study of factors affecting accuracy', *Roads, Road Construct., London*, **43**, 37–43.

Lomize, G. M., 1954, 'Nakhozheniye opasnoi poverkhnostii, skolzheniya pri raschotye ustoichivosti ostokov', *Gidrotekhn. Stroit.*, No. 2.

Maag, E., 1938, *Grenzbelastung des Baugrundes*, Erdbaukurs der ETH, Zürich.

Maslov, N. N., 1950, *Prikladnaya Mekhanika Gruntov*, I.M.S.I.M., Moscow.

Meigh, A. C., and Skipp, B. O., 1960, 'Gamma-ray and neutron methods of measuring soil density and moisture', *Geotechnique*, **10**, 110–26.

Meyerhof, G. G., 1950, 'The ultimate bearing capacity of foundations', *Geotechnique*, **2**, 301–32.

Mindlin, R. D., 1936, 'Forces at a point in the interior of a semi-infinite solid', *Physics*, **7**, 195–202.

Moos, A., 1956, 'Die Diemensionierung der Strassen bezüglich Sicherheit gegen Frost', *Strasse und Verkehr*, No. 9.

Newmark, N. M., 1940, 'Stress distribution in soil', *Proc. Purdue Conf. Soil Mech. and Its Application, Purdue Univ., Lafayette, Indiana*, pp. 295–303.

——1942, 'Influence charts for computation of stresses in elastic foundations', *Univ. Ill., Eng. Expt. Sta., Bull.*, No. 338.

Ohde, J., 1938, 'Zur Theorie des Erddruckes unter besonderer Berüksichtigung der Erddruck Verteilung', *Bautechnik*, No. 16, 150.

Packshaw, S., 1946, 'Earth pressure and resistance', *J. Inst. Civil Engrs. (London)*, **25**, 233–56.

Penman, A. D. M., 1969, 'Instrumentation for earth and rockfill dams', *Bldg. Res. Sta., Current Paper*, No. 35/69.

Polish Standard PN–59/B–03020, 1959, *Grunty Budowlane, Wytyczne Wyznaczania Dopuszczalnych Obciążeń Jednostkowych* (*Engineering Soils, Directives for Determination of Allowable Bearing Stresses*), Wydawnictwa Normalizacyine, Warsaw.

Polshin, D. E., and Tokar, R. A., 1957, 'Maximum allowable non-uniform settlement of structures', *Proc. 4th Intern. Conf. Soil Mech. Found. Eng., London*, Vol. 1, pp. 402–5.

Poulos, H. G., 1967, 'The use of the sector method for calculating stresses and displacements in an elastic mass', *Proc. 5th Australia–New Zealand Conf. Soil Mech. Found. Eng.*, pp. 198–204.

Reynolds, H. R., and Protopapadakis, P., 1946, *Practical Problems in Soil Mechanics*, Crosby Lockwood, London.

Road Research Laboratory, D.S.I.R., 1955, *Soil Mechanics for Road Engineers*, H.M.S.O., London.

Rückli, R., 1950, *Der Frost im Baugrund*, Springer-Verlag, Vienna.

Russian Standard N and TU 127–55, 1955, *Standards and Technical Conditions of Design of Foundations for Buildings and Industrial Developments on Natural Soils*, Ministry of Building, U.S.S.R.

Schultze, E., 1952, 'Der Wiederstand des Baugrundes gegen schräge Sohlpressungen', *Bautechnik*, No. 12.

Schaible, L., 1954, 'Über die zunehmende Gefahr der Frostschäden für unsere Verkehrswege', *Bautechnik*, No. 9.

Shahunianc, G. M., 1945, 'Protivorechiya v suschestvuyuschikh metodakh rascheta ustoyichyvosti ostokov: sposoby ikh ustraneniya', *Tekhn. Zheleznykh Dorog*, No. 9.

——1953, *Zemlynoye Polotno Zheleznykh Dorog*, Gostranszheldorizdat, Moscow.

Skempton, A. W., 1951, 'The bearing capacity of clays', *Bldg. Res. Congr. Div.*, 180–9.

——1961, 'Horizontal stresses in an over-consolidated Eocene Clay', *Proc. 5th Intern. Conf. Soil Mech. Found. Eng., Paris*, Vol. 1, pp. 351–8.

Skempton, A. W., and Hutchinson, J., 1969, 'Stability of natural slopes and embankment foundations', *Proc. 7th Intern. Conf. Soil Mech. Found. Eng., Mexico*, 'State of the Art' Vol., pp. 291–340.

Skempton, A. W., and MacDonald, D. H., 1956, 'The allowable settlements of buildings', *Proc. Inst. Civil Engrs.* (*London*), 5, Part 3, Dec., 727–68.

Śliwa, P., 1955, *Osuwisko Bachledzkiego Wierchu w Zakopanem*, Wydanictwa Geologiczne, Warsaw.

Sokolovsky, V. V., 1960, *Statics of Soil Media*, Butterworth, London.

Sowers, G. F., Rob, A. D., Mullins, C. D., and Glenn, A. J., 1957, 'The residual lateral pressures produced by compacting soils', *Proc. 4th Intern. Conf. Soil Mech. Found. Eng., London*, Vol. 2, pp. 243–7.

Steinbrenner, W., 1936, *Tafeln zur Setzungsberechnung, Bodenmechanik und neuzeitlicher Strassenbau*, Volk und Reich Verlag, Berlin.

Terzaghi, K., 1934, 'Large retaining wall test', *Eng. News Record*, Feb. 1, Feb. 22, Mar. 8, Mar. 20, Apr. 19.

——1943, *Theoretical Soil Mechanics*, Wiley, New York.

——1954, 'Anchored bulkheads', *Trans. Am. Soc. Civil Engrs.*, 119, 1243–80.

Terzaghi, K., and Peck, G. B., 1967, *Soil Mechanics in Engineering Practice*, 2nd edn., Wiley, New York.

Tettinek, W., and Matt, F., 1953, 'A contribution to calculating the inclination of eccentrically loaded foundations', *Proc. 3rd Intern, Conf. Soil Mech. Found. Eng., Zürich*, Vol. 1, pp. 461–5.

Vasiljev, B. D., 1955, *Osnovaniya i Fundamenty*, G.I.L.S.A., Moscow.

Ward, W. H., Burland, J. B., and Gallois, R. W., 1969, 'Geotechnical assessment of a site at Mundford, Norfolk, for a large proton accelerator', *Bldg. Res. Sta., Current Paper*, No. 3/69.

West, J. M., Moseley, M. P., and Bennett, D. H., 1971, 'The stability of a valley side in weathered shale', *Quart. J. Eng. Geol., London*, 4, 1–23.

Whitman, R. V., and Bailey, W. A., 1967, 'Use of computers for slope stability analysis', *Proc. Am. Soc. Civil Engrs.* (*J. Soils Mech. Found. Div.*), 93, No. SM4, 475–98.

Wiłun, Z., 1955b, 'Badania geotechniczne podłoża PKiN', *Inżynieria i Budownictwo*, July, 237–41.

——1958, *Wyznaczanie Dopuszczalnych Obciążeń Gruntów*, Arkady, Warsaw.

——1963, 'Standsicherheit von Boschungen', *Soil Mech. Found. Eng. Conf., Budapest*, Panel Discussion.

——1969, *Mechanika Gruntów i Gruntoznawstwo Drogowe*, 3rd edn., Wydawnictwa Komunikacji i Łczności, Warsaw.

Witun, Z., and Rogoziński, Z., 1953, 'Osiadania nowowznoszonych budowli', *Inżynieria i Budownictwo*, Oct.

Żénczykowski, W., 1949, 'Walka z żywiołem zsuwu na wzgórzu kościoła św Anny w Warszawie', *Przegląd Budowlany*, 7—8.

Relationship Between S.I., Metric, and Imperial Units of Measurement

The *basic units* of the S.I. system (Système International d'Unités) commonly used in Civil Engineering are as follows:

(i) Length: metre (m)
(ii) Mass: kilogramme (kg)
(iii) Time: second (s)
(iv) Temperature: degree Kelvin ($^\circ$K) equal to the commonly used degree Celcius ($^\circ$C).

Unit of	S.I. units		Metric units	Imperial units (1 foot = $\frac{1}{3}$ Imp. yard)
	Basic	Recommended sub- and multiples		
Length	10^{-9} m	1 nm (nanometre)	1 mμ (millimicron)	} metric units usually
	10^{-6} m	1 μm (micrometre)	1 μ (micron)	} used
	10^{-3} m	**1 mm (millimetre)***	1 mm	0·03937 in (inch)
	10^{-2} m	not recommended	1 cm (centimetre)	0·3937 in
	1 m	**1 m (metre)**†	1 m	39·37 in; 3·281 ft (feet)
	10^3 m	1 km (kilometre)	1 km	3281 ft
Area	10^{-6} m^2	**1 mm^2***	1 mm^2	1·550 x 10^{-3} in^2
	10^{-4} m^2	not recommended	1 cm^2	0·1550 in^2
	1 m^2	**1 m^2**†	1 m^2	10·764 ft^2
	10^4 m^2	1 ha (hectare)	1 ha	2·471 acres
Volume or capacity	10^{-6} m^3	**1 ml*** (millilitre)	1 cm^3	0·061 in^3
	10^{-3} m^3	1 l (litre)	10^3 cm^3 or 1 l	61·025 in^3; 0·220 gal 0·2642 U.S. gal
	1 m^3	**1 m^3**† or 10^3l	1 m^3 or 10^3l	35·315 ft^3

Unit of	S.I. units		Metric units	Imperial units (1 foot = ⅓ Imp. yard)
	Basic	Recommended sub- and multiples		
Velocity, rate	10^{-3} m/s 10^{-2} m/s 1 m/s	1 mm/s‡ not recommended 1 m/s†	10^{-1} cm/sec 1 cm/sec 1 m/sec	0·03937 in/sec 0·03281 ft/sec 3·281 ft/sec
Rate of flow	10^{-6} m³/s 10^{-3} m³/s 1 m³/s	1 ml/s* 1 l/s‡ 1 m³/s† or 10^3l/s	1 cm³/sec 1 l/sec 1 m³/sec or 10^3l/sec	3·531 x 10^{-3} ft³/sec 0·03531 ft³/sec 35·315 ft³/sec
Mass	10^{-3} kg 1 kg 10^3 kg	1 g* (gramme) 1 kg‡ 1 t† (tonne)	1 gm or gr 1 kg 1 t	2·205 x 10^{-3} lb (pound) 2·205 lb 2205 lb, 0·9842 T (tons) 1·1023 short tons
Density	1 kg/m³ 10^3 kg/m³	1 kg/m³ † 1 kg/l or 1 g/ml* or 1 t/m³ †	1 kg/m³ 1 kg/l or 1 gm/cm³ or 1 t/m³	0·06243 lb/ft³ 62·4 lb/ft³
Force	1 kgm/s² 10^3 kgm/s² 10^6 kgm/s²	1 N* (newton) 1 kN† (kilonewton) 1 MN (Meganewton)	0·101971 kgf 101·971 kgf 101·971 tf	0·22481 lbf 224·81 lbf 117·40 Tf
Stress, pressure	1 kg/ms² 10^3 kg/ms² 10^6 kg/ms²	1 N/m² 1 kN/m² ‡ 1 MN/m² ‡ or 1 N/mm²	1·01971 x 10^{-5} kgf/cm² 101·971 kgf/cm² 101·971 tf/cm²	0·02088 lbf/ft² 0·14504 lbf/in² 20·885 lbf/ft² 9·3238 Tf/ft²
Unit weight (specific weight)	1 kg/m²s² 10^3 kg/m²s² 10^6 kg/m²s²	1 N/m³ 1 kN/m³ ‡ 1 MN/m³	1·0197 x 10^{-4} gf/cm³ 0·10197 gf/cm³ 101·97 kgf/m³ 101·97 tf/m³	6·3657 x 10^{-3} lbf/ft³ 6·3657 lbf/ft³ 2·8418 Tf/ft³
Temperature	1°K (Kelvin)	1°C (Celsius)	1°C	9/5°F

* Recommended for laboratory work.
† Recommended for design work.
‡ Recommended for both above uses.

Gravitational acceleration (standard average) g = 9·80665 m/s² = 32·174 ft/sec²

Approximate Conversion Factors

1. Length: 1 mm ≈ 1/25 in; 1 in ≈ 25 mm; 1 m ≈ 10/3 ft; 1 ft ≈ 3/10 m.
2. Volume: 1 gal ≈ 4·5 l.
3. Mass: 1 kg ≈ 2·2 lb; 1 t ≈ 1 T (Imperial).
4. Density: 1000 kg/m³ = 1 g/ml = 1 t/m³ = 62·4 lb/ft³; 125 lb/ft³ ≈ 2000 kg/m³.
5. Force: 1 N ≈ 1/10 kgf ≈ 2/9 lbf; 1 MN ≈ 100 Tf (Imperial) ≈ 100 tf; 1 Tf ≈ 10 kN.
6. Stress, pressure: 1 lbf/in² ≈ 7 kN/m²; 1 Tf/ft² ≈ 100 kN/m²; 1 lbf/ft² ≈ 1/20 kN/m².
7. Unit weight: 1 kN/m³ ≈ 100 kgf/m³ ≈ 6·5 lbf/ft³.

S.I. Units in Foundation Engineering

1. Linear dimensions.

   (a) Laboratory work, details of apparatus, etc. – mm.
   (b) Foundation and earthwork details – m.

2. Density.

   (a) Laboratory calculations – g/ml.
   (b) Foundation and earthwork calculations – t/m^3 or kg/m^3.

3. Unit weights – kN/m^3.

4. Seepage.

   (a) Coefficient of permeability – mm/s or m/s.
   (b) Rate of flow – ml/s, l/s, or m^3/s.

5. Stress and pressure.

   (a) Normal and shear stresses in all calculations – kN/m^2.
   (b) Deformation and stiffness moduli and modulus of elasticity – MN/m^2.

6. Consolidation.

   (a) Coefficient of volume compressibility – m^2/MN.
   (b) Coefficient of consolidation – mm^2/s or m^2/s.

Notes for American Readers

For American readers of this book the authors have included a list of ASTM Standards relevant to the material contained in the text.

It must be emphasised, however, that the book is based on sound engineering principles which are universal in character, and therefore, it is in no way restricted to any one country. In fact the book presents an unusual combination of the experiences of two authors who have studied, taught and practised the subject in countries in which its development proceeded on fairly independent lines.

Z. Wiłun and K. Starzewski

List of American Society for Testing and Materials (ASTM) Standards Relevant to the Material Contained in this Book

The first number (e.g. D420) indicates the fixed designation of the ASTM Standard or Tentative; the number immediately following the designation indicates the year of original adoption or, in the case of revision, the year of last revision. A number in parentheses indicates the year of last reapproval. Tentatives are identified by the letter T.

A. ASTM Standards Relevant to Classification of Soils and Determination of their Physical Properties

D 2487–69	Classification of Soils for Engineering Purposes.
D 2488–69	Rec. Practice for Description of Soils (Visual–Manual Procedure).
D 653–67	Def. of Terms and Symbols Relating to Soil and Rock Mechanics.
D 2607–69	Classification of Peats, Mosses, Humus, and Related Products.
D 421–58 (1965)	Dry Preparation of Soil Samples for Particle-size Analysis and Determination of Soil Constants.
D 422–63	Particle-size Analysis of Soils.
D 423–66	Test for Liquid Limit of Soils.
D 424 59 (1965)	Test for Plastic Limit and Plasticity Index of Soils.
D 427–61 (1967)	Test for Shrinkage Factors of Soils.
D 854–58 (1965)	Test for Specific Gravity of Soils.
D 1140–54 (1965)	Test for Amount of Material in Soils Finer than the No. 200 Sieve.
D 2049–69	Test for Relative Density of Cohesionless Soils.
D 2216–66	Laboratory Determination of Moisture Content of Soil.
D 2217–66	Wet Preparation of Soil Samples for Grain-size Analysis and Determination of Soil Constants.
D 2419–69	Test for Sand Equivalent Value of Soils and Fine Aggregate.
D 2434–68	Test for Permeability of Granular Soils (Constant Head).

B. ASTM Standards Relevant to Strength and Compressibility of Soils and Rock

D 2166–66	Test for Unconfined Compressive Strength of Cohesive Soils.
D 2435–70	Test for One-dimensional Consolidation Properties of Soils.
D 2664–67	Test for Triaxial Compressive Strength of Undrained Rock Core Specimens without Pore Pressure Measurements.
D 2850–70	Test for Unconsolidated, Undrained Strength of Cohesive Soils in Triaxial Compression.

D 2938–71   Test for Unconfined Compressive Strength of Rock Core Specimens.

C. ASTM Standards Relevant to Soil Investigation Work and *In Situ* Testing

D 420–69   Rec. Practice for Investigating and Sampling Soils and Rock for Engineering Purposes.

D 1452–65   Soil Investigation and Sampling by Auger Boring.

D 1586–67   Penetration Test and Split-Barrel Sampling of Soils.

D 1587–67   Thin-walled Tube Sampling of Soils.

D 2113–70   Diamond Core Drilling for Site Investigation.

D 2573–67T   Field Vane Shear Test in Cohesive Soil.

D 2944–71   Method of Sampling Peat Materials.

D 1194–57 (1966)   Test for Bearing Capacity of Soil for Static Load on Spread Footings.

D 2487–69   Classification of Soils for Engineering Purposes.

D 2488–69   Rec. Practice for Description of Soils (Visual–Manual Procedure).

D 653–67   Def. of Terms and Symbols Relating to Soil and Rock Mechanics.

D. ASTM Standards Relevant to Compaction and Control of Compaction of Soils

D. 698–70   Test for Moisture-Density Relations of Soils, Using 5·5 lb Rammer and 12 inch Drop.

D 1556–64 (1968)   Test for Density of Soil in Place by the Sand-Core Method.

D 1557–64 (1968)   Test for Moisture–Density Relations of Soils Using 10 lb Rammer and 18 inch Drop.

D 1558–63 (1969)   Test for Moisture–Penetration Resistance Relations of Fine-grained Soils.

D 1883–67   Test for Bearing Ratio of Laboratory-Compacted Soils.

D 2167–66   Test for Density of Soil in Place by the Rubber-Baloon Method.

D 2168–66   Calibration of Mechanical Laboratory Soil Compactors.

D 2922–71   Determining the Density of Soil and Soil-Aggregate in Place by Nuclear Methods (Shallow Depth).

D 2937–71   Test for Density of Soil in Place by the Drive-Cylinder Method.

Subject Index

Author Index